BROOKLYN'S SCARLETT

SUSAN HAYWARD: FIRE IN THE WIND

GENE ARCERI

Published in the USA by:
BearManor Media
PO Box 1129
Duncan, Oklahoma 73534-1129
www.bearmanormedia.com

ISBN 978-1-59393-028-8

Printed in the United States of America.
Cover design by Christopher Jones.
Book design by Brian Pearce | Red Jacket Press.

TABLE OF CONTENTS

DEDICATION

A postman's delivery brought with it an introduction to Diana Adams. Fate interacted. A creative exchange evolved. Diana became a writer's hope, a colleague who was honest, intelligent, intrepid, dependable, encouraging and humorous. If I faltered, she persisted until the job was completed. I proudly dedicate this book to Diana with love and admiration.

ACKNOWLEDGEMENTS

I can almost hear their voices; see their faces. Throughout this book, you will meet them all. Though so many are gone now their words remain. They opened their homes — and hearts — to share their memories of Susan Hayward: Brooklyn school mate June O'Brien. Susan's brother, Wally, offered me a place to stay while in Hollywood. I slept on a rose covered sofa bed that Susan had bought so she could stay with her brother when he needed her. In Hollywood I sat by pools, met people I would interview in coffee shops, hotel lobbies. I went to Bel Air for a visit with Henry Hathaway, Danny Mann's office on Sunset Boulevard, and Nolan Miller's salon. I would go anywhere at anytime when and if they would see me. My travels led me to Baltimore to meet Father Thomas Brew–to Atlanta to see Father Morrow. In Carrollton, Georgia, I was the houseguest of Mary Williams and slept in Susan's bedroom where she would stay with Mary on occasion. A wonderful nostalgic journey walking through the town, stopping in the stores Susan frequented. I visited the church she built across from her home and Father McGuire.

All of this has been revisited on the following pages. Back in San Francisco, I was driven up to spend time with Ed Montgomery and his family. Over lunch at the SF Press Club Graham Kisinglinbury could not be more supportive. And I will never forget Curlee, Susan's housekeeper and confidant, who fixed a dinner for me and her family in the kitchen. My only wish is that I could not do it all over again. Still, as I read this book, a tribute to all those involved, in so many ways — I have!

PRELUDE

Her name was up in lights for the last time. The large unevenly placed faded red plastic letters SUSAN HAYWARD hung innocuously on the front wall of an undistinguished building along West Hollywood's La Cienega Boulevard.

The building at 526 No. La Cienega Boulevard in Los Angeles was not a movie house, nor a theatre, but the Arthur B. Goode Auction Gallery with its folksy slogan 'Buy or Sell the Goode Way.'

There was to be a Sunday afternoon session on June 13 and two evening sessions, June 14 and 15, 1976, with refreshments served and 'programs' printed on deep orange paper bearing an unmemorable photograph of the actress, wearing a very uncharacteristic wig, from her only stage appearance as Mane.

The Oscar Susan Hayward had won for *I Want To Live* sat on the top shelf of a locked display case along with her other awards. The David di Donatello from Italy, The Golden Gaucho from Argentina, the Silver Bear from Germany, The Mar del Plata from the South American Film Festival, Foreign Press Golden Globe for the World's Favorite Actress, and dozens more stacked up below on shelves in the main showroom of the auction gallery.

A Not For Sale sign had been scotch-taped under the Oscar making it, and the other awards, the only Hayward possessions in the place that didn't have price tags. The alloy objects, seemingly impervious to time, would escape the fate of the boxes of Christmas ornaments, kitchen utensils, books, prescription glasses, and such sentimental items as framed poetry readings and all the worldly goods left behind to be disposed of. The auction had been commissioned by the heirs and the probate division of the superior court of the State of California.

Her films had been packing them in for a long time and the Gallery was filled to the walls for each session. Some had known her or worked with her in one way or another, others were fans — but most were the curious, anxious for a look at what had filled her closets and dresser drawers. There were also the losers in the acting profession, people who had never made it — certainly never in the way she had. They came because they knew no matter how she had beaten them out during her lifetime they had finally won — because in June of 1976, they were still alive and Susan Hayward's life was over.

One lady faintly resembling the late star may have wondered silently alone among the numbered pieces — looking, touching, remembering — it would have been her older sister Florence Marrener, who was a stranger to her at the end of her life. Certainly one person who was there to inspect the assemblage was her brother Walter Marrener.

Walter, totally unknown to anyone, would be left to contemplate sadly where it would all go — as it did eventually; scattered around by the auctioneer's gavel as the vestiges of his sister's life went on the block. Green and yellow living room furniture, and earth toned clothes, a box filled with Bibles, towels with signs of the Zodiac on them, a fishing reel, jump rope, sewing box, espresso maker, a jade ring, and a plaque with a quote by Goethe — 'Nothing should be more highly prized than the value of each day', showed something of the fabric of her passage through life.

Arthur B. Goode, a tall heavyset man with a receding hairline and an auctioneer in Hollywood since 1936, boasted that his first memory in life was of his mother washing his mouth out with soap. Despite his 68 years, he conveyed the energy of a used car salesman and the patter of a stand-up comedian.

Eventually all the movie star estates seemed to end up at an Arthur B. Goode Auction. He had sold the remaining lifetime accumulations of Valentino, Bogart, Hedda Hopper, and John and Lionel Barrymore, to name but a few. For the movie stars who wanted to completely dispose of their pasts (like Hedy Lamarr who walked out of her house one day in 1950 and never went back) he listened to their weary instructions over the telephone to 'sell everything' and just took over from there.

Arthur B. Goode, who lives off the memorabilia of faded and fallen stars, is by default, a bit player acting out their last scenes. As for his nebulous audience, he bragged while chomping on a cigar: "People come to have fun. They don't know what they're doing, so I help them enjoy themselves. I also make money that way. I joke and laugh with 'em. And I never use a script. My secretary told me I'm the only guy who can get high without grass or liquor. I just turn myself on. We have X rated auctions." Goode added that most of his customers were upper middle class curiosity seekers.

Among the customers was a fussily dressed woman in the front row that eagerly chattered: "Auctions are one of the games people play, and I love to play it! It's an expensive hobby but my husband makes lots of money and it's something to show guests before cocktails."

A young couple had been there for the entire auction buying towels and pictures — the husband said sheepishly, "My wife has this thing for Susan Hayward and when we saw the estate sale advertised in the paper she just had to come down and get some keepsakes."

A couple of young men sat in the back row, nudging each other as pieces of Susan's life filtered through the auction, throwing out a bid for a dress, a pair of gloves, shoes, a handbag."

A serious man in a three-piece suit bought a ginger jar and some art supplies. An obese open shirted auction pro said, "This is the rag sale tonight. Oh I did pick up a few things for my kids to horse around with."

A woman wandering around the showroom was looking for bidder number 49. "Number 49 got a box of Hayward's panty hose for $4 and I bid $5. It was a good deal — I mean, they're all unused. I'm not here because I want a part of Susan Hayward. I'm no exhibitionist. In fact, I can't see why anybody would want to wear one of her wigs. That stuff gives me the willies. You know, she was completely bald from that tumor."

A meek young man bought a lovely chiffon green gown and red wig for his mother.

Standing off to one side behind a calculator was a tall blonde man watching everything with computer-like eyes, making notes, adding figures and giving nods of affirmation or denial to the auctioneer; squeezing every cent from the bidders with silent encouragement and smiling at Goode's tasteless jokes. A reporter went up to him, he was Timothy Barker, one of Susan's sons. But Barker was too preoccupied with the calling out of bids and the action going on to break his rapt concentration. He brushed the reporter aside as his wife came rushing up to him and in a thick German accent told him she had just gotten another parking ticket, which seemed to annoy him and he took her away to admonish her.

Near the close of the auction, members of the audience were still in a buying mood. They were like trick or treaters, and Goode had run out of candy to give them. No doubt about it, they were still hungry.

As the evening wore on, a carnival like atmosphere began to develop, particularly when the wigs went on sale.

The wigs were luxurious and red. Susan Hayward, one of the most famous titian-haired performers in the history of films, had been completely bald for the last painful years of her life.

"Come on kids," the auctioneer cajoled, "Somebody start the bidding. You too can be a Susan Hayward look alike. Remember that. And remember Halloween's coming."

"It'll be Halloween before you know it..."

The curtain came down. The lights dimmed. The audience left — and another lifetime of collecting was unraveled. It was finished; the show was over.

In a dimly lit corner, unnoticed and unsold, remained a stainless steel framed poster of soaring seagulls bearing four lines of poetry:

Hold fast to dreams,
For if dreams die,
Life is a broken-winged bird,
That cannot fly.

Sixteen months before on March 15th, 1975, Susan Hayward had departed Hollywood forever.

Susan had made a name for herself and finally came home. The name was Mrs. Floyd Eaton Chalkley, and home was Carrollton, Georgia — population 10,973. The girl who almost became Scarlett O'Hara was to be buried not fifty miles from that heroine's creator, novelist Margaret Mitchell.

At one time, Susan had reflected on becoming a southern 'lady' — making a home in the South. "This belle from Brooklyn had to be forty-five years old before she became a 'detoured Scarlett O'Hara,'" she quipped. "Mrs. Chalkley...and that's what I want to be called..."

Now she had come back to her adopted hometown, to her final resting place, to be buried beside her husband in a simple tomb honed from Georgia granite, designed and created by Susan herself with the aid of Georgia sculptor, Julian Harris.

The pink marble headstone was a sculptured head of the Agonizing Christ, bought by the Chalkleys in Italy. The plot, surrounded by pine and holly, overlooked the expansive rolling lands where she had spent 'the happiest years of my life' and now, with every dream she could have ever have dreamed come true, her last wish was to be laid to rest in the obscurity of rural West Georgia.

For Susan, the ten years with Eaton were the contented years. She had loved the 6'1" Chalkley far more than anyone Hollywood could have dreamed up for her. Chalkley was a Virginian who had made good as an FBI agent, a Washington lawyer, a gentleman farmer, and finally as the owner of the Chalkley Motor Company, adjoining the Carroll Theatre on Newman Street.

It was during their marriage that she had won the elusive Oscar…
something she had been within Excalibur's reach of through five nominations before finally grasping it.

Susan was flown home to Carrollton — and Eaton. There was no
fanfare. This time no crowds lined the path to the incoming plane. No
motorcade of home folk led the parade toward the rolling green hills of
Carroll County. There were to be no great speeches, no eulogy, no applause,
and no laughter.

Susan Hayward Chalkley came home to Carrollton on her last earthly
journey in peaceful dignity. The day ended in a rich sunlit glow that bathed
the hills and etched the stark late wintry trees into a canvas of rare beauty.

On Sunday, March 16th, 1975, the day of the funeral, the people of Carrollton, following their tradition, baked cakes and hams. Ann Moran, a close friend of the Chalkleys, baked a special banana cake — their favorite.

They lined seven miles of highway between the funeral home and the cemetery. The message on the Village Theatre's marquee expressed the feelings of all Carrolltonians; SUSAN WE'LL ALWAYS LOVE YOU.

It was a gloomy, rainy, Sabbath morning as the townspeople assembled in the chapel of Our Lady of Perpetual Help Catholic Church. After the service, officiated by Father Thomas Brew from Baltimore, the mourners filed slowly past the coffin, which was heaped high with yellow roses — Susan's favorite flowers — and white orchids. The local grocery clerk paused and remembered seeing her in pedal pushers with her red hair tied back and driving a pick-up truck with CHAL-MAR (Chalkley-Marrener; Susan's given name) FARMS painted on the side. A country woman, with a small baby in her arms, recalled the day Susan sat on the back steps of her home, drinking cold buttermilk, and talking about 'so many things.' A bank teller remembered her standing patiently in line. People waved and she would return their greetings — almost saluting — as she passed them by dressed in her bandanas, western shirts and khaki cotton slacks.

Curlee Crowder, a Carrollton woman who had worked for the Chalkley's for many years, spoke about her: "Mrs. Chalkley liked the simple people. 'They were more sincere,' she used to say. She was bored by bridge, gatherings, teas and socio-charitable company."

Now, outside, a crowd gathered around the small Catholic Church in the misty drizzle. Only the clicking of television news cameras indicated that the rites being said there were for someone of international status.

Some 18 years had passed since Susan Hayward had made her home in Carrollton, following her marriage to Eaton Chalkley. Until his death in 1966, some ten years later, she was much a part of the local community 'as down to earth a person as anyone else.' She had only wanted to be with Eaton, in their home together, and the reason she had left that home was because of memories of him.

She was to be buried today, beside her husband, across from the home where they had lived; her last request. Although the wind was cold and the drizzle was turning to rain, the grass was green and the flowers, surrounding the grave, cast a brilliance of color against the granite marker placed there after Eaton's death.

The group seated underneath the canopy protecting the gravesite was small. Movie stars, jet setters, and dignitaries were noticeably absent at the gathering. Only Susan's immediate family attended, including her twin sons, and a brother. Onlookers kept a respectful distance, some no doubt disappointed by the lack of celebrities.

The Chalkleys had arranged for the building of the Chapel of Our Lady of Perpetual Help, in granite matching the rock of their own home, on a hill in the heart of their property and given the land to the parish.

Now, at graveside, before a tombstone engraved simply Mrs. F.E. Chalkley, the local residents knew they would not see the handsome couple dancing at the Carrollton Country Club again or share the small dinner parties for close friends, which Susan preferred.

The beautiful, willful, Mrs. Chalkley, born June 30, 1917 in Flatbush, Brooklyn as Edythe Marrener to Walter and Ellen Marrener was now buried beneath the red clay of Georgia. Mrs. Chalkley, dead at 57, survived by her sons, a grandson, a grand-daughter and millions of fans around the world, the star of more than 50 motion pictures and winner of numerous international awards…could it have been only 36 years ago that a young girl of 19 looking over her shoulder, red hair blowing in the wind, smiled to the future from the cover of the Saturday Evening Post…a color photograph that would take her to Hollywood, and, after much heartbreak, to fame and fortune.

To Eugene best regards Susan Hayward

CHAPTER 1

June 30, 1917 — worldwide newspapers carried headline coverage of World War 1 from the North Sea to the Mediterranean; President Wilson ordered 10,000 of our aircraft to fly to France to bomb the German lines. The War Department issued lists of casualties in the American army in France. Pope Benedict XV led the free world in prayers for peace, and King George and Queen Mary were approaching their silver wedding anniversary. Mary Pickford's latest picture *How Could You Jean* opened at the Strand and the Follies headlined W.C. Fields, Marilyn Miller, Will Rogers and Eddie Cantor. At battle outposts, with our boys in the trenches darkened by night against air raids, the sound of a newborn baby howling for attention in a railroad flat in Brooklyn could hardly have presaged the future headlines she would occupy.

The baby's mother just dreamed of 'getting out.' She had heard the clang of the Church Avenue trolley too many times, walked past the Jewish candy stores 'til she was sick of them, smelled the stale beer odors of the Irish bars and the sweet sticky ones of the German bakeries so often that they made her gag. But Ellen Marrener came from Swedish stock and the Swedes were clean, practical people and looking in a mirror in her drab, fourth-floor flat at 3507 Church Avenue, Brooklyn, she could plainly see that she was not quite young and no longer pretty.

As for Walter, her husband, she knew that there was no way to count on him. He was a slight, ineffectual man, who preferred words to action and drinking to either of them. He was a wireman for the Interboro Rapid Transit Company, the I.R.T., and the most exciting thing that happened in their lives these days were their fights when they both had too much to drink. (President Wilson had repealed the prohibition of beer and wine, and a pail of beer from the corner bar was a luxury they needed, to forget.) Walter would threaten her if she didn't stop nagging him and Ellen would go on nagging, safe in the sad knowledge that Walter could never do anything, not to her, and not for her either.

So much for herself. And Walter. That left the children. Florence, her girl, was beautiful and from her first steps displayed a talent for dancing. Along with her cornflakes, Ellen fed the child the notion that she was going to be a star.

Then there was Wally, two years younger, slight like his father, with an impish and adorable grin. He too danced like a dream. Her real hopes

This page, facing page: The Brooklyn Apartment Building where Susan grew up —
2568 Bedford Ave.

were with Florence but there was no telling — Wally might very well make it, too. After all, her kids had talent in their veins.

Walter was half-English and half-Irish but the Irish side was pure starshine. His mother had been an actress in the Old Country and was still known by her stage name of Katie Harrigan. His sister had been one of the original Ziegfeld Girls and one brother was a musician. The closest Walter himself had ever come to 'show business' was when he worked as a barker for a Coney Island rollercoaster. But Walter — what the hell!

At least he'd given them something — the gift of Katie Harrigan's blood. Lots of the Irish who lived around them in that corner of Flatbush still remembered her. And someday, Ellen Marrener was determined, every one of them and everyone else in the world, too, would know the names of Florence and Wally Marrener.

All she had to do, Ellen told herself, was get through the winters that were cold and drab and the summers, when the heat that gathered on the narrow streets steamed up towards her fourth floor 'penthouse', and the

only cool spots anywhere were on the fire escapes or on the roof of the building; where you could look across the East River, past the Brooklyn Bridge to the skyscrapers of Manhattan.

CHILDHOOD

*This I was born with: an imagination
and a natural talent for lying.
The perfect ingredients for an actor.*

CHAPTER 2

Flatbush, covering approximately three and a half square miles, is located in the center of Brooklyn, about thirty minutes from midtown Manhattan by car, train, or bus. Indians had once lived there and now it was the home of many ethnic groups to which the Marreners could claim affinity with English and Irish stock on the father's side and Swedish on the mother's, although both Ellen and Walter were born in America.

Ellen's third and last child, little Edythe Marrener was born on the 30th of June 1917 Saturday — 'Saturday's child has to work for a living.' She was a tiny baby with bright hazel eyes, long brown lashes, with a tilt to her nose and her father's flame colored hair.

After her birth, Walter and Wally moved into one bedroom and Ellen and the girls stayed in the other, and that was the end of any further additions to the Marrener family.

On the day she was born Wally and Florrie ran in and out of the flat giddy with excitement, as they showed friends their new sister. Right from the beginning, there were people who called her 'Red' or 'Carrot top'. With that hair, there was no way to avoid it, just as there was no way for the beautiful baby to avoid Ellen Marrener's dreams.

Edythe's first summer was so like so many summers in Flatbush. The horses and wagons clattered up the hot street, the kids, on vacation from school, ran bare-foot and the canaries, perched in their cages in front parlors, chirped along with the clang of the trolley car bells, sounding as they passed along the street.

For grownups, their neighborhood was drab and unfulfilling but for children it had its attractions, however temporary.

Years later, Wally Marrener would recall; "a block from where we lived, Church Avenue turned into a dirt road and even further out there was farmland. You could walk just a little ways and come to a farmer's market."

Walter Sr. who worked in the subways from four p.m. until midnight rarely came home before early morning, and he treasured the little time he had with his children. On his occasional days off, feeling like a visitor to the unfamiliar daylight, he would take them to an empty lot for one of his favorite activities.

According to Wally, "My father loved kites. Loved to make them and loved to fly them. And E — I always called Susan (Edythe) that, just plain E — and I would go along and watch them soar up into the sky."

Walter also understood his children in a way that Ellen who was pre-occupied with turning Florrie into a star never could.

When little Edythe began to attend P.S. 181, she took a lot of teasing because of her bright hair and sometimes words would turn to blows. Edythe quickly developed a defensive chip on her shoulder as a result of certain incidents, and it remained with her for the rest of her life.

One day walking home from school alone a boy teased her, she answered back and he socked her.

Gripping her schoolbooks, she sat down on the front steps of her building with tears in her eyes. Her father, coming downstairs on his way to work, sat down beside her. Fighting back tears, she told him what had happened. He looked at his youngest, detecting the fighting spirit and hot temper of his Irish forebears.

"Always hit back," he said to his daughter, "and remember this, the harder they hit you, the higher you'll bounce — if you're a good ball to start with. If you're not, you might as well give up anyway."

The thin, tired man brushed back her hair from her eyes, got up and walked away.

She sat, staring after him.

As back up to his advice, he urged her to practice sparring with Wally. Soon the schoolmates who called her 'red' and 'pepper pot' were surprised at the fierceness with which she fought.

When Edythe was seven, she lived through the first significant event of her life. Just barely.

Late one afternoon — her father had already gone off to the subways — she was standing at the window in their flat, watching her brother and some friends fly kites on the sidewalk in front of the house.

Eager to join them, she ran to her mother and asked for 3¢ to buy a paper plane at the neighborhood candy store. Mrs. Marrener thought carefully, along with everything else milk had just gone up to 12½¢ a quart and every cent mattered. She looked at her seven year old, who looked back at her hopefully.

Ellen carefully counted out the pennies and gave them to the little girl, who whooped happily, as she dashed down the four flights of stairs to the street.

"I'll be right back Wal," she announced as she crossed to the candy store.
Out of habit, Wally said, "Be careful, E —"

But she was too excited at the prospect of playing with Wally and the big boys to be careful and as she dashed back across the street, a speeding car turned the corner and tossed her to the ground.

"Lying there, she looked just like a broken doll," Wally would remember many years later. "On the ground next to her was that paper plane of hers just soaked with her blood. The driver of the car picked her up in his arms and ran up the four flights of stairs to our flat. Then," he added wryly, "he ran down the stairs, straight to his bank to withdraw all his savings."

Doctors at the Free Clinic where Ellen took the girl told the distraught parents that they must expect the worst. Edythe would probably not live. But the little red-haired youngster was tougher than anyone realized. She hung on, and hung on; finally, painfully, pulling herself out of death's reach. The doctors marveled.

"Yes," they finally told her parents, "She will live. But prepare yourselves. She has two fractured legs and a broken hip and she will be a cripple for the rest of her life. She will never walk again."

For six months, Edythe was a prisoner in a complicated structure of plaster casts and traction lines, unable to move, unable to do anything more than look out the window of the bedroom towards Manhattan.

The temperament that would so ably portray the courage of Jane Froman (herself crippled by a plane crash) in the screenplay *With A Song In My Heart* may have begun to take shape on that sultry day in Brooklyn, when a little girl, against all medical advice and odds, struggled to walk again.

But it was not a totally unhappy time. What had happened to the little Marrener girl was shocking enough to have touched a nerve in the entire neighborhood. The car that ran her down could just as easily have broken the bodies of any of their children. That's the way those things happened.

"After she was back from the hospital," Wally remembered, "the ladies from the church brought over a big bag of toys and she was allowed to open one each day that she was laid up in bed. She got a big kick out of that. It added a little surprise."

The reward for the pain and the suffering was her first taste of fame — and she liked it.

"Then when she got out of traction, we were able to take her out. But she still couldn't bend one leg and she couldn't walk at all, so my folks bought her the longest wagon they could find, and we used to pull her around in that."

The little girl in her wagon, with her crown of shining hair became a neighborhood favorite, a slum princess pulled through her streets by willing and loving hands.

Eventually, the wagon gave way to crutches.

"And those she hated. So she began spending most of her time alone in the flat, mostly in the kitchen — that was her favorite room."

Looking around her, at the tawdry furnishings, she began to be acutely aware of the drabness of her surroundings and looking out the windows of the kitchen, at the pole where all the washlines were attached, she realized that she hated the view. More and more the sheets on those washlines became curtains, which rose on the private dramas she began to act out in her imagination.

At the end of six months, she went back to school but she had changed. Always aloof, she became even more so, offering her friendship to very few of her schoolmates.

Edythe, even then, was not just a regular kid on the block.

"E was choosy in picking friends, if she didn't like you she would have nuthin' to do with you. The neighbors thought she was snobbish," said Wally. "I used to watch after E and after she got a little older she had her own friends. She brought kids home to do homework on the kitchen table, Martha and Sarah Finkelstein and Ira Gossell (who later became actor Jeff Chandler); he was a little fat kid from around the corner, about half a block away."

And she began to lie.

"I can still remember walking home from school," she was quoted as saying years later, "telling the other children about all the beautiful dresses I had at home in the closet — lying through my teeth! I guess that's when I first began acting, or at least getting interested in it. Pretending, making believe, using my imagination. This I was born with; an imagination and natural talent for lying. The perfect ingredients for an actor."

The accident brought with it another foreshadowing of the 'Susan Hayward' to come. As a result of it, her hips were unbalanced and one leg was a quarter of an inch shorter than the other. For the rest of her life, she wore a lift in one shoe. But even with the lift, she was left with an odd, rolling gait. At the time that it happened, it was one more part of her ordeal. Later on, it became the 'sexy' walk that characterized her to the world.

As a child, she was drawn to the bizarre and the dramatic. Sometimes when Ellen Marrener was busy, Edythe's sister, Florence, was forced to mind the two young ones and she would often take them to a nearby cemetery where they could wander through the grounds, pausing here and there to read a tombstone or two. Sometimes they would watch, spellbound, as a funeral procession moved slowly past them.

On days when they tired of reading who was resting in peace, Florence would take them to the Kings County Hospital; known throughout the Borough of Brooklyn as the place they put the "crazies." Standing safely outside the huge iron gates, they would make faces at the patients on the lawn inside until they finally caught someone's eye. When he or she came towards them, they would shriek in horror and run away.

The trips they enjoyed most were to nearby farms, not more than a five to ten minute walk away. They would pick tomatoes and eat them sprinkled with salt taken from their kitchen or try for a handful of corn stalks, until they were caught and chased out of the field.

Most of the time, Florence was too busy to bother with the other two. As she grew up, she remained pretty and proud of her good figure and her golden-reddish hair. Ellen Marrener had sold her own faith in Florence to a relative more solvent than the rest of the family who believing that Florence could indeed make it in the professional world, paid for her dancing lessons and encouraged her to devote all her time to preparing for a career.

More and more, Wally became responsible for entertaining Edythe.

There were places she disliked violently. One was the public swimming pool, which, to most slum children, was a glorious escape during the sweltering days of summer. To Edythe, it was disgusting, with towels that remained gray and dingy no matter how often they were laundered and a smell of sweat clinging to the locker rooms no matter how carefully they were cleaned.

She much preferred going to Coney Island with Wally, ambling down the boardwalk, smelling the cool salty air, listening to the waves, then finally going into Steeplechase 'the friendly place' as it was billed. The vast entertainment park with its rides and food stands and fun houses was the pride of Coney.

Once inside, the two youngsters would seek out 'the friendly people' with the Combination Tickets. Very often, when the happy possessors of these prizes left the park, they would turn over their tickets to Wally and E. The combination offered 10 rides for 50¢ and most of the time there were a few unpunched, and the two Marrener children would remedy that immediately.

She also loved going to the neighborhood library and almost as soon as she learned to read, Edythe developed an insatiable appetite, going through everything on the shelves, even the encyclopedias.

A few years later, she would discover Thomas Wolfe and devour every word he wrote. To her it seemed incredible that the North Carolina writer had actually lived in Brooklyn at the same time that she did. So deep was her devotion to him that the neighborhood librarians gave her a nickname. Privately, they called her "the Wolfe girl."

But true heaven was in the theatres — The Brooklyn Paramount, Fox, Flatbush and Kenmore. At the crack of dawn, she and Wally would stand in line and willingly trade in their hard-to-come-by 15¢ for admission to the First Show. When it was finished and the auditorium cleared, they would hide in the bathrooms, and then sneak back into the auditorium. By the time the theatre closed at night, they were heady not only from hunger, but from seeing three complete shows.

Vaudeville performers began to recognize them (whenever they could they sat in the front row) and they began to ask 'the little redheaded girl' to climb on stage to help with the magic tricks.

'The little redheaded girl' got another turn in the spotlight when she and Wally won an amateur dancing contest. They were there courtesy of Florence, who, at seventeen, was entering all the dance contests and talent competitions she could find in Brooklyn, Queens, Long Island and New Jersey. At one of them, there was a special competition for 'amateurs' and the two little ones, who'd picked up some of her routines, entered and won.

Florence, who had never actually won anything herself, shrugged it off. Let the children play if they wanted to. Florence was headed for more important things than "prizes."

Being a woman of limited emotional range, Ellen Marrener focused almost all of her attention on Florence. Though little Edythe talked all the time about being an actress, her mother paid no attention. To her it was just "child talk." As far as she was concerned, the accident had retired the girl permanently from the great game of success.

Besides making kites, Walter also made radio sets and on his few evenings away from his job, he would plant himself at the kitchen table and put sets together. Edythe and Wally would sit next to him, looking on in absolute fascination. When he had finished, he would give each of them a turn at the headset, letting them listen to music and voices that came in "out of nowhere."

Edythe's sense of responsibility was implanted at twelve years old, when she helped her brother deliver his newspapers for the Brooklyn Eagle.

"Years after the accident, she used to help me with the Sunday editions — they were so big. We'd pile the papers in the wagon and she'd help me deliver 'em. I used to give her money to go to the movies, and get ice cream — things like that," Wally explained, "she never tried to get out of it, even if it was cold and raining or snowing hard."

On such days, Wally would sometimes stop to cup his hands around his mouth and blow some warm breath through his fingers that were numb from the cold. E would wait a minute or two and say, "Come on Wal, let's get goin', sooner we'll get home," and give the wagon a push from behind.

Actually, she was learning many things. One was the fact that her family was poor, another that the neighborhood was poor. When the country ran crashing into the Depression, the Marrener's became even poorer. They had to move from their red brick 'penthouse' on Church Avenue to a shabbier, smaller and more crowded place at 2568 Bedford Avenue. Just hanging on became harder and harder.

Edythe and Wally, like a lot of Brooklyn kids, collected junk — mostly paper — in a wagon made from a wooden soapbox with solid wooden wheels. They would get about a penny for ten pounds of paper but pennies could be changed into nickels and dimes to buy a 10¢ gallery seat at a matinee.

Sometimes Ellen Marrener would give Edythe a few household chores, which she would try to get out of by offering to go to the stores for her mother. It was more fun to go to the bakery for a ¼ loaf of Jewish rye bread — 'and see that it's fresh' — , smell the fresh baked poppy seed rolls that she loved, and gaze longingly over all the trays of raisin and cinnamon buns with icing on top. And 'day olds' were always cheaper. At the butcher shop she would ask for a nickel's worth of tongue 'the end of the tongue' she would say. Then on to the local grocer.

"Hi, red," they would greet her. Her face burned at the name and seeing her reaction, they quickly became serious about her order. It would then be penciled in as a charge and a subtotal given, to be paid on a Saturday when Poppa got his bi-monthly paycheck.

On her way home she would go through Woolworth's Department Store, passing the perfume counters, 'just to smell it,' and look at the rhinestone jewelry and clothes racks. Walking slowly home, she would stop in front of store windows, to press her upturned nose against the glass and wonder what it would be like to have money.

Her arms filled with grocery shopping bags, she would pass the other little girls in ragged dresses, and scruffy boys in straggling knickerbockers and peaked caps.

Sometimes she would stop in front of a house to admire a shining brown gelding with black mane pulling a small wagon, with an old Italian man holding the reins. There were horses too, on the outskirts of her Aunt and Uncle's place in New Jersey, where she would occasionally be sent for a summer visit, which was as close to being in the country as she ever came.

"Birthdays at the Marrener home were no big deal. Mom baked a cake or pie, and that was it," Wally said, "at Easter time we'd get a chocolate egg, or a rabbit or something. On Thanksgiving, we used to dress up in a masquerade, fill up socks with chalk and whack people with it. Flo didn't go; didn't do much of anything except stay in her own little word, dancin' mostly."

"E loved Christmas," Wally continued. "She'd be makin' all kinds of things, paintin' pictures, cards; we hadn't any money for real gifts. We'd do our Christmas shoppin' in the 5 & 10, typical of families in Brooklyn in those days. We'd wait 'til Christmas Eve to get a free tree from the stands — 'cause you knew if they didn't sell the trees they were goin' to reduce them to practically nothin'. When it got to a certain point in the evening they figured they might as well give 'em away. We used to wait 'till the last minute, when they were throwin' trees away, and go down the street and pick one up and haul it home."

"Our parents gave us what presents they could. We'd always hang up stockings. We didn't have a regular fireplace, a mantle piece or something would do. As we got older, we got less and less. We used to get apples, oranges, candy and nuts. One time I got a bottle of medicine I had to take this fish oil, to build myself up, Scott's Emulsion."

One Christmas they got a sleigh. Bundled up they went to Prospect Park not too far away, where there were some hills. Then finally, there were only gift-wrapped lumps of coal. In the language of poverty, they said, "that's the end — no more toys for you."

No more toys for Edythe instead there were her own private pleasures that she began to seek out. Riding on an open-air double-decker bus, for instance, that could take her for a nickel, from the Battery in downtown Manhattan, past the lions of the Main Public Library, up Fifth Avenue and past Central Park.

Sometimes she'd get off at the library, go in and wander around, browsing through the books and soaking up the atmosphere of learning, which was later to become so much a part of her own life.

And sometimes — best of all — she'd walk along 42nd Street or Broadway, past the wonderful new Roxy Theatre that glittered and shone like no other place in the world.

She said from the beginning, that she intended to be an actress and she was diligent in pursuing the theatre, Flatbush style. No club, church or society in the neighborhood could start casting a play without the little Marrener girl turning up for it. When she wasn't cast in a part, she would volunteer to do costumes, begging and borrowing material to make her creations.

As she approached her teens, Edythe began to think again about her grandmother, Katie Harrigan, her aunt, the Ziegfeld girl, and her uncle who played in a combo in Coney Island. They had all made careers in show business. She would, too.

She was aware that she needed to study and learn, so she sought out a local drama 'coach' and told him that she was interested in taking lessons.

Looking at the youngster, it was clear to him that the only way she could take lessons would be as a "scholarship student." Nevertheless, he told her to recite something for him.

Although she'd acted in a number of shows, Edythe suddenly found herself on the verge of panic. This was serious business! This could make a tremendous difference in her whole life! The more she thought about it, the more nervous she became and her normally high voice pitched even higher.

After a few minutes, the coach indicated that she could stop.

"You have a bad voice," he told her. "It's high. It's squeaky. And you have an accent."

"What kind of an accent?" she asked.

"A Brooklyn accent."

"But *this is Brooklyn.*"

"The students I work with do not have Brooklyn accents."

Then grudgingly accepting reality, he added, "Or if they do, they lose them quickly."

Edythe refused to be put off. Sitting down, she pleaded her case. Her voice was steady but the handkerchief she kept twisting and untwisting, and her legs, which she kept crossing and uncrossing, indicated what was going on inside her.

"Well, that's why it's so important for me to study with you. So I can learn to speak right. I'm going to be an actress — a professional actress," she ended in an unusual burst of confidence.

The coach smiled thinly.

"I wouldn't waste my time if I were you, Miss…"

"Marrener. Edythe Marrener. Why not?"

"Because you're never going to make it. It's bad enough not to speak well. But even worse, you don't understand the basic responsibility of every actress."

"What do you mean —"

"You must be meticulous about your personal appearance."

She looked at him in amazement. She had dressed carefully putting on each newly laundered piece of clothing as if it were part of a nun's habit.

"You have a hole in your shoe."

Edythe nodded, too proud to explain that she had only one pair of shoes and the cardboard in them had just worn through.

Now that he had systematically destroyed the girl, the coach smiled — "Actually, you're a very pretty little girl and I'm sure there are all sorts of things in the cards for you — "

Without another word, Edythe got up to leave. His inability to evoke a subservient reaction irritated the coach.

"The most amusing part of this," he said, "is that you obviously came here expecting to win some sort of *scholarship.*"

In those days, daughters of the poor could put their time to more profitable use than going to High School. But when she graduated from grammar school, Edythe was determined to go on with her education, and she enrolled at Girls Commercial.

Here again, she was standoffish to the other students. Although she was scholastically eligible for the Arista, the Honor Society, she never made it because it required endorsements from all the other members. Edythe's often prickly tongue kept her from having many friends.

"What's she got to be so stuck up about?" the other girls asked each other, seeing in her nothing more than another product of the Brooklyn slums, no better than they were. If anything, she wasn't even as good as they were, with her one blouse that she wore every day and washed every night. Everyone was poor, but it seemed that the Marreners were even poorer.

What few people saw was that underneath the almost ludicrous snobbery was a very frightened youngster, mistrustful of everyone and constantly on her guard against ridicule.

"The only way I knew how to protect myself," she later explained, "was to try to scare people before they scared me."

At Girls Commercial, she spent a great deal of time in the library, letting herself get caught up in the shining web of words that Thomas Wolfe spun for her. It was also in that library, she read for the first time, George Bernard Shaw's play about Eliza the flower girl who becomes a great lady.

When she read Pygmalion, she might have wished for some Professor Henry Higgins to come into her life and turn it around but she knew that the chance of that was not too likely. What of it! She would be her *own* Professor Higgins and make herself into someone the whole world would know and admire.

No question about it. She would be an actress.

One of the women in the Dramatics Department was named Eleanor O'Grady. After she heard Edythe read for the first time, she called her into her office.

"I believe you have real talent," she told the girl. "Have you ever thought about making performing your career?"

Had she ever thought —!

If she hadn't been afraid to reveal herself to anyone, she might have told the nice looking middle aged woman that she had thought of nothing else since she was a little girl playing Cinderella at P.S. 181. She might have told her about Katie Harrigan, and about the times she'd been called onstage by the magicians at the Vaudeville Theatre.

She might have said that hearing someone else tell her she had talent had finally made it real. Instead, she said in a tone that was almost too self-assured, "I'm going to be an actress, Miss O'Grady. I decided that a long time ago."

Miss O'Grady was perceptive enough to see through the emotional armor Edythe wore as regularly as she did her one blouse.

She saw to it, from then on, that Edythe was given leads in school productions. Her undemanding faith finally paid off. The girl permitted her to become a friend.

She'd always been selective about her friends.

In grade school, one of the few kids who fit her standards for friendship was Ira Grossell, whose family owned a candy store. They'd been cast together in Cinderella. Ira had been the Prince until the onset of puberty suddenly made his voice crack and turned the Prince into a silent Stage Manager.

He was a chubby boy with warm, sensitive eyes and a sweet smile. The thing they had in common was their love of movies and plays and the fact that both planned to act for a living.

When Edythe went off to Girls Commercial High School, her friendship with Ira ended. Now and then, she would see him in front of his family's candy store, and though she was aware that he was getting taller and quite handsome, they never fell into the 'dating' pattern of most teenagers.

Both of them were too busy 'getting out' and in a hurry to do it.

For in those days, in her mid-teens, Edythe was very much a young girl in a hurry.

The boys who had called her 'red' as a child, the ones who had tied tin cans to her bicycle when she was a twelve year old tomboy, suddenly became more aware of her long flaming hair and her pretty face. They began calling her 'red' again but this time there was something different in the way they said it, something taunting and a little nasty. After all, she was a redhead, and everyone knew that redheads were fiery, selfish, mean — and sexy.

"You find, as you approach the dating age," said Susan, "that men are divided into two divisions; the curious and wary. The latter seem to give redheaded women a wide berth, probably figuring they're too hot to handle. The former take the attitude that inasmuch as there are fewer redheads than blondes or brunettes, they must be different somehow. And if you want to find out check with one of the curious type; pinned down, he'll admit it!"

But if you noticed her and sought her out, she couldn't care less. There was no place in her life for the likes of them. She had no intention of ending up in a Brooklyn tenement, tied down with children and a husband who worked in a dull routine job.

It was much safer, and more satisfying to concentrate on celluloid lovers. There were a series of them, but the object of her special adoration was Ronald Colman. Elegant, gentle and world weary though he was, perhaps the most appealing thing about him to the Brooklyn girl was the beautiful way in which he spoke English, turning words into music. Someday, she told herself, she too would speak like that.

Focused as she was on herself and her future, it was a shock sometimes to look up from studying at the kitchen table and look at her family for a moment.

Ellen Marrener's brown hair was almost entirely grey. Her father seemed even slighter than his five feet five and one hundred and forty pounds should make him. His flame-bright hair had turned white and the glasses that kept slipping off his nose made him seem almost a sad figure.

Florence had quit High School long ago. Though she had slipped and fallen, and hurt her tailbone, she was determined as ever to keep on dancing. Wally had quit High School too and was working full time during the day.

But she, Edythe, would never quit. Not High School. Not anything. The mirrors in the Marrener's flat told her she was young and healthy and beautiful. And whether the world went through a Depression again — or another War, from the way people were beginning to talk, didn't really matter to her. She would get through it just fine.

It was Saturday, June 30, 1934, and after three days of temperatures hovering near 100 degrees, the mercury mercifully dropped. That morning Edythe Marrener joined her mother and sister at the kitchen table.

Mrs. Marrener was talking to Florrie about Mrs. Anna Antonio, the twenty eight year old mother convicted with two men for the murder of her husband. For the second time in twenty-four hours, the condemned woman had won a reprieve from Governor Lehman. Florrie read the morning's headlines — Woman Again Gets Stay of Execution In The Final Hours.

"Mom, can't we talk about somethin' else, it's my birthday remember?" Edythe reminded her, "I'm seventeen today."

Edythe Marrener couldn't possibly know that twenty years later she herself would portray the role of another convicted murderess, suffering similar circumstances, in a performance that would shock the movie going public around the world.

A few years before, far away from Brooklyn in Atlanta, Georgia, an unknown woman of thirty-six, had been grinding out a manuscript for over ten years, despairing with it and stuffing chairs and cupboards with chapters wrapped in brown paper. When finally assembled it became one of the great classics that the 30's produced — *Gone With The Wind.*

If it had not been for that one (and only) book written by the Atlanta housewife, perhaps the destiny of Edythe Marrener might have taken a different path. For certainly, *Gone With The Wind* changed the lives of both women.

Something about its characters; Scarlett O'Hara, the beautiful willful Daughter of the Confederacy; Ashley Wilkes, the man she pursued; Rhett Butler, the romantic rogue who pursued her; Melanie Wilkes, the kindest and gentlest of women; captured the minds and hearts of the American public as no book had since perhaps, *Uncle Tom's Cabin* almost a century ago.

When it was announced that *Gone With The Wind* was going to be made into a film, the country went crazy and the search for a girl to play the stunning, half-Irish Katie Scarlett knocked almost everything else off the front page.

Her final starring role at High School…

Wally, her mother and her father sat in the audience. Florence, who was practically the financial mainstay of the family at that point, was out dancing professionally.

But it was she, Edythe, the one her mother never took seriously and the one with the lift in her shoe, who was center stage.

Even though she wasn't making a cent as an actress — yet — she was sure that someday soon she would be making real money. Then she'd show Florence who the star of the family really was.

Unfortunately for the poor, 'someday' doesn't pay the rent or put food on the table. The Marreners reminded her that they'd sacrificed enough just to keep her in High School long after other girls were working in shops or factories, or for the telephone company.

Susan under studio contract.

CAREER

If I were starting out in this day and age, I don't think I would choose an acting career. The motion picture has all changed so tremendously. I think I'd be much more attracted to a career in something like archaeology or geology. Acting, no.

CHAPTER 3

"Susan lived at home until she went to Hollywood," Wally told me. As for the boys she left behind — "There was only one boy who used to come down to the dances that she was interested in. He went to the same church as we did, Lenox Road Baptist Church. The boy was a piano player. Susan had a little crush on him but it didn't last. There were other boyfriends but her mind was on her career."

Graduating from Brooklyn's Girls Commercial High School, the highlight of her school days was a $75 prize she won in an art contest when she was eighteen.

She took the money to invest in a career on Broadway. Producers and directors weren't exactly waiting for her. Acting upon the advice of a friend, she enrolled in the Feagan School of Dramatic Arts in Rockefeller Center, New York City. She went after the much talked about 'experience.'

Lack of money resulted in her looking for work as a model. At this time, there was a big boom in color photography and a natural redhead would be in.

Edythe (she changed the spelling of her name to have a 'classier' sound to it) had grown up 'hand-me-down-dress-poor' in the shadow of her mother's favoritism toward her sister Florence. Ellen Marrener still dressed her in what she considered demure high school clothes. Her eyebrows weren't plucked, she wore no trace of make-up, lipstick or rouge, yet determined as she was, she started the rounds of modeling agencies.

As usual, always in a hurry and with her red hair flying she walked fast and furiously to save money. Her hip rolling gait was not affected by a reminder of her pelvic fractures, which had knit incorrectly when her mother had taken her to a free clinic instead of an orthopedist.

Edythe checked the yellow pages of the Manhattan phone book tearing off the listings for model agencies. On a hunch, she picked out what she thought were the best by their addresses. Acting impulsively on that same hunch she walked into the Walter Thornton Agency and asked for a job.

One of Edythe's girl friends from Astoria, Long Island, Margaret Lane reminisced about those days back in 1938.

"We had to break into modeling the hard way then. Armed with a folio of our pictures and a scrapbook, we'd call on photographers, artists and fashion directors — and there were about 500 of them on the list."

"When we waited in reception rooms together, clutching our scrapbooks and hoping, Susan was scared, but she was wise enough to concentrate on the positive — the strong belief she had in herself. She became artist Jon Whitcomb's most beguiling cover girl when he began to draw her wistful, saucy loveliness, and that was the start of her climb as a model."

Edythe not only found favor with the well known illustrator Jon Whitcomb but the Walter Thornton Agency needing a true red head, and not having one, they became interested.

With her red hair, hazel eyes, good teeth and small but well proportioned figure, she was registered.

"As a model," she said later, "I didn't get more than a few days work a month. At $35 a day, from ads — bread, cereal, toothpaste, soaps and appearing in mail order catalogues. I was always the other girl at the picnic."

Thornton himself said of her, "She was a real lone wolf, a girl with no time for friends or social life."

As a photographer's model, it was the color photographs taken by Ivan Dimitri, illustrating a national magazine article in the *Saturday Evening Post* that first got her attention.

Titled 'How Models Come To New York', Edythe was quoted as saying, 'in my case, by subway.'

"After the article came out," Wally remembered, "agents came to the house in Brooklyn. My father was in the hospital at the time, he had had a heart attack at work — so he had no say in the matter. My mother had to give her permission for her to go to Hollywood."

Edythe read everything about David O. Selznick searching for an unknown to play Scarlett O'Hara. Although the book emphasizes Scarlett's dark hair — this time the studio wanted some red heads. And she believed it all. She read the book. She was half-Irish like Scarlett and a redhead and wanted to get in on it somehow. Besides, she was no stranger to the camera, having done a Vitaphone short scene as a hat model.

Agents from the Warner Brothers New York office offered her a $50 a week contract. There were other offers but the one that most excited her was from the David O. Selznick New York office. The story goes that director George Cukor was thumbing through the magazine when his eyes lighted on Susan. Another was that Cukor saw her on the cover of the *Saturday Evening Post*, which would have been difficult as that issue with the Marrener model in color came out October 7, 1939 when *Gone With The Wind* had completed shooting.

Finally, George Cukor, bored with the 'discovery' story said over the phone, very succinctly — "She was brought to my office by her agent."

The only person available to go with 18 year old Edythe to California was Florence, 6 years her senior. Florence felt this was her chance too; she might get a test and break into the movies once they got to Hollywood. Edythe really wanted her brother Wally to go with her, but he was needed at home.

Edythe and Florence took the train to California. They found cheap rooms and began the rounds of agent's offices. The names vary, but Benny Medford's name appears more than any other, as the agent who brought her to George Cukor. She would be just one more girl in the hundreds who would get a test for Scarlett, in the biggest publicity gimmick of the year. There were girls from all over the country waiting for even a second look.

Streetwise Edythe sized up the situation — it was tough for girls trying to break into the movies.

Never, it seemed, had there been a place on earth where men enjoyed the privilege that they did in that community. The cause was obvious. Hundreds of the most beautiful girls in American — the majority sadly deficient in talent and worldly experience — flocked to Hollywood each year. Never more so than in the year of the casting for *Gone With The Wind*. The line stretched from the studio lots through every agent's office, to any party given by any man with some free money who wanted to provide someplace for food and drinks and, most importantly, contacts.

At these parties, most of the lovely girls met a few unattractive men with little influence. There were hundreds of pretty girls waiting to be discovered, but few with Edythe Marreners real talent, who through sheer perseverance and ability got up every time they were slapped down and finally literally demanded recognition.

On September 20, 1937 at $50 a week at the Warner Brothers Studios in Burbank, she began working as an extra on her six month contract.

In her very first film, *Hollywood Hotel* Louella Parsons, the powerful Hearst columnist would play herself in a movie based on her radio show. Edythe Marrener was put on the film as an extra.

Warners wanted to change Edythe's name and she was holding out for her grandmother's name, Katie Harrigan, but they laughed her down. From now on, it would be Susan Hayward.

The newly christened Susan Hayward made an important and influential contact on the set of *Hollywood Hotel* — the self-acclaimed Queen of Gossip, Louella Parsons.

Next at Warners, she did a small bit as a telephone operator in the Bette Davis — Erroll Flynn potboiler *The Sisters*. The unbilled Susan Hayward in the film would be billed over the formidable Miss Davis the next time they were in another picture together.

Following this, she was assigned to *Girls on Probation* putting her 10th in the credits under the up and coming Ronald Reagan. She was back to no billing again in *Comet Over Broadway* before her option was dropped by the studio. During this time, in between filming, she posed for cheesecake pin-up stills, which she disliked so intensely she would never agree to do the same again.

"Susan really got kicked around and I think it got to her," producer Marty Rackin said, "Jack Warner, the head of Warner Bros., used to say that an actor on his ass, was worth two on his feet and he kept them that way. Susan was shy and very insecure then and after the Warner treatment she never let down her guard."

While waiting for her chance to test for *Gone With The Wind*, Paramount OK'd a test for her at their studio, to be directed by Henry Hathaway.

Contrary to popular opinion, this, in fact, was her very first screen test, not the one for *Gone With the Wind*; "As a matter of fact I took her very first screen test. She was 18. I did the test that got her into Paramount. She chose a recitation *Alter Ego*, by Arch Obler. She recited that for the test. It was made in color because of her red hair. She was marvelous, just sensational. It was 15 minutes, a whole reel; it was made on nitrate (which disintegrates). She was not nervous or in awe. She wasn't in awe of anybody in her life, except maybe, Selznick. I wasn't around to know but maybe him. But he would be the only one that I would imagine she might be in awe of. Her *Gone With The Wind* test came *after* that," he repeated. "She did that *Alter Ego* test and eventually it got her a contract at Paramount."

Alter Ego was the story of a girl with a double-personality one good, one bad, with the evil one fighting to take over the weaker good side. It was a female version of Jekyll and Hyde and was made into a feature film in 1945 called *Bewitched* starring Phyllis Thaxter.

At 19 years of age, Susan did finally test for Scarlett, and then did over 100 other tests with young actors who were trying out for the part of Ashley Wilkes. While testing she held out hopes for Scarlett and resisted other studio possibilities.

Glenn Langan was one of the young actors who tested with Susan for the role of Ashley Wilkes. "The scene from *Gone With The Wind* used for my test was the one during which Scarlett, after the death of her second husband, washed her mouth out with cologne so Rhett Butler will not know she had been drinking." Langan believed Susan looked right for Scarlett, however inexperienced.

While she was awaiting word, Susan's father died in a Brooklyn hospital at the age of 59. "When he passed away," her brother said, "Susan called and asked us, "Why don't you come out to California? So I quit my job and my mother and I took the Greyhound bus to California, it was her first trip anywhere, her first time out of Brooklyn. That was early in 1938."

Meanwhile, Wally remembered, "Her agent told her, 'If you can hold out a little longer I'll get you a better deal on the contract.' She could have had a contract at $75 a week but this agent was holding out for $350 to start with, we all wanted it for her. She said, 'Once you start low you might stay low.' She had a good mind and she was pretty cagey with a buck."

Then, on November 18, 1937, in a memo to Mr. Daniel T. O'Shea Selznick wrote; "I think we can forget about Susan Hayward... we don't need her anymore as a stand-in for Scarlett, or to work with people we are testing for the other role, what with others around..."

According to Henry Hathaway, "The biggest disappointment in her life, that maybe set her off, was she thought she was going to be Scarlett. She was shook by it. They wanted some new person — what the hell! Vivien Leigh was unknown. She would have been equally as good as Vivien Leigh playing that part. Selznick didn't care at that time who it was, just so she was beautiful, brilliant, and full of belligerence — and she was. She was Scarlett! If ever there was one she was an instinctively good actress, she could have handled it."

Asked by a reporter about it years later, Hayward said, as if excusing herself for not getting the part; "It would have been the shortest career on record. I was 16½ (19) years old and I didn't know where the camera was. I was just one amongst many who were brought there — sort of a publicity thing. I think they knew all along who was gonna play Scarlett."

AT EASE

Some people have to be constantly amused. I don't. I don't have to be surrounded by people or "entertained."

CHAPTER 4

For quick money and because she had heard you got cases of the product, Susan anonymously took a posing job again for a Shredded Wheat advertisement. About this experience at that time, she said, "I glanced out of the window at the cheap bungalow court where we all lived, my mother, brother and sister. I studied the worn couch with broken springs, the splintering chairs causing runs in my nylons and all the free samples of Shredded Wheat from the company we had to eat..."

It was six months later that she landed her contract at Paramount, in 1939, cast in a small part replacing Frances Farmer who was tied up in a play in New York, or in a sanatorium as believed.

At Paramount, as one of the new starlets, she recalled; "What I remembered most was the mop closet (the dressing room) all the studios were crowded in those days and they stuck many of us brash upstarts into cubbyholes which barely gave us room to turn around in let alone change costumes and clean up."

At a starting salary of $250 a week, she made her first appearance in *Beau Geste*, with Gary Cooper and Ray Milland. She received fifth billing but no mention in the reviews. From there, she went up to second place for *Our Leading Citizen*, a minor effort, and dropped to fourth place in another poor film *$1,000 A Touchdown*. She began a new year and a new picture- *Among The Living*. This part, as a small town vamp, seemed to portend the role of a vixen, which she was to portray so well throughout her career.

The Scarlett test had an adverse effect on her when she was new at Paramount. She had preconceived, stubborn notions of her ability.

The studio gave a party to introduce all the young hopefuls and all the super-stars and successful actresses were there, Claudette Colbert, Paulette Goddard, and Marlene Dietrich, the studio's biggest box-office names of the time.

To Susan it was a learning experience: "All my life I've been terribly frightened of people. At the studio, it was the casting director, the cameramen, reporters and publicists who asked endless questions. I thought everyone was so brilliant and I felt so inadequate. At this party, those famous stars seemed so poised, so sure of themselves. Or so I thought. That's when I got the idea that I should try to be like them."

People at the studio advised her to change because her attitude was wrong. She stopped being herself and tried to copy everyone else. She got so mixed up and became more confused than ever. The ones who tried to help her make changes approached her the wrong way. They criticized her and as a result, she became belligerent.

"Her agent tried to get her to put on more of a front," Wally said, "he told her that she should have a house with a swimming pool and a big car."

She objected to this, "If you keep me working," she told her agent, "when will I be able to enjoy all of that. I don't need a swimming pool so all the drifters can come in while I'm working and use it." Later on when she could afford it, she would by herself Christmas presents, like a fur coat one year, a diamond ring the next. She enjoyed spending money but she was still careful.

Louella Parsons did not forget the little redhead who apple-polished her with attention while at Warners. She chose her along with a few other promising players, including Jane Wyman and Ronald Reagan to begin a Vaudeville Tour on November 13, 1939, in Santa Barbara; then on to the Golden Gate Theatre in San Francisco, Philadelphia, Pittsburg, Baltimore, New York, Washington D.C. and Chicago. Throughout the tour the cast did 4-5 shows a day of songs, dances and skits. Susan did sketches with Reagan in which she slapped his face after an innocent remark he made. She hit him hard enough for him to remember to this day. It was believed that Susan and Jane Wyman were enemies from the start, over Susan's interest in Reagan, who was Wyman's fiancé. Mostly Susan did an 'is anybody here from Brooklyn' routine. She endeared herself to Louella for the rest of the columnist's life, and when they returned to Hollywood, Louella would start the publicity ball rolling for the ambitious starlet."

Items began to appear with regularity in her column, usually telling the studio they should give her better parts. Meanwhile Susan's elocution lessons were laying on a finishing school accent over her pure Brooklynese. She joined the dozen promising players at Paramount — The Golden Circle.

One of that group Richard Webb has not forgotten their first meeting; "I met up with her around 1940. She was a beautiful gal with a husky voice that turned me on. I would say she was a 'ballsy' gal. I was under contract there and the guy who handled Veronica Lake's and my publicity was

Cecil Perril. They were trying to push their new actors all the time and Cecil arranged some things. Susan and I did some publicity poses around the pool of the Beverly Hills Hotel. One week they had me engaged to Martha O'Driscol in print, the next week to Ssan Hayward. Susan was highly intelligent, very alert, and had a tremendous character. I thought of all the girls, that she would make it."

Susan with Ronald Reagan.

Susan's advancing movie career affected her mother who became increasingly pretentious. Ellen Marrener still believed that when Florence got her break she would outdistance her younger sister. After all, Florrie was beautiful compared to Susan and she could dance whereas Susan could not. Florence was a hit in Holly wood with all the men who turned around for a second look at the lovely girl. While she looked back, Susan only looked straight ahead for better jobs and bigger parts in the business.

Susan took an increasing interest in astrology; looking for answers or guideposts to help direct her life. Commenting on this she said, "I've been interested in it for years. I have all the books and read them from cover to cover. I'm a Cancer with a Leo rising, which gives you a tip. I'm very much as my sign says, moody, the sensitivity and all that — but otherwise I'm much more a Leo."

Whether it was the planets or her intuition that moved her to step out of line in front of a studio sales convention for exhibitors she took the opportunity to speak her mind. Chosen to say welcoming words, Hayward said compulsively; "Several of you have asked why I'm not in more Paramount Pictures and that's a damned interesting question."

Then addressing herself directly to studio chief Y. Frank Freeman. "Well, Mr. Freeman do I get a break or don't I?"

"Things became easier after that," she said, "Anyway I always saw the thing as a job. I was never late. I always learned my lines and I did what the director told me to do because he was the boss. I didn't party. I went home and read or studied. I didn't romance anybody for work, no way. I wanted to make it right."

Susan fancied herself older than her years when she hit Hollywood. One evening, on one of her rare evenings on the town, at the nightspot Macambo, she was sitting with two overbearing young men who were giving her the full treatment in open admiration. Reporter Harry Evans spotted her and getting an introduction told her he'd like to do an article on here.

"Why?" Susan asked.

"Because I admired your work in your last picture very much," he replied.

"Oh yes," she said. "My latest non-starring film. If you decide to do this article, I have some special photographs to illustrate it — snapped from the neck down. You can reach me through any unimportant press agent at Paramount. And thanks for the compliment," she added, dismissing him. "I didn't know I looked so young and naïve."

To her he was just another aggressive Hollywood character trying to get her phone number. Her belligerence that night at the Macambo had become her natural reflex, developed as a kid from Brooklyn with a chip on her shoulder and a determination to beat every male Hollywood smarty. In all, she had become overly suspicious and very pugnacious. She would not be like some of the others who had their spirit beaten down to the point where they would play ball with anybody.

Henry Hathaway, among others, agreed with that comment; "She never slept around, not at all, she wasn't a flirt."

Susan handled men on their own terms, as she said, "I've been fortunate. I've always been liberated, but circumstances differ with each woman. I think that if a woman does the same job as a man, she should get the same respect but I personally don't want to be in competition with a man. I would rather have him lead the way, with slight encouragement from me, of course. And some nudging to make sure he leads me in the right direction. But I have no desire to go out and run some man's garbage truck."

Louella Parsons gave her another boost in her column when she told Paramount Studio that they had a young Bette Davis on the lot. Now she practically demanded they put her in a decent picture. So they loaned her out to Columbia.

Director Gregory Ratoff tested 35 girls for the Robert Sherwood production of *Legacy* before he found his Hester in 23 year old Hayward. The film was released under the title *Adam Had Four Sons* and in it, Susan as Hester, was hot for every one of them. As the nymphomaniac home wrecker, it was her best role to date and she took advantage of it. She got third billing to Ingrid Bergman and Warner Baxter. The New York Times critic wrote; "Susan Hayward so coyly overacts the romantically unlicensed mischief-maker that often she is ridiculous."

Susan was grateful to director Ratoff for her chance and she never forgot Bergman's professional manner and kindness toward her in helping her gain screen time and experience, as Bergman threw many scenes her way. Invariably, she said, Ingrid Bergman was her favorite actress and meant it. As for the critics: "I don't like critics very much; I don't read them. I have much more respect for my own opinion. If the work I've done pleases me, nothing a critic says is about to change my mind."

The Hollywood grapevine gossip was out. Hayward was good. One of the people who studied her work in the film was producer Walter Wanger. It was Wanger's opinion that Susan darned near stole the picture from a darned good actress, Ingrid Bergman. A fact that seemed never to have been publicized to any extent was that Susan was nominated for best supporting actress because of her work in the film.

Why didn't her employers do something then about this recognition? Why didn't they buy a special story for her and give her a star build up? *Adam* was produced at Columbia. Why did Paramount treat the whole matter as it were a freak of fortune and wasted her proven ability for another five years? This is one of the mysteries of the film business. Anyone can be ignored in Hollywood.

Possibly one answer was Hayward was a curious standout at Paramount. She displayed a flare for histrionics in front of the cameras, as she modified her artificially throaty voice into dramatically convincing inflections. More experienced actresses, noticing her fiery competence, felt threatened and pleaded with their directors not to be cast opposite her. Susan, without being arch or in any way showy, inspired a nervous watchfulness in her fellow starlets and either desire or impotent fear in the young men of the Golden Circle.

People seemed to be always angry with her, a condition of life that she not only tolerated but actually appeared to thrive on. Her world, inside and out, was one of ire.

Her career had hardly begun when she was sued by the Walter Thornton model agency in New York and her first agent in Hollywood, in both cases for breach of contract.

Thornton claimed; "I made her famous. When she left for Hollywood on a contract I got for her (Warner Bros.) her name was Edythe Marrener then and she was a very discouraged looking little girl. She came to me in 1937 after having been tested and turned down by several movie studios. Then I went to work to build her into a star. I taught her make-up, grace, gave her confidence in herself, spent lots of money getting her good publicity, and my wife and I helped her with her clothes to make her look smart when she went for jobs. We made contacts for her career. Then came a contract for Hollywood, which we got for her. When she left she kissed us good-bye and swore she would never forget all we had done for her and cried when the train pulled out."

Possibly Susan was too busy now to try to remember or too young at the time to give it much more thought or attention than the casual remark that almost anyone might make in similar circumstances. Who has not made similar promises on an emotional parting?

While other girls were going right to the top, she was given the parts nobody else wanted. Susan, now back at her home studio, was shipped off to the lower rated Republic Studio for a B picture, *Sis Hopkins*, with Judy Canova and Jerry Colona.

At Republic, she met studio contract player John Carroll, a Rhett Butler type, who made a play for her and this time she let herself get caught — just briefly.

The country was at war that December of 1941 and Susan was in a war-ring mood at the studio. Things went from bad to bedlam. Then suddenly she was called into the front office and told they would be loaning her out for the important lead in *Dark Waters*. Louella was pleased and gave her readers the scoop. Susan's faith was restored, but just as swiftly as it came, it went.

Unexpectedly, Merle Oberon was available. Hers was a box office name, so the deal was called off. Hurt and humiliated she stormed into the front office demanding to know the reason why. Why hadn't they protected her when the contract was already signed? A top executive then told her he had deliberately okayed the cancellation to teach her a lesson. She knew then in some way she would have to start all over again.

Paramount sent her to Kentucky to judge a horse race. She went coop-eratively. They loaned her a creamy beige molded-to-her-figure gown to wear. It was originally made for Carole Lombard. When she returned to Hollywood there was a studio wardrobe woman waiting at the station to take the gown back. She took score of the incident and one day would give back as good as they gave.

Cecil B. De Mille, the king of showmanship at that time on the lot, was preparing *Reap The Wild Wind*.

Jesse L. Lasky, Jr. had never forgotten his experience with her on that film; "I met her and knew her through *Reap The Wild Wind*. I was fortunate to be one of the writers on it and there was a day I remember, I was working on some sort of scene. De Mille read the scene; it was a rough draft. They were going to test Susan and De Mille said, 'Jesse I'm interested in this girl, because you know, the moment in the film is coming when the divers go down and they open the chest, and the first thing they see is this great streaming blaze of red hair coming out of the chest at the bottom of the sea in this wrecked ship. She has the right color hair. Whether she has the right color acting, we must learn. Now you go out Jesse and work the test with her."

I went out and I worked the test with them and read with her, rehearsing. I thought she was quite promising even then and I went back afterward and told De Mille, which was dangerous. Saying someone was marvelous could have been the kiss of death — 'writer's don't cast pictures my dear boy,' De Mille would have said. It could have been that way but in this case he looked at the test and he was very moved, very impressed. That was her first break at Paramount."

Lasky continued, "I certainly couldn't have imagined how far she would go. When I saw her, I thought she was very promising and cer-tainly a beauty. I had no idea she would become the actress that she did."

"I had to learn to channel my energy very early in my career," Susan had said, "In the old days of movie making, when a director said 'Action!' and he meant for tears or laughter or whatever mood was needed, you had to be ready — or they'd get someone else to do the job. You couldn't take time to get in the mood; you were paid to *be* in the mood."

"You had to have your emotions right on tap, to turn it on — snap!

Reap the Wild Wind.

Like that. I got my early training with some very good directors, William Wellman *(Beau Geste)* Gregory Ratoff *(Adam Had Four Sons)* De Mille *(Reap The Wild Wind)* — and they weren't about to sit around and wait for me or anyone to get in the mood. I didn't spend time between scenes joking with the crew or playing poker with the wardrobe women. I saved my energy so that when they said, 'Action!' I was ready. I learned it because it was part of my trade. And by the same token, I learned to turn the emotions off just as quickly."

Reap The Wild Wind opened at the Radio City Music Hall that March in 1942. Hayward got 6th billing below John Wayne and Paulette God-dard, with whom she had competed for the role of Scarlett just a few years before.

She was so effective that Paramount gave her *The Forest Rangers* again with Goddard — competing with her for Fred MacMurry, the male lead.

I Married A Witch and *Star Spangled Rhythm* with an all studio cast, in which she sang with her voice dubbed, completed her 1942 film schedule.

Republic released *Hit Parade of 1943* with Susan and attentive John

Ray Milland, Paulette Goddard, Susan Hayward and John Wayne in Reap the Wild Wind.

Carroll, a comedown for her that was most discouraging. Louella wrote, "redhead Susie Hayward and John Carroll will soon announce their engagement."

Susan, however, called the whole thing off when she found Carroll to be a cheapskate. It appeared to be a wise decision in light of Carroll's later troubles; when a lawsuit by a seventy year old widow demanded the return of $228,000 she claimed to have loaned him.

The studio publicity departments tended to inspire a sexual laissez faire attitude among the starlets in those days, with their constant inventions of romantic liaisons, and the gossip columnists ate it up.

Susan, fitting into this 'norm', began having romantic attachments. Ellen Marrener, dependent on her daughter for support, could say little about Susan's conduct, which was discreet enough and in a way, almost expected by her peers and superiors. If she was going to make a career by playing mean little sex kittens on the screen, there had to be a certain amount of real life initiation.

William Holden and Susan began a lengthy affair during the making of *Young And Willing*. After they finished the film, they went to Paris, passionately inseparable for the time.

Eddie Bracken who was in *Young And Willing* with Holden and Hayward recalled a scene between Susan and himself off camera; "Everybody was telling dirty jokes and she walked into the dressing room. I had told a joke and everybody was on the floor laughing at it. It had a four-letter word in it. They asked me to tell the story to Susan and a couple of others. When Susan heard the four letter word, she slapped my face. It was such a stinging blow; I can feel it to this day. I didn't realize it, but I hit her. After that Susan and I were fastest of friends, maybe she liked to get hit, I don't know. I had never hit a woman, never would. I felt terrible, but because of my alertness, of hitting in the prize ring, I just reacted too fast."

Susan was receiving mail from her brother who was now in the army. "That was a sad portion of my life," he recollected, "you had to be at least five feet. I just made it. I got into a transportation outfit, driving jeeps. Susan joined a nanny outfit down at Long Beach. She had a uniform and everything. She would go and spend a few hours there each week. She did volunteer service and sold war bonds."

Wally had a picture by his bunk from his sister inscribed: "To Wally from his little sister Susan, also known as Edythe, Momma, movie actress, Miss Hayward and hey Red! Love and kisses — Susan." All of his buddies in the army wanted autographed photos from him when they found out Susan Hayward was his sister. As Wally said, "Getting those pictures of Susan to give around kept me outta a lot of K.P."

In 1944, after Susan returned from San Francisco for the premier of *Jack London*, in which she played Charmian Kittredge, the sweetheart of the author. She began volunteering some evenings at the Hollywood Canteen as part of the war effort to help servicemen's morale. She was serving behind a snack bar at the canteen when she saw a young Leslie Howard type emceeing the show. The tall blonde actor's name was Jess Barker.

Jess Barker, born in Greenville, South Carolina in 1912, was a better than average athlete during his High School days and aspired to a baseball career. An opportunity came for Barker to go to New York; here he made the acquaintance of several theatrical people, and an inflated ego prompted him to take 'a fling at acting.' A course of study at the Theodora

To Wally – from his little sister Susan also known as "Edythe" – "mama" "movie actress" "Mrs Barker" "Miss Hayward" and "Hey Red!" Love and kisses

Irvine Studio for the Theatre in New York, led to stage engagements. For a dozen years, he trouped in New York and on the road, playing opposite such luminaries as Ina Claire, Tallulah Bankhead and Lenore Ulric. Plays in which he appeared included such hits, as *You Can't Take It With You*, *Allure*, *Magic* and so on. Then came a low period, between seasons in 1940-1942 during which time Barker was out of work because of a dearth of theatre productions.

So, he made the acquaintance of several Hollywood people and an increasingly inflated ego prompted him to take 'a fling at movies.' Under a studio contract, he got work in Hollywood because being 4F, he was available and the crop of Hollywood leading men was lean; the six foot, blue-eyed blonde actor of Irish-English descent made his screen debut in *Cover Girl* at Columbia Studios opposite red-headed Rita Hayworth.

Oddly enough, Susan had wondered at one time if she should have changed her name because of Rita Hayworth who occupied an adjoining dressing room at Paramount, thinking the public might get their almost similar sounding names confused.

Later, as movie magazine columnists would say, "He (Jess) found his heart at the Hollywood Canteen — in Susan Hayward."

nother version is that Gregory Ratoff who had just completed *Adam Had Four Sons* with Susan was on a trip to New York and caught Jess in a stage show. Seeing him, he thought that Barker would be the ideal leading man to play opposite Susan in real life.

But whatever fates brought her and Jess Barker together in 1943, soon there was no turning back. She became pregnant by Barker that same year.

While Susan was attracted by the up and coming actor, she didn't consider him stable husband material and for a time toyed with the idea of having his child out of wedlock. When she finally went to the studio heads and told them of her condition, they informed her that if she didn't marry Barker her contract would be terminated. The studio had told her who to date, how to dress, what to say to the press, and now they were telling her whom she should marry. Determined to become a movie star she never defied the studio's dictatorial hold over her life. She married him.

Jess hardly knew the emotional hurricane he was marrying, and little suspected the furies that would engulf him over the next ten years of his life. He should have been forewarned when Susan, acting on her mother's advice, insisted that they sign a prenuptial financial agreement in which they each waived their right to community property should there be a divorce.

"My mother won't come to the wedding unless you do (sign)" Susan pleaded to Jess.

Mother Marrener went to the wedding without protest, as Jess had signed the document. Susan judged correctly that she, the more ambitious one, would outdistance her husband professionally and wanted her future bank account protected.

The marital storms between the Barkers began almost immediately. After three months, they broke up, only to have the studio decree that they reconcile for the sake of appearance.

On February 19, 1945 at St. John's Hospital in Santa Monica Susan gave birth to non-identical twins, Timothy and Gregory. Gregory was named after Gregory Ratoff who gave Susan her break as a shrew in

Barker Family.

Adam Had Four Sons. (She remembered he chose her from among the 35 actresses trying out for the part.)

The span of the time between the marriage ceremony and the birth of the twins, seven months, was just long enough for the studio to issue a news release about the 'premature' birth. To Paramount's relief, none of the columnists had guessed the hoax. Susan's forced marriage to Barker was just an opening to the shattering circus of publicity that would later sweep over the couple.

Louella, who was at the wedding in St. Thomas Episcopal Church in Hollywood stuck up for her protégé when she and Jess started to battle. "Susie said they are temperamentally unsuited to each other." She added, "Susie led a sheltered life up until her marriage."

Susan got lost in *The Fighting Seabees*, again with John Wayne and again on loan to Republic. She did get second billing to the increasingly popular box office star.

"John Wayne is my favorite leading man of all time," she would repeatedly say, "He's so big and rugged and so strong and can do practically anything, yet he's so gentle. I've always adored him, always, but then so has the whole world."

In her next picture, Eugene O'Neil's *The Hairy Ape*, she got second billing next to William Bendix. A reviewer wrote, "Miss Hayward who is achieving a type of ultimate odiousness, resorts at times to artificiality, but generally contributes her full share to the picture."

Louella kept mentioning Susan for several leads at Paramount, in fact several in a week, but they generally went to someone else.

The Barkers rented a modest house in Beverly Hills, then Columbia Pictures dropped Jess and his agent signed him up with Universal. Susan's contract was to end with her next film, *And Now Tomorrow*. She had several offers at this point and one was from David O. Selznick, the mogul who memo'd her out of work in 1939.

Louella spoke for Susan in her column when she wrote, "Susie says Life is beautiful, my career is moving along and you should see my babies, you've never seen anything so cute. Jess has been a good boy. I believe we're making a success of our marriage."

Susan had decided on an offer, 'because, she said, the moon was right.' But first, she had to do one for Howard Hughes' studio RKO, *Deadline At Dawn*. She would play a dance hall girl who helps clear a naïve sailor of a murder charge.

Director Harold Clurman spoke enthusiastically: "The whole experience is very vivid. Susan Hayward was very nice, but she was not in the best state there, because for some reason they (Paramount) had lost interest in her. One thing the film did for her was to make her rise again, until she became a star, as we all know. Clifford Odets wrote some good lines, it got good notices, and it's played all over the world. Considering it took only about $500,000 to make I am sure the studio made a lot of money on it."

Bill Williams, her co-star, who played the sailor in the movie couldn't forget something that had happened; "She was a heck of an actress and a lovely human being. The last shot in the picture was when I was sitting in the bus with her; remember she was going to go with me. We had to kiss and it wasn't right. Either I was holding her too tight or was a little too innocent about it. It went on about 3-4 hours. I said, "Gee Susie, it's been a long time kissing you hasn't it?"

"Bill," she said, "I gotta tell you something, you didn't do anything for me, either."

One of the reasons was probably Barbara Hale. After the premier of *Deadline At Dawn* in Rockford, Illinois, Bill Williams married Barbara Hale on June 22, 1946.

Susan went to Universal Pictures under personal contract to producer

And Now Tomorrow.

Walter Wanger.

As Susan told publicity director Graham Kislingbury at Universal, "I had two opportunities. Selznick offered me a contract but he had no definite plans for me. Wanger said, you come in and do this picture for me, and sign a contract and I will build you into a star. That's why I went with Wanger."

Susan now had someone who believed in her and she had great confidence in him. That was all she needed.

Wanger said, "They've sprung a redheaded Bette Davis on me. She reads every book written, printed and pesters me to buy stories for her. If Susan had her way, I'd own more literature than the public library."

"I have an insatiable appetite for reading," she admitted, "I'll read anything that comes along, even the encyclopedia if I run out of other things.

I consider it all grist for the mill; it all goes into the burner and something worthwhile is bound to come out."

Wanger first put her in a technicolor Western *Canyon Passage* with Dana Andrews. The world premier of *Canyon Passage* was held in Portland, Oregon, home of its author Ernoe Laycox — which is possibly why the movie out grossed *Gone With The Wind* in the State of Oregon.

Smash Up: The Story of a Woman.

But it was her next Walter Wanger picture that was the turning point for Susan. Wanger bought a property, tailored made for her untapped talents. *Smash Up: The Story of a Woman.* In it, she would portray the neglected wife of a crooner. It was said it was based on the life of Dixie Lee, the wife of crooner Bing Crosby.

Susan really needed a big hit because by this time she was supporting her unemployed husband, her mother, and giving handouts to her sister.

Wanger had an original screenplay written for Susan from the story by Dorothy Parker and Frank Cavett. Miss Parker's reputation speaks for itself. Cavett was one of the most proficient and successful writers in Hollywood. The original title of the Parker-Cavett opus, written for Susan, was 'Angelica.' It was later changed to *Smash Up*.

She was being given the chance of a lifetime as the dipsomaniac and she reached out for it with both hands, determined to make every scene count in her favor. As the unhappy alcoholic wife, Hayward worked on her part every second she had on and off the camera.

Wanger's former publicity man, Graham Kislingbury said on the making of *Smash-Up*; "Mrs. Marty Mann, who was director for National Education on Alcoholics, and her assistant came out as technical advisors on the picture, both of them having been alcoholics. My wife and I took Mrs. Mann and her assistant to Lucy's, which was a famous place for dinner in those days in Hollywood. Mrs. Mann gave Susan a lot of background for the film."

Susan commented to the press; "Women should not drink. Women are not constituted like men; they're too emotional and can't take a lot of liquor. A woman spends hours making herself beautiful and then after two drinks her face falls."

Her director on *Smash-Up*, Stuart Heisler, became wise to her method of whipping up her emotions: "Susan had so many emotional crises on tap that she arranged a set of signals, like a lifted finger or a nod of her head, to let me know when she was in the proper mood to start the scene."

She was afraid to speak, for fear it would break her emotional pitch. Heisler became so sensitive to her vibrations that he shared every moment of anguish with her, he said, "What an ordeal that picture was. I was limp as a rag every night."

So was her co-star Lee Bowman, but for different reasons. He found her cold, difficult to relate to and remained bitter about the whole experience. In later years, he said he would not even speak of it to anyone as long as she was alive.

Marsha Hunt, an excellent actress, co-starring as well in the picture recalled: "Sadly she had absolutely nothing to do with me. I never understood why. I finally realized it wasn't personal, I couldn't have offended her. This was a person so private and so closely involved with her job at hand that all relationships with others were nonexistent. After the scene (in which she attacks Miss Hunt in the powder room — giving her a beating) she went back to her dressing room. She would turn on her heel and walk away. I don't think I ever worked with anyone more private, more excluding. Maybe she felt it might break the spell."

After the picture was in release, Miss Hunt met Susan in a department store in Beverly Hills.

"She was dressed as for a garden party. I don't mean she was badly dressed; she was extremely feminine, in a floating chiffon gown, wide picture hat, and little white gloves. She was gorgeous, a beautiful woman, and so gowned that your eye was fastened on her. She was standing in front of can openers, strainers, utensils, and kitchen supplies. When I glanced up from the counter where I was shopping, there she was facing me, without a sign of recognition."

Someone who knew Susan well said, "She was painfully shy, a trait which takes the form of brutal frankness. She is almost sullen with strangers, making no effort to please them. She goes out of her way to make an unfavorable impression. She used to say, 'you have to accept me at my worst or not at all.' She didn't want to wear glasses, and half the time she couldn't make her way without them. That's why she didn't recognize people — she couldn't see them."

Graham Kislingbury had further recollections on *Smash-Up,* "I remember when the picture was completed. I came up with an idea that if I could get Susan to Sacramento, we would screen the movie for the Legislators at a midnight preview. I was sure we could get it presented before the assembly in the Senate, before the Governor. We then could probably get some good wire breaks out of it. I talked Susan into going. I found out that somewhere along the line, somebody must have pushed her around, maybe they pushed too hard. I never did. So maybe she trusted me?"

We went to San Francisco first and had a press conference with the critics at the St. Francis Hotel. (Susan sipped sherry — publicly). Later we were driving from San Francisco up to Sacramento and Susan said to Jess on the way up, 'I think I'm gettin' too old for this sort of thing.' She was 30 years old."

At a dinner party before the preview that night, for the leaders of the assembly and the Senate with Governor Earl Warren there, and other dignitaries, Susan made a little speech before dinner.

"It's just wonderful, to meet you men who run the State. This is my adopted State, I come from Brooklyn. It's a beautiful State, but there is just one thing I wish you gentlemen would do. I wish you would remove those atrocious billboards from our highways."

Fru Morton, the lobbyist for Foster & Kleiser, the big outdoor sign company turned red as a beet.

During dinner, two highway patrolmen came in and put handcuffs on Jess Barker and arrested him for impersonating the husband of Susan Hayward.

"This beautiful girl couldn't be married to a guy like this," they admonished as they hauled him off.

"You bring back my husband, bring him back," Susan shouted. They all broke up laughing, as the assembly was in on the gag.

Susan wasn't laughing, and neither was Barker.

The New York Times film critic Bosley Crowther wrote: "Susan Hayward performs the boozy heroine with a solemn fastidiousness which turns most of her scenes and drunken fumbling and heebies into key burlesque."

Life magazine gave the film a four page spread. The public went for it and found Hayward's performance very sympathetic and other critics singled out her performance as one of the most revealing character portraits of a woman alcoholic as one of the most memorable of the year.

Susan Hayward got her first 'best actress' nomination from the Academy of Motion Pictures Arts & Sciences.

She was headed for triumph and disaster.

Loretta Young, who won the Oscar (1947) as Best Actress for *The Farmer's Daughter* said, "I personally voted for Susan Hayward, because I was absolutely stunned by this performance, and when I saw it, I knew I couldn't do it as well. I knew that woman had done that part magnificently. And I voted for her because I think she deserved it."

Loser, Susan Hayward, kept her chin up for the press. "I'll be nominated for an Oscar again," she swore. "Maybe not next year. Maybe I'll have to wait until the fifties. (1958 exactly) But I intend to win someday."

GOSSIP

I have no interest in gossip. I think people who repeat tales about other people should have their mouths taped.

CHAPTER 5

Susan's career was ignited by her mentor Walter Wanger, and really caught fire after her performance as an alcoholic wife in *Smash-Up*. As Susan's star rose, Jess's burned up. His yearly income from his acting would usually be counted in the hundreds of dollars, not the thousands. His first few films shortly after his marriage to Susan were hits with the bobby soxers. Yet soon afterwards, he seemed to take a back seat to his ambitious wife, looking after the children in the daytime and not particularly looking for work. Was Jess lazy or was he merely becoming what he felt Susan needed to become a success herself — who can really say? Could Susan have stayed married to a driving, self-realizing, ambitious male? Or was she too competitive?

She had little or no time to be a good mother, giving every waking moment over to her career. Jess became both mother and father, taking the boys out shopping and on outing sprees while his wife spent long hours at the studio.

About her ambition Susan was quoted as saying, "I feel sorry for anyone who doesn't have some drive or ambition. If you don't have it, you're nowhere and going nowhere. You have to have a purpose in life, a reason for being. Otherwise why be here?"

Susan who said she needed very strong men in her life, contradicted herself by falling for their weaknesses, and then resented them for it.

She was a moody creature and became very aggressive during periods of strenuous work. There were continuous arguments with Jess over his failure to find work, and sometimes they became violent. What she may have failed to realize, were the boys to lose the one steady parent they had, and Susan's 'masculine' ego would have been damaged if Jess had donned the normal worldly role of a husband. In this, she was like her mother in her neurotic refusal to face up to her true feelings about her husband and children. As a result of all this Jess drank more and more and the boys became confused. Susan lied to journalists, spinning her quaint homey stories of family togetherness with as much conviction as she read dialogue in front of the cameras.

To ease his sense of lost confidence, Jess would invite his other 'at liberty' actor friends over for cocktails around the pool. Susan, coming home after a hard day at the studio, would go to her room and stay there until he got rid of them.

When he didn't and arguments ensued, she fled from their home and sought sanctuary with understanding friends who would hide her from Jess. She slept on their couch. On one occasion, she spent two weeks in the small apartment of a girl press agent. There she cooked her meals (usually pot roast) washed the dishes, cleaned the house, and spent half the night sitting on her friend's bed pouring out her troubles.

When her friend suggested a divorce, Susan replied, "When there's a divorce, it's the woman who gets it in the neck…"

Her friends asked naturally enough, "but why go back to him?" "Why did she keep going back when there was so much friction in their lives?"

"The answer is a question," she told her friend, "Have you ever been lonely?"

Susan didn't need a crowd around her in her free time at hone, "When I'm not working I do as little as possible. I read, I swim, I go to new places and travel. But my idea of relaxing is just doing nothing. Stretching out and looking at the sky. I can do that for hours. Some people have to be constantly amused or entertained. I don't."

Graham Kislingbury commenting on a long and friendly association with Susan recalled one particular incident: "Susan and Jess and her two sons were living in a rented home in Beverly Hills. They were being evicted and they were going around separately in different parts of the area they wanted to live, looking for an apartment where they could live with their kids. Eventually they moved into a hotel in Santa Monica. The telephone rang in my office and I answered.

"Are you Graham Kislingbury, this is Hedda Hopper — look you, I understand that Barker and Hayward have split up, he's looking for an apartment."

"I said, 'I don't know anything like that at all.'

"'Where's Susan?' she demanded.

"'I don't know where she is right now.'

"'You don't know where Hayward is? What kind of a press agent are you anyway!'

"'I truthfully don't know. They moved out of their house because they were evicted.'

"'Where's she staying,' said Hopper impatiently.

"'I don't know.'

"'You're one hell of a press agent. Look you find out where she is and you call me right back, you understand' — and she slammed down the phone.

"I called Susan at the hotel and told her about the conversation," Kislingbury said.

"Just ignore her and if she calls you back hang up on her," she told him.

Jess, Susan and the twins.

Susan resented this scandal hunter rummaging around in her closet looking for skeletons. She liked Louella Parsons, Hopper's rival, but couldn't care less about Hopper because Hopper was only out to hurt her, ready to break a scandal, which wasn't happening.

The truth was that the lease on their rented house was expiring, and the place was being sold for a huge amount of money. Susan and Jess moved four times in two years. She refused to pay black market rentals and she would definitely not pay cash under the table.

"The Barkers had been house hunting for weeks," said Kislingbury, "Walter Wanger backed them for a loan and they bought a house out in the Valley."

The house was a simple two-story affair on an unfashionable street in the San Fernando Valley, with two garages for their medium priced cars. There was a small lawn in front of the house with a swimming pool in the back yard. Their neighbors had nothing to do with the movie business. The price was $25,000, which was considered quite high in 1946. According to the newspapers on the day following the sale, it was reported that when it was discovered that the perspective buyer was Susan Hayward the price was jacked up by another $10,000.

Susan must have reflected at that moment on the Brooklyn drama coach who years before took one look at her and rated her below the crowd because of a hole in her shoe. Today, the mere mention of her name to the real estate salesman had rated her above the crowd — by $10,000. The ivy covered, English cottage in the Valley meant so much to her as it was the very first home she had ever owned.

Graham Kislingbury had to make frequent calls at the house to discuss things they were going to be doing. "They had no furniture in the living room at all," he remembered. "Susan made it clear that 'we're not going to put a piece of furniture in here until we can afford it.'"

Gradually they furnished the house, 'at least we are better off now than when we moved in Christmas Eve. About all we were able to set up except for the beds, was the Christmas tree,' she said.

"When they were married they were just about on a par — in their careers. Then Susan began to go and Jess didn't move. I asked Wanger to give Jess a role," Kislingbury said, "and Susan tried to help."

To the press, she stated that she would not permit her husband an experienced theatre trained actor to take inferior film roles. She added she felt handicapped by having never been on the stage. Barker pursued his hobbies, photography, horse racing and drinking, and Susan began another picture.

Alfred Hitchcock's associate Joan Harrison borrowed her for *They Won't Believe Me* and Wanger then put her into *The Lost Moment*. Susan got a chance at an *Alter Ego* character in *The Lost Moment* playing the schizophrenic lead, Tina Bordereau. She also fought frequently with its director Martin Gable.

"He," said Susan, "was a great genius — he thought. You couldn't even walk into the room properly for him. I had a long difficult speech in a long scene. It was going well, but he stopped me at the same point, each time I got to a certain word. It was some simple word. I've even forgotten what it was, but he insisted I was mispronouncing it. By the twelfth take, I thought surely I had said it the way he wanted, but it still didn't suit him. I told him, "If you stop me once more, I am surely going to haul off and hit you. He answered, 'Ho, ho, ho!' Sure enough in the middle of the next take, he stopped me again. Well, being a lady, I didn't punch him. Instead, I picked up a lamp. It connected. Oh, yes I paid for the lamp! Of course, it was just one of those things; emotion building up until it is released like a typhoon — and over just as quickly."

Director Martin Gabel, who came from the New York theatre, went back to it after this one film, as a character actor.

One day Kislingbury called Louella to get a Sunday feature story on Susan's role in the film and she asked to see the children. Kislingbury and Susan gave each of the boys a little bouquet of posies to give to Louella and they prompted them as to what to say. When they arrived at her front door and rang the bell, it was opened by the black maid and the kids said, "These are for you Miss Parsons." While Susan doubled up laughing, Kislingbury, restraining himself, instructed them, "Not yet, not yet."

Louella wrote about it for her readers, "My adopted daughter Susie brought the twins over. They sang and did their little routines. You know, Tim is the serious one and Greg the comedian and Susie said, 'I think Greg will be an actor and Tim will write the scripts.'"

Hayward, the dark horse in the Oscar race that year, 1947, lost to the venerable Loretta Young. The nomination did however advance her career. Susan was determined to try harder.

"Susan came into my office in the rickety old writers' building at Universal one day," Kislingbury recalled. "It was down at one end of the studio. Every time you walked up the stairs, the building shook. As she came in I said, 'isn't this awful?'"

" 'It's all right', she smiled, "some day you'll have a good office, you gotta have faith, it sure carried me a long way.' She always had just a little bit of that Brooklyn manner."

Susan, going from one picture into another, barely had time to keep in touch with her mother. Her sister, Florence was married and Wally, just out of the army, went to work for the Race Tracks in Santa Anita and Hollywood, where he would be for the next 30 years.

"Susan was a hard worker", Kislingbury recalled. "We went up to North Carolina to make *Tap Roots* and she would have to be up at 5 o'clock in

Susan and her brother Wally.

the morning to be at the hairdresser and into make-up before we drove 50-60 miles to location that day. She did not party at night, though the rest of the cast did. Sometimes she would get back from location at 7 o'clock at night. She would call me 2 or 3 times a week. She knew I was going back and forth from the location to the studio and she would ask me to take her out to dinner when the rest of the cast went off partying. We would try to find a new place to eat each time. I remember one time we got a cab to go somewhere to some restaurant we had heard about, up in the mountains there. The cab driver kept looking in the rear view mirror, and finally turned around."

"You're Susan Hayward," he blurted out.

Then he whirled the cab around, turned down a side street, and start speeding off.

"Where are you going?" Kislingbury said, but he wouldn't answer.

Susan shouted at him, "What are you trying to do?"

He drove up to a house in a nearby small town and grabbed the ignition key and ran inside.

Kislingbury turned to Susan, "You know what he's going to do? He's going to bring the whole family out to meet you."

"You're kidding!" she said.

Sure enough, out came the whole family—"you're our favorite star," exclaimed the cab driver, and Susan had to meet the entire family.

"We have a very tight schedule, and I asked him, 'can we go now?'" the publicity man said. "He drove us out to the restaurant and he wanted to come back to pick us up."

"Oh, no, thank you," we replied quickly. "We have a limousine coming." We weren't going to get caught again.

Susan confided in a trusted friend during the North Carolina shooting of *Tap Roots*, "I'm having a rough time with Jesse. I wouldn't care if he got a job in a department store as a clerk; he just lies around the house all day. He criticizes me constantly. If he was working this wouldn't happen. He's very down, he hasn't been able to get acting work and he won't do anything else. What the heck, if I couldn't make it in this business, I would do something else."

Jess did do something else — he applied for unemployment insurance.

Susan's brother very often went over to the house to check up on the boys who had to be looked after when their mother was not at home. One mid-day when Jess came down from his bedroom, having been awakened by the twins on the front lawn circling around on their bikes, he was very upset about getting up so late, and having missed his appointment at the unemployment office. Wally was fixing lunch for the boys, and Jess wanted him to stop and squeeze some fresh orange juice for him. Wally refused. Jess went back to bed.

In November of 1947, Susan sued Jess Barker for divorce but just before Thanksgiving they reconciled, Susan couldn't go through with it so close to the Christmas holidays because of what it would do to the family.

Interviewed by the press, she said, "When I start a picture, Jess and I study the script together. If I give a good performance, he is greatly responsible. I could never have played the role in *Smash-Up* if it weren't for Jess. Not because he drinks, but because he's a fine actor. Even the best talent has to wait for a chance to make good. That's the routine in this town. Jess will get his". Who was Susan trying to convince — herself?

While on location for *Tap Roots* Susan wasn't needed for one particular days shooting and she didn't have anything to do, so as Graham Kislingbury was going to the airport, to pick up cast member Ward Bond, Susan decided to go along just for the ride. While waiting at the airport a middle-aged society woman approached Susan.

"Oh, you're Susan Hayward," she gushed. "Well, I'm having a party at my home, tomorrow night, and I want you to come."

"Thank you," Susan replied. "But I am working very hard and while I'm working, I just cannot accept social engagements."

"Well!" snapped the woman, "Of course movie stars mean nothing to us out here. I just thought it would be nice for you," and walked away in a huff.

Susan blew a puff of smoke from her cigarette. "You'll find one in every town", she said to Kislingbury.

After *Tap Roots*, the British froze the pound sterling and the film companies couldn't get their money out of England. This threw Hollywood into a real tailspin towards the end of summer of '47.

"We were just winding up Tap Roots when Wanger announced out of the blue, that he was going to leave Universal and go to Eagle Lion. Of course that meant that she would go with him," Kislingbury related, "and Wanger wanted me to go to Eagle Lion too, but my wife and I had enough of Hollywood, so we decided to go back to San Francisco. When Susan heard the news she called me. 'Can we have lunch?' she asked. 'Sure!' I replied and we went across the street from the studio.

"'Gee,' she said over lunch, 'I feel terrible — you're the one person I really have gotten along with.'"

Susan, who had responded easily to the soft, spoken Kislingbury, felt protected with the publicity front man who gave her fatherly advice and the warmth of his presence. His like were not replaceable.

"One day I got a call from Dave Lipton at Eagle Lion," Kislingbury continued. "Susan had moved to Eagle with Walter and was making a picture called Tulsa. He said she didn't want to go to San Francisco to plug the premier of Tap Roots and could I go down there and try to persuade her. I flew down to the studio and Dave and I drove out. She was working in the picture and didn't know I was coming. We went to the sound stage and she was in her dressing room so I knocked on her door. The door opened. 'Graham!' she screamed and threw her arms around me and took me inside. She wanted to know what I was doing and I asked her if she liked it there. 'one studio's like another,' she sighed.

"I asked her about the opening of Tap Roots in San Francisco and told her that Boris Karloff was going, Julie London and Dick Long and some more of the cast but without her, it would be a flop.

"Why don't you come up, and we'll have some fun.

"She though a moment, 'O.K. Graham, I'll do it.' And that was that."

During the filming of Tulsa, she had a scene in which she was supposed to crack up with remorse. The way the scene was planned, the camera followed her across a room until she went out, slamming the door behind her. During rehearsals, she raved and ranted at that door. She kicked it, and slammed it and yelled at it, while most people watched in astonishment. Director Stuart Heisler, her director from Smash-Up, merely sat back in his chair, waiting for the tears to come. To whip up her emotions she had to have something to get mad at, he was wise to her technique.

Tulsa was to be her last picture with Walter Wanger under his personal sponsorship. She went, on loan, almost immediately into another picture, The Saxon Charm at Universal.

Susan collapsed on the set of The Saxon Charm — reported Louella in her column. She, however, would not hold up production and forced herself into a quick recovery.

"Days off get me out of the rhythm and take the edge off my characterization," she stated.

Walter Wanger, who had controlled her professional destiny up to this point, sold her contract to 20th Century Fox for $200,000. Wanger felt a mixture of relief and regret. Although his contract with her had more than 2 ½ years to go he felt it was time for Susan to move away and go ahead; but it was believed he simply needed the money.

Susan signed a 7 year no option contract at a sliding annual increase salary beginning at $150,000. It raised the eyebrows of the economy-minded industry. From now on, Susan really got the star treatment.

"I couldn't care less — and I never did care — about the A number one treatment, the star's dressing room, the limousine. That's all junk," she declared. "Oh, it's nice if you can have it, but it was never important to me. I never cared if I had to dress in a broom closet or a tent as long as I had privacy to change my costumes. Some performers wouldn't work if their dressing room wasn't as posh as someone else's and that's junk. Just externals; it means nothing. The only thing that's important is what you put on film and what it does to your audience. Of course now that I've said that, the next time I work they'll probably make me dress in a broom closet."

What Hayward did put on film in her first picture for 20th Century Fox was *House of Strangers*. Director Joseph L. Mankiewicz and Susan battled from the start. The fireworks were over her red hair. Mankiewicz said there was too much of it and wanted her to cut it.

"Every other producer and director wanted me to cut my hair and my answer was 'No!'" Susan said defensively her first day at work. "I refuse to be led around by fashion dictators who say women have to have short hair. I know I look better with a long bob and I'm going to keep it!"

Susan's proudest possession was her long, luxurious red hair. She regarded it as an identifying trademark. No studio hairdresser was allowed to touch it and her present contract prevented Fox from ever calling for any change in her hairdo without her consent.

The veteran actors in the cast of House of Strangers, working with her for the first time, were taken aback by her coldness. During the production, she thoroughly upset Joe Mankiewicz — a director noted for his informal approach to life — by calling him Mr. Mankiewicz. He called her Susie. As the picture was winding up, Susan completed a scene and asked, "How was it, Joe?"

Mankiewicz, startled by her sudden familiarity, replied, "It was fine, Miss Hayward."

Samuel Goldwyn wanted Hayward for the lead in My Foolish Heart and made a deal with Darryl Zanuck at Fox studio. Having seen the script, Susan wanted the part, feeling that it was a perfect part for her. During the shooting of the picture director Mark Robson was amazed at her stamina, which enabled her to remain in front of the cameras for nine weeks of non-stop shooting. As she appeared in all but two scenes, it was a tremendous physical task.

"Susan may look frail," a friend commented. "But she's got the constitution of a truck driver."

Susan was up at 5 a.m. each day to keep up with the increasing schedule of films lined up for her at Fox, leaving her non-acting husband in bed to sleep until noon. She left money around the house, in a handbag or bureau drawer, to get what was needed in the way of groceries, etc. She was becoming increasingly successful, and more moody and unhappy with her personal and home life — what was left of it.

Her brother didn't bother her, knowing how hard she was working. Her mother was off to Reno and Vegas on gambling trips, sponsored by Susan. Florence, by this time was completely out of the picture, with a husband and children, struggling to make ends meet.

In fact, Susan's life now seemed to rotate entirely around the studio. She was now 33 years old and had been working steadily for the past 15 years.

My Foolish Heart opened on New York City's Radio City Music Hall and for her performance in this film; she would be up for her second best actress academy award nomination. The movie going public took her to their hearts as the unhappy girl caught up in an ill-starred wartime romance, and she became bigger box office than ever before.

Her new home studio then gave her an inconspicuous little comedy entitled *Stella*, which she rightfully refused. They signed another redhead Ann Sheridan to replace her.

It was, to her, a decided comedown with the possible Oscar staring her in the face. Now that she knew what her box office draw was the ambitious and riled redhead went to the front office and asked why she wasn't being given better parts.

It was the same old story but one she was familiar with. She had learned one hard method of competition; to get your way frighten your peers with arrogance, and pretend submission to your bosses.

To her co-stars, during the making of films, she was frigid — coldly detached — never mingling and only friendly to non-threatening lessers like hairdressers and make-up artists. For top directors, she was always admirably efficient, doing difficult scenes in fewer takes than it took other actresses. To lesser-known directors, who were intimidated by her on-set frostiness, she behaved like a shrew, losing her temper and issuing ultimatums. When told a hairdresser she wanted was in London on an assignment, she told the director, "Well, bring him back!"

Her coldness, mingled with her usually superior work in front of the cameras, inspired a fearful awe.

True, most actors wanted to keep their distance from her, seldom putting her on dinner party lists, but they also rarely dared to compete and often moved aside to make way for her to go on to increasing success.

Her climb to become America's biggest grossing actress, during the early 50's, was as much a matter of steely and unscrupulous will power as of talent.

Veteran director Henry Hathaway, who was a pioneer in the industry and learned his craft from the days of silent epics like *Ben Hur*, was a tough taskmaster.

A Hathaway picture was done on time. He was a company man who didn't tolerate any temperament and he was tough, but he was good. The studio knew Susan needed an iron hand at times and that Hathaway couldn't be browbeaten. He was also an expert Western director and a man's director. Wayne, Cooper and others of their like worked with him and became lifelong friends. It was Hathaway's direction of John Wayne in *True Grit* that landed him an Oscar.

"She was a bitch!" said director Hathaway. "Anybody who is a bitch to work with has got to be a bitch to live with. That's an inherent thing, a part of your make-up, to be an obstruction to everything. She was a little twisted, she was twisted in her walk, she always walked a little sideways, stood a little sideways, it's a thing that was in her nature. It was in her head, her look, her walk, in the way she stood, that girl was twisted."

Susan's first film back at Fox after they had suspended her for refusing *Stella* was *Rawhide* to be directed by Henry Hathaway, and co-starring Tyrone Power.

But Hathaway said emphatically; "There was not a speck of trouble with her on that picture. In the beginning, in her earlier pictures she was never any trouble. Oh, she was aloof and went off by herself, didn't mingle, didn't go out to the cafés or join in on anything. Up in Arrowhead on location, the cast and crew — all of us — went to the San Louie Café and we'd all sit together, but she would go with her maid or hairdresser to some other place. It sort of bothered her to be friendly, she didn't want to get into any traps or make any commitments. I think her children were a disappointment and I think her marriage to Barker was a disappointment. She had a lot of inherent hurts, the same thing happened to Gene Tierney."

"She spent all her free time up in the mountains with those two kids of hers looking for arrowheads", Hathaway mused in mystification, "always going up to Lone Pine and Bishop, taking the kids on trips when she could have taken them up to Arrowhead and Big Bear where we were working."

20th bought the play rights to *What Makes Sammy Run*, a hard hitting play about the New York garment industry and the ruthless Sammy

Glick. They changed the sex of the anti-hero to that of Harriet Boyd, a hard-shelled dame, especially for the Hayward talents. It was tailor made for her.

The studio sent her to New York for location shooting. With the boys in school and looked after by their grandmother and uncle, Jess went along for the ride. They stayed at New York's Hampshire House on West 58th street and made the most of their visit; with Susan leading the way now very much back on home ground, but with a much different perspective than the one that she had departed Brooklyn with some years earlier.

Following the New York location, the studio planned to send her to Dawsonville, Georgia. She would replace Jeanne Crain in the film *I'll Climb The Highest Mountain* as Miss Crain had become pregnant.

Here Susan met restaurateur Harvey Hester, who owned Aunt Fanny's Cabin where the crew often went for dinner, and finding him as comfortable as an 'old shoe' she struck up a meaningful friendship with him which was to last the remainder of her life.

Harvey Hester, a large, very rotund man, took a small part in the film as one of the local characters.

Susan enjoyed the location and rural scenery, and made headlines May 31, 1950, in Georgia when she lost her footing while trying to take snapshots of the 729 ft. Amicola Falls. She was saved by 20th Century Fox chauffeur Will Gray who caught her, but almost went over the Falls with her while doing so.

Fellow actress on the picture Lynn Bari when asked of their working relationship could only comment; "She had nothing to say to me."

Susan endeared herself to her fans again, as the backwoods minister's wife. However, when a reporter told her it was one of his favorite films, she scoffed, "You gotta be kiddin'. I never saw myself as much of a preacher's wife. I didn't like wearing all those pretty dresses or having to be so genteel."

Cast next as Bathsheba to Gregory Peck's *David*, Hayward commented that she would have preferred it if the film were called Bathsheba and David, instead of the other way around. Either way, on investment alone 20th proved that she was their most valuable player. They tied up $12,500,000 in her films that year alone (1951) a quarter of the studio's annual production budget.

The one memorable thing to her about the biblical technicolor opus was that she caught a cold during the famous bathing scene, when she had to stand up all day on the sound stage in a waist high tub while a female slave poured water over her.

Susan had to cancel plans for a European trip with Jess when Fox gave her what she really wanted. The Jane Froman Story, 'I'll See You In My Dreams,' changed finally to *With a Song In My Heart.* Jeanne Crain was originally cast, but lost to her Brooklyn opponent; and this time Miss Crain was not pregnant.

Two of the dancers in the musical biography with her were Herman Boden and Frank Boden told this version, "Susan preferred tall fellows, we were all over six feet. She was just 5'6" in heel. She worked very hard, and she was a perfectionist, a real pro. No matter how many times they wanted her to re-do anything, she did it; she wanted people to help her. I remember the first tine she came into the rehearsal hall; she looked at everybody and wanted them to like her. She was warm and natural. We then rehearsed with the piano…"

On the other hand Frank commenting on the same movie told his version, "When we met her she was pleasant, but quiet and not particularly warm. She didn't know anyone and was standoffish. She sang along with the soundtrack and we thought she must have had coaching prior to her coming onto the sound stage, because she fell into the dance steps pretty fast. It took between 3-5 days to film the 'Song In My Heart' sequence. Herman and I did a lift with her and she was tense and Froman was there, watching from a wheelchair. She liked what she saw (in Susan playing her). Susan would ask 'is this right? — Am I holding myself correctly? — Doing this the right way?'"

"Even to me," he said. "Susan became Jane in the movie. Jane also mentioned Susan visiting her in New York and how they preferred the same perfume, hair color, clothes, etc. to a point it was like a psychic experience. They got along beautifully.*

"It was an elaborate set on a big stage, and Susan often sat with Billy Daniels, the choreographer (who was later to commit suicide) and Richard Allen, Her dancing partner in the sequence (who now works in a massage parlor). It was a very subdued atmosphere and we kept our distance. When they were finally ready to shoot the number she was very serious, and they must have really practiced to get to that point. After we shot the number, she thanked everyone and left at 6 o'clock, she didn't like to shoot after 6 p.m. It wasn't like working with Betty Grable, which was fun, Betty broke us up constantly."

The story was about Singer Jane Froman who surmounted crippling injuries in an airplane crash in 1943 while going overseas to entertain the troops.

Susan spent hours in her dressing room with Jane Froman going over the script, scene by scene. She asked her about her childhood, she wanted to know what kind of clothes she wore, what her drives were, her tastes, and interests. How she felt after the Clipper crashed finding herself in the water.

Every time Froman looked around the darkly lit recording studio during the recording sessions of the 26 song soundtrack, she would see Susan sitting somewhere in the back watching her every move, every gesture.

With a Song In My Heart.

Jane Froman's husband Rowland Smith of Columbia, Missouri, mentioned a conversation he held with his now deceased wife about the movie, "I remember Jane telling me how impressed she was with Susan Hayward. Susan watched her as she recorded, dubbed the soundtrack, and she copied so many mannerisms of hers that it was uncanny."

Costumer Charles La Maire created "the most expensive wardrobe I have ever designed and we used colors that went with Susan's red hair."

While Susan had made four pictures in that year (1950), Jess had a bit part in a B movie *The Milkman*.

Susan, who herself had stepped into the footprints of other stars in the forecourt of Grauman's Chinese Theatre when she first arrived in Hollywood, now immortalized herself by putting her own footprints and signature in cement that same year.

She received her third Oscar nomination for Best Actress for *With A Song In My Heart* and garnered many awards from magazines but most importantly, from the public. The Foreign Press gave John Wayne and Susan Hayward their award in 1952 as the World's Favorite Actor and Actress — the most popular stars in the world.

The American Beauticians Congress voted her "the most beautiful

With a Song In My Heart.

redhead in the world" and the National Florists Association crowned her their Queen.

Susan spoke contemptuously of her screen allure, calling it gimmicky, and in tossing her long red mane, exclaimed, "I feel like whinnying when I do it."

But for all that, at night Susan went home to her English Ivy covered cottage exhausted to an inebriated husband, sleeping children and loneliness.

Movie making is a business normally involving enormous costs, much elaborate equipment and complex inter-relationships among gifted and talented people, with profit usually as the motive. Susan was used as a yardstick for measuring profit and while she was on top she was kept working constantly. In the film industry, the profitable was generally the beautiful, but the beautiful was not necessarily the popular.

Susan at the top was an easier target for those a step below and her detractors were waiting, hoping for her to topple, and again there were those who with praise and smiles who were working to dislodge her.

She had entered the film industry as a teenager, and through hard driving, competition, and versatility she had fought to get where she was and now had to fight to stay there.

"My life is fair game for anybody. I spent an unhappy, penniless childhood in Brooklyn. I had to slug my way up in a place called Hollywood where people love to trample you to death. I don't relax because I don't know how. Life is too short to relax," she said.

The climb took its toll on both her and her family. She stayed home at nights, reading books, searching for screen parts. There was enough fighting on the set and to unwind she took those few extra drinks at night.

She couldn't beat her husband at his hobby so she joined him. If the Barker's drank heavily and fought, they did it at home; they seldom went out in public.

Now whenever she was approached by anyone seeking favors she fired first before they could ask, "Whatever it is, the answer is *no!*"

Darryl Zanuck put her next into Ernest Hemingway's *The Snows of Kilimanjaro* along with Gregory Peck and with Ava Gardner borrowed from MGM to co-star.

Famed astrologer Carroll Righter did her daily charts while she was filming the picture: "I'm like a doctor; they come to me when they have problems. I would do 40 pages a month for her. I was on the set of *The Snows of Kilimanjaro*, doing her chart and Hildergard Neff's, she was a typical Moonchild, moody, up and down that is why she was such a fine actress. Jess Barker was a Gemini, and the twins, Pisces. She needed a Taurus."

When Susan was undecided about whether to take a long-term contract at Fox as opposed to freelancing, I advised her as her astrologer to sign the contract, as her chart imposed this direction. I could foresee a slide in her career if she were on her own. She wanted to know what time of the day she should sign it. I gave her 3:23 a.m. She set her alarm, awoke during the early morning hours turned on her bedside lamp and signed the contract and then went back to sleep."

Susan was warned by her astrologer to be cautious. The studio giving some of the best scenes in the picture to Ava Gardner were careful to shoot them all after Susan was off the lot and Susan piqued at Fox over this turned down a series of their next scripts.

Howard Hughes wanted her back at RKO and got her for *The Lusty Men* with Robert Mitchum. However, she was happier on *The President's*

Lady with more her kind of man, Charlton Heston, on her Fox schedule. But she still felt they weren't treating her properly and she did not like the next script *White Witch Doctor*, set to co-star again with Robert Mitchum.

Henry Hathaway, on directing *White Witch Doctor:* "She would sulk if they tried to make her do something she didn't want to. And when women get angry about something and get a chip on their shoulder they're never good in films then and it's true with men too. Suddenly there would be one person she would get mad at, or the studio, and then she would slack off a little bit. You know what happens to some of these people then, they don't want to do this picture or that one. That was why Wayne was such a big guy, a big star (he didn't do that kind of thing).

"I got a call from Zanuck's office and he said, "I have this picture, it has to start and both she and Mitchum came in here and said they will not make the picture, and it has to start in two weeks. They said it was a terrible script they just wouldn't do it. Besides, they didn't have any faith in the director. Will you read it and see what the hell's the matter with it."

A worried Zanuck went on, "I have a commitment with these people and if they don't make it, I have to pay them."

"I read the script and called Zanuck — 'Jesus, Darryl. I don't blame them. It's a lousy, awful, unbelievable script.'"

Zanuck called off the picture temporarily, cancelled the director and debated the situation, having spent over 600 thousand dollars in one of the units for exteriors with a million tied up in the production so far, including pre-production costs. Shortly afterwards Zanuck called Hathaway.

"Henry, do you think you can do anything with it at all. I'll give you a couple of writers. I can't lose a whole million if I make this picture. There's no way to lose with those two people in it."

Hathaway was given the script assignment, and total directorial control. He rewrote the script in two weeks but he said, "I didn't do it as good as it should have been done."

"There was no romance between the two of them (Hayward and Mitchum). As soon as you said 'cut,' she went off to her little cabin and went either right inside or sat in the doorway — or the chair outside the doorway. I think she got along with Mitchum because anybody can get along with Bob. He's such a sweet man; he's on a level with Cooper.

"She had no sense of humor — none. She would stay where she was and wouldn't crack a smile, then turn around and walk away and never say anything. She was a fully competent actress, capable of any kind of emotion, and doing it well. She never had to be prodded into doing anything."

Director Hathaway elaborated, "You could talk to her about what should be done and that was it. She was camera-wise and always tilted her face in her favor. She had a way of standing and always ended up in the same position no matter what the hell happened, she would end up with her hand on her hip. Very characteristic and a little awkward, I thought."

With a Song In My Heart.

June O'Brien of San Jose, California was almost 18 years old in 1952 and a senior at Girl's Commercial High School in Brooklyn, "One of my warmest memories," she said, "was in the spring of that year. *With A Song In My Heart* was about to open in New York City at the Roxy Theatre and there was quite a fuss being made. Susan Hayward was coming back to visit her old alma mater. The assembly hall was jammed with maybe, 1,000 students, and we were all singing 'With A Song In My Heart' as she walked in.

"She was truly the most beautiful woman I had ever seen. It wasn't make-up either. It was a look on her face. As she reached the stage, tears were running down her face. She looked at us all with such feeling. Jess Barker was at her side. When all the excitement died down, our principal started to speak and pay much tribute to Susan. She began to list her accomplishments while a student there. In the middle of it the principal mentioned Susan had been a member of the Arista Society, which was the Honor Roll Society for students who managed an A average all through school.

"Susan stood up and interrupted the principal at this point and brought

With a Song In My Heart.

the house to its feet when she said, 'I never made Arista once during my years here.' The girls just ate it up.

"She then spoke to us of her memories of her school days and how she was so torn between her schooling and costume designing, and her tremendous desire to be an actress. She told how she had this wonderful English teacher who had encouraged her in her acting and talked to her many times, continually encouraging her, and Susan gave all the credit to this wonderful teacher, her true friend in High School. This teacher had told her to leave school and try her hand at acting in Hollywood. Then Susan pointed up to the balcony in the assembly hall and said, 'There she is sitting right up there, now.'

"It was Miss O'Grady, the little white haired teacher sitting in the back off to the side. It was really a tear filled moment when the teacher got up and slowly made her way down the stairs to the center aisle and up on to the stage.

"Susan moved towards her, helped her up the steps and embraced her with such love. It was really a tear filled moment.

"Outside in front of the building Susan standing in her mink coat, pressed her heel hard on the cigarette she had dropped to the sidewalk, stepped into her limousine and sped off, leaving it all behind, without looking back."

Susan picked up awards everywhere; The *Photoplay* Magazine Award; at the Del Mar Club for International Good Will; the Gold Medal for *With A Song In My Heart* (along with Gary Cooper who accepted his for *High Noon*). Not only was her performance nominated for best actress but the picture brought in over 10 million dollars at the box office.

She felt she deserved a vacation so she and Jess left for Europe in May leaving the twins in the care of her mother and brother.

Upon her return and in spite of her contemporary look in *David and Bathsheba*, for which she and the film were accorded poor reviews, Fox assigned her to *Demetrious and The Gladiators*, a super cinemascope technicolor biblical potboiler. She was cast as the wicked Messalina and she sneered her way all through the film.

Louella Parsons quoted Susan as saying, "I'm (practically) a split personality. Through my screen roles I live many lives in one; here at home I'm happy to be just Mrs. Barker who goes shopping at the supermarket like any other housewife."

Then the night of July 16, 1953, Susan ran shrieking into the night, 'Don't kill me! Somebody help me!' she screamed as she fled naked from her home in the valley, with her husband hot on her heels.

In court, Jess explained what had happened preceding the escape that Susan believed had threatened her life.

After dinner that evening (July 16, 1953), he and Susan were sitting in front of the television set and browsing through the newspapers. There had been a discussion between them about families in Hollywood and during the conversation, Susan brought his mother into it.

Questioned in court Barker said, "Well, it wasn't very pleasant. It was about an incident when I was a child that I had told her about."

"Possibly," she had retorted, "that's what's wrong with you."

Jess said that he had then sat in stunned silence while Susan told him all the worst things she could about him. Then she had leaned across him to reach for a cigarette and said, "Besides, I think you're queer."

Jess then slapped her and the struggle began. As he tried to quiet her down, she bit him in the left arm, and then ran outside. He brought her back inside and gave her a spanking, picked her up and put her to bed. He told her, "to be quiet, the children were upstairs."

Susan got up and ran outside with Jess threatening her that if she didn't keep quiet, he would cool her off. He caught up with her, picked her up and threw her into the pool. The robe that Susan was wearing slipped off. Jess went back to the den and Susan back to her room. He then decided to take a walk and was in front of the house when Susan appeared fully dressed, carrying the dog in her arms.

She was heading down the street. He tried to get her back and asked Susan's friend, Martha Little, who was staying with them convalescing from an illness, to get her inside and put her to bed.

Susan then told her story: It was late at night because Jess had gone to get the late edition of the papers. She said she had been studying a script and Jess was watching television. They were in the living room when the argument started. She asked him for a divorce, as she felt it was the only solution to their problems. He said "never."

"If you don't love me, and don't want to do what I consider right, why do you want to hang on?' she asked him.

"You're a good meal ticket," he replied.

Susan looked at him and said, "I don't understand you. I think you're very queer." And he walked over to her and slapped her in the face.

Susan told the court that he then threw her on the floor, pulled off her robe and beat her. She managed to get free and ran into the back garden. He caught up with her but she broke away again and reached for the phone to call the police. He came after her, knocked the phone from her hand and dragged her outside into the garden and up the steps to the swimming pool and threw her in. She was panicked as she was pulled down into the water by the heavy pink terry cloth robe. She struggled to the surface and started screaming for her life and he pushed her head under the water. When she came up for the second time, she remained silent and he allowed her to climb out of the pool.

She, considering that he might have become deranged, quietly went indoors, leaving the heavy wet robe by the pool.

Once inside her room Susan just wanted to run and dressed swiftly to make her escape. She opened the side door of the bedroom and walked quietly past the den and out to the garden, then around by the kitchen door, which lead to the driveway — and freedom.

Barker intercepted her by the kitchen door and grabbed her, pulling her inside with such force that she arrived practically effortlessly at the front door, which she opened and ran down the driveway. He caught up with her and started to beat her, as she screamed for help.

"Don't kill me. Somebody help me!" she cried into the night. The critically ill Martha Little ran out and begged him to stop as Susan ran into the house and called the police. He chased her and grabbed the phone out of her hand. Then suddenly there was a commotion outside. Someone had called the police.

Susan asked them to get a cab and they offered to drive her but she refused. The cab came and Martha Little and Susan sped away, to Ellen Marrener's house.

The next day, Susan returned with her brother and Martha to ask Barker to leave. She had also called her business manager Mr. Wood to have him meet here there.

Susan described her injuries in court, "I had a black eye, bruises on the left side of my face, on the temple, the jaw, the nose and I thought my jaw was broken. The eyeball was injured — it was all bloody. My body was covered with bruises, mostly on my fanny, and my feet and legs were scratched and bleeding from being dragged up and down the steps and knocking against things."

A witness was called to describe the incident. She was a maid at the house next door to the Barker's and her room overlooked their garden and pool. Dodee Hazel Swain said she had been awakened by screams, a woman's screams, in the early morning of July 17th. "From the lights in the backyard I could see a woman running, her hair was kind of red — reddish like — and I hear a big splash and a man mumbling, 'you goin' sign that deal' and the woman says, 'no-no.' She ran over to the back door, close to where I am — she was naked. I hear some slaps and her screamin', 'don't kill me — somebody help me!' Then I hear the man voice, 'you're goin' to sign that deal' an' he throwed her into the pool. I didn't call the police 'cause I didn't want to interfere. It went on quite a while because I went and laid down."

Whichever version is closer to the actual happening, this you can be certain of; Susan and Jess had been drinking and started another fight that this time got completely out of control. The dunking and the swimming pool splash were heard around the world. The Hollywood press had a field day, and Susan Hayward's image as a tempestuous fiery woman was enhanced.

Following these proceedings that Labor Day weekend Susan returned from Hawaii where she had taken her sons for a respite and Jess called to take the boys out for Labor Day. Susan agreed.

She had guests at the house, a Mr. and Mrs. Dorsen, when Jess and the twins returned at 6 o'clock. They were all out by the pool having drinks and Susan politely asked Jess if he would like a drink. He said he would like to talk to her, and the Dorsen's left the pool and went indoors.

"Please, Jess," Susan said, "will you please be sort of quick about it, dinner is almost ready."

He started to speak of reconciliation but she flatly said that it was impossible, and he made it clear that he wouldn't leave. This caused delays in the kitchen for her guest and the children, who ate at this time every day and wondered what was happening. Susan tried to persuade him to go suggesting another time to talk about it.

He would leave when he was ready he told her. There was an argument and a scene and Susan said in court, "Well I was furious. I tried to get him to leave peacefully. He was sort of standing near me and I had a cigarette in my hand; it was lit, and I have a temper and I said, 'I would like to push this cigarette right in your eye.'"

"You haven't got the guts," he challenged her.

She then shoved it in his face. He smacked her across the mouth and Susan yelled. Then Thelma Dorsen came running out holding a drink in her hand — which Susan grabbed, throwing the contents in Jess's face.

The next day Susan called her lawyer Martin Lang, "I want that divorce, and fast!"

Susan who gave glowing reports of her marriage to movie fan magazines appeared in court in a chic black dress and dark glasses, to cover the bruises and commenting about all the false quotes, said, "After all, I am an actress and wanted things to look right."

Following the filing of her suit for divorce, on September 10, 1953, Susan left on November 22nd for Mexico to go on location for *Garden of Evil.*

Regarding the marital agreement, which Barker had signed, forever separating their income, he later said he was too busy buying the wedding cake to really read the agreement.

Henry Hathaway met up with 'her' again in Mexico when he directed *Garden of Evil,* "I never found her to be friendly, cooperative or anything. I never did have a good relationship with her, even down in Mexico with *Garden of Evil.*

"She was very objectionable and nasty. For instance, I like to start early, with energy. I like to shoot what I call my master shots in the morning and catch up with some close-ups and take a little time, and quit early.

I have always done that because mostly I have worked outdoors and the very early morning light is the best light to photograph — anyway, before the sun gets in right up ahead. We were all ready, not too early, at 8:30 in the morning. I saw that she was sitting in her dressing room and I said to the assistant director, Stan Huff, 'Stan, go over and tell her its time to work, that we're ready.' She was all ready, so Stan went over and came back.

"I don't want to tell you all this but she looked at her watch and asked if it was 9 o'clock. It wasn't."

Hathaway walked towards her, "I went over to her dressing room and said, we're ready to work and I see you're ready."

"Is it 9 o'clock?" she asked.

"No!"

"My contract says I work at nine!" was her snappy answer.

Hathaway now, with barely unrestrained anger, spoke with strong deliberation; "Your contract also says you work from 9 to 6, and I want to tell you something, Miss Lady. I am going to work you every fucking night until 6 o'clock. You've been getting off at 4:30 and 5 and you don't say 'I have to work until 6,' when you leave early. What else can we do?

"I am not only going to do that," he continued. "I'm gonna shoot every fuckin' close up of you after 5 o'clock at night. How do you like that?"

"You can't take a joke can you?" she looked up at him exhaling her cigarette.

"Fuck you!" he said and walked away.

"Then," he went on. "She came over and said she was ready to work. She's just nasty. Like there is something about her that she can't help; for no reason.

"Gary Cooper, Richard Widmark and Cameron Mitchell were all part of the cast. She never got along with anybody. Cooper was the sweetest man in the world and so is Widmark and I'm not hard to get along with either.

"We were all invited by a friend of mine Bruno Pagliai down to Cuernavaca (Bruno later married Merle Oberon) to his place New Year's Eve. He's a genteel man, an aristocrat. When he arrived, there was this great big long table and on both ends were silver buckets of ice with caviar, champagne and other things. She came in (Susan) with the assistant director, Stan Huff, a sweet guy. She picked up with him right away and I think she did it out of protection. She went over and looked at the table and said, 'When the hell do we eat?'

"Pagliai said we would be eating later.

"'Look I eat at 7:30 to 8 o'clock and if this is all you got to eat — good-bye!' and she left.

"She raised a stink about when and what she wanted to eat and they don't eat there in Mexico until 10:30. She wasn't drunk — she's just god-damn mean, and she may be sitting up there listening too!" the director said looking up.

"Later on, New Year's Eve, just before midnight, we went down to a café, and she came back after she had had her dinner, and sat down. We were sitting around the tables and midnight comes and a couple of the guys, Cameron Mitchell was one, went around kissed several of the dames. Mitchell wished her Happy New Year and reached down to kiss her. She reached up and clawed her nails down his face and drew blood."

Hathaway shook his head, "We had to lay off shooting for two days because his face was full of scabs — and that for no particular reason. She's just a mean son-of-a-bitch."

"I have a scar on my face from Susan, runs right down here," Cameron Mitchell pointed out, "We were doing a film in Mexico. It was lovely." According to Mitchell, "you couldn't leave Mexico if you had a work permit at the time, unless you saw the president."

Susan had left the children in the care of her mother and brother to go to Mexico, during the months following her separation from Jess Barker. At Christmas time, she flew back to spend a day and a half with the family. To make this trip, Susan fought with the studio brass and got a special dispensation from the President of Mexico to break the period of her work permit to leave Mexico and re-enter.

Mitchell continued his story, "Susan was having a big love affair then with Jeff Chandler and she wanted to go back and see him. She got permission and left. The rest of the company all wanted to go home for Christmas too. They thought it was not too nice of Susan to do that. So they excommunicated her for a week when she got back. The thing with Jeff was not a happy one and poor Susan incommunicado — she was blacked out for a week. On New Year's Eve, I couldn't take it anymore 'cause I really liked her. I had a crush on Susan and I went up to her to wish her well, the Happy New Year stuff. She had had a few brandies and she went just like a cat — (Mitchell clawed and made sounds) just like that and blood came out, in front of 900 Mexicans."

Mitchell told of another encounter, "Another time we were in a very primitive place called Paracutine — that was the volcano — you've heard the story about the peon who was pounding the fields with his bare feet, felt the earth get warm and this huge volcano sprang up. It was that way with Henry Hathaway. I'm sure you've heard stories about him too, a nice man, but on the set, he's a maniac. He couldn't drink coffee in the morning and he resented other people drinking it. We were in this primitive location and Hank, the generator man, who was Italian, would make this marvelous coffee. Susan was the drinking coffee and with that long beautiful hair and that feminine way of hers. Hathaway would never yell at her, he would yell at Stan Huff, our assistant, who is now married to the ex Mrs. Howard Hughes, Jean Peters. Anyway, Hathaway yelled at Stan, 'Stan I told you we won't have any goddamn coffee drinking on this set, anyone drinks coffee they can get their ass off my set, and when they finish they can come back and go to work.' So Susan very quietly took her cup of coffee and went to Mexico City for a week. Every time they called her, she said she wasn't finished with her coffee. She was lovely — like little children.

"Hathaway took her out dancing one night with his friends, Richard Widmark and Gary Cooper, 'Let's take her out,' they told me, but when Widmark danced with her, after the dance he came back and said, 'I can't dance with that dame, she leads.'" Hathaway broke up laughing, "She'd grab a guy and away she'd go. She was gorgeous."

Susan once said — on being difficult: "I've never been difficult to work with, just ask any director I've ever had. I'm difficult only to myself and I'm very hard on me. I think I've learned a great deal — patience for one thing — but I still have a tremendous amount to learn."

At about the same time of the filming of *Garden of Evil* in Mexico Susan was very upset over the imprisonment of her champion Walter Wanger, who was now serving a jail sentence for the shooting of Jennings Lang over Lang's attentions to Wanger's wife, Joan Bennett. She realized now that Walter had sold her contract to Fox to pay off creditors against the multi-million dollar fiasco of his independently produced *Joan of Arc*.

He had given her a strong boost to the top. She had made it and he'd fallen off the heap, and now she was looking for a way to help him out. Wanger had reshaped her whole professional life, pointing her in the direction of what most would have considered Utopia.

"Utopia, the word should be struck from the dictionary," said Susan, "Do you know of anybody who's every found it? Anyone who's even visited it or been there? I don't. The politicians all guarantee it but I don't think there is any such thing; if there were we'd probably all get tired of it very fast. Life seems to be a constant battle with a few moments out now and then for relaxation. If there is a Utopia, you probably find it only when you're dead."

For all her success she was desperately lonely, "I know it well," she said.

On being asked to comment about a book on Susan Hayward, Henry Hathaway could only say, "The only way I could see a book about her would be about a woman who destroyed herself. Like the movie about the drunk she played — everything she did was destroying herself, her marriage, her children, her mode of living, her attitude, and to spite all that she survived. Just to destroy herself many times over. The only kind of book about her that would make any sense would be like the part she played, of a person who absolutely destroyed herself. It should be called 'Self-Destruct!' That's a good title, 'Self-Destruct!' There is nothing good you can say about Susan — except that she was a good actress."

---

* The one time Rowland Smith saw his wife perform, it was in Germany during the war. She took the stage on crutches, a 50 pound cast from her hip to her toes, to perform for the wounded and dying. Smith was an officer of war information.

When Froman died, at 72, in her Columbia home, Rowland spoke about her life. She was born in University City in St. Louis County on November 10, 1907. Although she wasn't a Roman Catholic, until high school she attended a Catholic convent school in Clinton. Her mother was a piano teacher. After graduating from Christian College, she enrolled in the University of Missouri, Columbia School of Journalism. "Actually she flunked out of the school of journalism so her mother whisked her off to Cincinnati Conservatory of Music. Her first paid performance was an ad for Tom's Toasted Peanuts.

However, her big break came as a singer for the Paul Whiteman band. From Cincinnati, she went to Chicago and landed a full-hour Sunday afternoon radio show. After four years in Chicago, in 1935 she was voted top girl singer on the air. Venturing into New York, she landed a job with the Chesterfield Hour until 1943.

Credited with being the first USA volunteer, she boarded a plane for Europe to sing for allied troops in a USO show, the plane crashed into the Tagus River near Lisbon, Portugal. She was saved from the wreckage by co-pilot John Burns, whom she later married and divorced. The scene became a highlight of a 1952 movie about her life called, *With a Song in My Heart.* With Froman's voice dubbed in, Susan Hayward won an Oscar nomination for the part.

After the plane crash, doctors wanted to amputate her crushed leg but she refused. More than 35 operations later, she was back on the USO tour. It was on that tour that Smith heard her sing. The US Congress promised to pay off her mountainous doctor bills- but reneged on it. In 1962, she married Rowland Smith. Although Froman stuttered throughout her life and feared the telephone, she never had any problems before an audience. Contributions in her name were to be made to the Jane Froman Foundation for Emotionally Disturbed children at the Menninger Foundation. She was a humanitarian to the end.

JOHN WAYNE

John Wayne is my favorite leading man of all time. Why? He's so big and so rugged and so strong and can do practically anything, yet he's very gentle. I've always adored him, always, but then so has the whole world.

CHAPTER 6

Susan's emotional life had all the security of a floating crap game. Now, of all the people to gamble on, she took a chance on Howard Hughes. Not even her astrologer, Carroll Righter, could have predicted what would happen in that relationship.

Choreographer Bob Sidney was called in by the director and ex-song and dance man Dick Powell to choreograph a sequence in *The Conqueror*, produced by Howard Hughes at his RKO Studios. He would spend over six million dollars on this epic story of Mongol King Genghis Khan, who would be portrayed by the totally unexotic John Wayne, who turned it into an oriental western. To assist him in making it even more unbelievable Hughes finally got Susan Hayward for RKO as Bortai, the Tartar princess captured by Khan en route to her wedding. As the plot churned, Genghis wants to honeymoon Bortai — first. The casting could not have been worse if Charlie Chan had been cast as Rhett Butler and Anna May Wong as Scarlett in *Gone With The Wind*. In the film, Susan defends her honor for almost two hours, but not before her misplaced Salome dance in which she wants to slice Khan's head off with a sword, between bumps and grinds.

Bob Sidney, who had worked with Dick Powell before has never forgotten the experience; "She did not want to do the picture. She wanted no part of it."

"It was thought that it was Hughes 'way of getting her', but Susan was a very direct person. She would have said; 'Look Buster, to take me out you don't have to make a movie.' She was a very defiant person, a strong lady. Hughes borrowed her and she was told by Fox if she didn't do it, they would put her on suspension. Hughes was powerful and the Zanuck clan and Hughes were very close anyway. That business of her not going to do *The Conqueror*, well it was not so much that the picture was lousy; it was more like 'OK Mr. Howard Hughes, you want a match!'"

She fought him to a point where he said she was going to do it or else. The only reason she did it, she said, was because they gave her a lot

of money. Susan was a businesswoman, she was not going to go on suspension and lose all that money. She was the top-notch star at Fox, too.

"Dick told me that Michael Woulf, the designer, was going out to see
Susan at her home in Sherman Oaks, and I went with him. She knew he
was coming and she opened the door herself.

"'I'm Michael Woulf,' he said.

"'Yes, and who are you?' she asked, looking at me.

"'Why, I'm Bob Sidney the choreographer,' I replied. I'll never forget
her next comment; this is exactly what she said:

"Why are you here, who needs you!

"I was shocked. 'Well, I was told once, that people are hospitable here,
and if I come to your house, you have got to be polite, don't you?'

"Susan broke up, 'Oh, come in.'

"Poor Michael Woulf, who was under personal contract to Hughes,
was a very important guy at the studio and he designed these wonderful clothes for her," Sidney carried on. "He knew exactly the kind of
things Susan like. She hated 'la-de-da' things, she had a very specific
taste, not frilly, she liked things that might cling. Woulf showed her each
sketch and with each one she said, 'Hate it! Hate it! Hate it! I don't like
anything!'

"When we got back to the studio, Dick Powell asked how it went. 'She's
a monster!' I said and told him what happened and he went hysterical.

"Powell finally had a talk with Susan, "Look Susan if you really hate the
clothes fine, but if they are any good at all, you can't say they're horrible.
There's a guy involved and he has a job to do."

"When she heard that she might jeopardize this guy's job, which wasn't
the case," Sidney went on. "She said that some of the designs were O.K.
Michael made them like sheets, they would cling, that's the only thing she
would wear. She never had good legs; they were thin and weak. Her hips
were good and she had this beautiful bust — that was real, she needed
nothing to support them."

On one occasion, when a female columnist purred that Susan aug-
mented nature with a bit of padding, La Hayward picked up the phone
and quickly set the lady straight, the columnist backtracked, "Darling,
can't you take a little joke?"

Said Susan, "Darling, I have no sense of humor about my bust!"

"Susan was very conscious of her legs, because they were thin and that's
why I think she always diverted your attention. She always insisted on her
left profile. In the early films, she looked wonderful no matter how you
shot her. Perfect face for the camera. Later, she always posed from that

left side and by doing that no one would look at her lower body. From the knees up she was damn good."

Sidney had to work up the dance routine for *The Conqueror*, in which Susan would be doing some motions in 'close-up' to drums, as they didn't know what the music would be. He met her again on the sound stage.

"She couldn't dance at all, but I thought from looking at her body that she had hips, so I tried to devise something which she as a non-dancer could do well as a dancer; something that was based on a certain line of her body. We showed it to her — she already said she would not dance — and she agreed to do two inserts, two close-ups. The dancer would do the long shots and Susan would come in for the close-up, smiling. I told her, 'when we say "close up" you do this with the knife.'"

She was supposed to get up from a reclining position in the scene when she sees the two knives hanging on a wall, about 18 feet high. She had to keep leaping in the scene until she got a knife and threw it at Khan.

"Did you read this thing," she said. "No pole vaulter can go that high — that's why I hate this dumb script."

"Well, anyway we lowered the knives," Sidney continued. "And she did the two close ups."

The professional dancer stand-in was waiting to do the full dance routine and Susan wanted to watch.

"Why, should I audition for you?" Sidney told her. "Then you'll do what you did to Michael Woulf's clothes. I was there and you tried to throw me out, too."

"You're a real son-of-a-bitch," she said. "Now if I'm nice and won't even tell you if I hate it can I watch?" (Of course she did.)

The girl, a very exciting dancer, did the number. When she finished, Susan asked where the close-ups went. Sidney brushed aside any further curiosity from her, "That's it, you can't help, I don't want any complaining about the dance. You didn't want to do it, now you don't have to."

"What do you mean I don't have to," she kicked off her shoes. "O.K. let's start!" she said. "But really, Bob, if I'm lousy, don't let me do it, let the girl do the long shots."

"Came the day of the shooting and the poor girl never even got lined up with the camera. I asked Susan to please, let her do it, just once; she wanted to earn her salary. She answered, 'Screw her! I'm doin' it. She'll get paid anyway.'

"She was fabulous for a girl who couldn't dance. She worked hard — we would rehearse every day (for six weeks). I gave her exercises and she'd say 'look at these legs, what can I do?' She looked forward to these exercises. She knew she was killing me during the sessions and she enjoyed it.

"I screamed, 'Enough!' she came back with, "you're supposed to have strong legs."

"'You know you never take me to the commissary,' I said to her one day. "I want to look glamorous going in there with a star."

"'Yeah, sure,' she'd say.

"For lunch she'd have a piece of cheese that she brought from home. 'It's lunchtime,' I always reminded her. 'No!' the same answer — but finally she went with me.

"All the dancing girls came on the set in costumes when they heard John Wayne was there, they could hardly wait to see him, and they were absolutely disenchanted. (Wayne wore pantaloons and was heavily mustached.)

"A fire broke out on the set and everyone ran screaming to put it out the crew, all the men, everyone but Susan. She thought if the set burned down it would take them days to rebuild it and they'd get extra money. She was afraid of nothing. She jumped the horse's side saddle, and she wasn't afraid of Wayne."

An amused Sidney related this episode: "Susan had this scene with John Wayne where he grabs her. She had all that red hair and another fall on top of her head to make her look taller. I asked her what she was doing with all that growth on top of her head 'You bitch,' she said. Wayne shook her so violently in the scene that this thing flew off her head. They reshot the take, and did it over and over, and then they were going to do it without her hairpiece. She said to me 'he's hurting me that son-of-a-bitch.' Her arms were black and blue. I said why don't you let him have it (in the groin) — she loved it!"

Sidney went over to John Wayne — "He's very macho and wanted every one to call him 'Duke.'"

"So I purposely said — 'Mr. Wayne.'

"He said, 'call me Duke.'

"I said, 'Mr. Wayne — this thing with Susan, well she's frail and she's not feeling well; its ladies day. I know she's the last person to admit it but couldn't you go easier, you're hurting her.'

"Wayne cried out, "Look she's so damn strong, she's stronger than I am. I don't want to come across as though she's putting me down.'

"He had a devil of a time controlling her, she raised her knee — you know where — and she let him have it. He really got it. They yelled, 'Cut!'"

"Susan respected talent," Sidney said. "She wasn't too fond of women. The women she liked were wardrobe women, hairdressers. Jokingly, she referred to herself as a nice Jewish girl from Brooklyn. She spoke very grand. She worked hard to get that deep, rich, low tone — then she would slip into Brooklynese kiddingly, she'd say, 'so wadda ya want ta do?'"

"When she came into a room she would give this furtive look, because she couldn't see, and she wouldn't wear glasses because that would give her the excuse to end up with the left profile. I told her I didn't like that profile, the other one was better, and she said, 'How much did they pay you to say that?' 'A lot!' I said, because it meant redoing a whole damn scene. When she was being fitted she would say — 'lower,' 'higher' — sharply. She was not coy. She never used her wiles. If she didn't like something she'd say it."

Sidney found this difference, "She never gave a party for the crew after the picture was finished, no presents, none of that. I asked her to give a party after this picture, but she wouldn't do it. Dick Powell didn't like to spend money either (ask June Allyson, his wife at that time.) Susan would say, "If you don't like what you're doing, why take the job. And as for a party? We're all working in the same business. They get paid.""

Sidney reminded her one day, "I had met you years ago at Dick Wyman's house when you were married to Jess Barker."

"You must have not made any impression," she replied. "I didn't remember you."

"You're sweet," he said. "The only reason I remembered you was because you had all this dyed red hair."

"It wasn't dyed — then," she said. Now she was angry, "You're going too far. If I hit you, you'll know it."

She liked Bob Sidney and they were to remain friends.

As for *The Conqueror*, she said, "I had hysterics all through that one. Every time we did a scene, I dissolved in laughter. Me, a red-haired Tartar princess! It looked like some wild Irishman had stopped off on the road to Cathay a few years back."

Although Susan had legal custody of the children, Jess Barker tried to throw up as many legal roadblocks as possible.

In March, he tried to stop her from taking them on location with her to Utah, where she was filming Hughes's technicolor bonanza *The Conqueror*, but he failed.

Barker's lawyer S.S. Hahn, pleading Barker's case, told the judge — "to melt the ice in the heart of that woman with the legal whip...a river of gold has blinded that woman to her responsibilities to her children and husband...that woman is an absent mother with an icy heart..."

That same month Jess Barker met bit player Yvonne Doughty when he visited the restaurant operated by her mother. On their second date, she became intimate with him in an apartment in Sherman Oaks.

Susan would be absent again, but not from her children as she took them with her when the cast and screw were scheduled to go for exterior shooting on the picture to St. George, Utah.

The site was the main fallout zone for America's worst nuclear accident, the explosion known as "Dirty Harry'; one of the 87 open air atomic tests conducted at the nearby Nevada range between 1951-1962. On May 19, 1953 a sudden wind change, as Dirty Harry was detonated at 5:05 a.m., carried a more intense cloud of radioactive fallout than had been measured in a populated area, even in Japan after the explosion of two wartime atomic bombs.

In between May and August 1954, Susan Hayward and John Wayne and members of the cast and screw shot scenes in the thick of the fallout zone, unaware of the dangers of radiation.

Tons of the red earth, which had absorbed lethal radiation doses, was loaded into huge carriers and carted back to Hollywood, where it was used to construct huge indoor sets. Hayward, Wayne and the others left St. George and followed the caravan of big trucks and trailers which began rolling back to the studio with the red Utah earth which was to be used to make exterior scenes filmed in the studio for the six million dollar production.*

Susan had found something of a match in Howard Hughes. Both were extremely independent and very much loners, and both had peculiar sex problems. Hughes was very much attracted to the unpredictable, untamed redhead. She at least fulfilled one of his sexual fantasies with the required attribute of well-formed breast. Hughes certainly had power and money and that appealed to Susan, but his enigmatic attraction soon bored her.

During the divorce trial, Barker's lawyers called Hughes to the witness stand.

Hughes testified that his visits to Susan's home in Barker's absence were strictly business; he wanted her for his film *The Conqueror*. Barker countered that as a result of Hughes' visits his sons' attitude toward him had changed since the break-up. They told their father that Mr. Magic — as Hughes was introduced to the boys by their mother — had promised to take them for an airplane ride. They said his name was Howard Hughes, but that 'Mommie said we shouldn't tell Daddy his name.'

Susan, called back to the stand, admitted that Hughes had been to her home but denied having told the boys to keep the meeting a secret. Why should she, he was there to discuss a contract. Besides, Susan felt

Hughes could distract the boys from the recent split between the parents by taking them on trips, plane rides and sport outings (making Howard Hughes sound like a Boy Scout Master). To add to all this, the Marrener clan encouraged the liaison.

With Hughes in the picture, Barker fought to regain custody of his sons.

Susan with Timothy and Gregory.

Herb Caen, in his column in the *San Francisco Chronicle*, reported his arrival in San Francisco to retain lawyers Melvin Belli and Kathryn Gehrels. Later, Barker dropped by Peter Arnesto's restaurant on Geary Street, ordered coffee and a bromo seltzer and signed an autograph for waitress Nela Kennedy, still a celebrity coasting on his wife's fame.

Hughes was always amazed that he could call Susan quite spontaneously and say they were going out someplace and she would say she would be ready in ten minutes.

One time, they flew to Las Vegas in his private plane. His reasons, never truly explained, seemed unimportant to her. Seated in the lounge of the Sands Hotel, with two bodyguards at the next table, Susan and Hughes ordered dinner. Brooklyn born opera singer Robert Merrill was currently appearing there. After his nightclub act was over, Jack Entratter

who books the acts brought Merrill over to the corner table to be introduced to the famous pair. Hughes did not look up or stop eating; Susan
however, commented on how much she had loved his show. Hughes
mumbled that the mike was too loud and Susan gave him a sideward
glare.

"That Pagliacci aria, it almost made me cry," she said.

"Opera leaves me cold," said Hughes.

Susan gave him a menacing look and said sharply, "We Brooklyn
people stick together."

Hughes, who was embarrassed by her putting him down in public,
ignored the remark and asked her if she wanted anything for dessert.

Susan shook Merrill's hand as he excused himself to get ready for the
next show. Hughes did not offer his hand and Susan was annoyed by his
rudeness.

At 3 a.m. that morning, one of Hughes aides phoned Merrill in his
room in the hotel.

He offered Merrill a contract at Hughes studio, RKO, almost certainly
resulting from Susan's intercession. Merrill fended the offer with a 'speak
to my agent' answer.

Hughes could counter act what he supposed was Susan's interest in
Merrill by tying him up under contracts with options and dangling him
for years, which could kill his operatic career. Whereas Jane Russell, Ava
Garner and Lana Turner would placate Hughes, Hayward would tell him
off and say that he was acting like a spiteful little boy. Afraid to fight back
and incur her rejection, he would then go around her back to retaliate. In
the end, Merrill refused the offer.

On September 2, 1954, Susan was awarded custody of the nine-year-
old twins, with visitation rights for Barker.

Susan continued to live at 3737 Longridge Avenue Sherman Oaks in
her San Fernando Valley home — which remained half-furnished — and
her old friend, Martha Little, continued to live with after the divorce
from Jess.

Though critically ill with cancer, and certainly a handicap during
this period, Susan especially wanted her friend to enjoy Christmas. She
secretly paid thousands of dollars in medical bills for the incurably ill
sister of one of her schoolmates. She planned the Christmas holidays
for Martha and her family. It was to be Miss Little's last Christmas with
Susan, as shortly afterwards Miss Little returned to New York.

On New Year's Eve, Susan planned to have dinner with Howard
Hughes in the Polo Lounge of the Beverly Hills Hotel and he arranged

for one of his chauffeurs to pick her up at home. Susan was beautifully dressed and might have expected on this special evening that Hughes would make some commitment about their uncertain relationship.

He was waiting for her in a private dining room dressed in sneakers, jeans and open nick white shirt. They ordered drinks and Hughes in his soft nervous voice avoided her attempts at a serious conversation to clarify her position in his life. She was interrupted anyway by an aide calling Hughes away from the table when the midnight hour struck amid loud screams of 'Happy New Year' and the sound of horns and bells bringing in 1955.

He returned and was very apologetic but became more restless than ever. He was beckoned once again by another of his men from the dining room entrance. Susan had had it. She was suspicious and furious by this time and got up from the table and followed him into the main dining room, where she saw him sit down in a secluded corner next to actress Jean Peters.

Absolutely enraged by this double date maneuver she pushed through the crowd and stood before the startled Miss Peters and the now shaken Howard Hughes. She denounced him with Brooklyn adjectives in a very loud voice and stormed furiously out of the room.

Howard Hughes was now struck out as any possible contender for the man she needed in her life.

Meantime, Jess, who was penniless, counter-sued for a community property settlement and custody of the twins. The courts found that because of the pre-nuptial agreement with his wife, he was not entitled to community property but eventually awarded him $10,000 to help him begin a new life.

"Susan was more fortunate than I," Barker told the divorce court judge. "She became a star."

The Conqueror would be in production for the next two years and Susan would be working in two pictures at the same time as she was back and forth between RKO studios to complete her scenes while working on her next picture for 20th Century Fox.

When asked about a possible reconciliation with Jess, she replied, "Not a chance in the world, I know now I should have left Jess a long time ago. He'll be better off without me to depend on and I'll be better off not having to worry about him."

As a divorcee, Susan became the target for every prowling caballero in Hollywood. According to a friend, one gallant phoned for a date and got this reply, "See here, my friend, why do you want to go out with me, besides the fact that I'm rich, famous and beautiful."

When he hesitated a second too long, she hung up. Susan appreciated a quick response and if he'd come across with one she might have made a date with him.

"I pity the poor devil who takes me out in public the first time," she said, "We'd both be miserable. I haven't had a 'date' in so long I hardly know how to talk to a man except career wise, and I'm sure he will be uncomfortable with all the romance rumors the most casual dinner engagements will bring forth."

When Susan got the news of the death of Martha Little she dropped everything and flew to New York for the funeral. She was very disconsolate and back in Hollywood after the funeral. Jeff Chandler offered Susan a shoulder to cry on. Chandler, Susan and Martha Little were all old friends from their Brooklyn childhood days, he was now separated from his wife and with their mutual broken marriages; it was one more bond to share.

---

* John Wayne, Susan Hayward, Dick Powell, Agnes Moorehead and most of the top production people on the same movie developed cancer later on. Character actor Pedro Armendariz, Carroll Clark died, production manager of the film, his wife, the make-up chief and so many others working on this film all died of cancer related illnesses.

THE DARK

I'm terrified of the dark; always have been.
I don't like the night and I keep the lights
on — all the time. I can remember the very
moment it happened when I was a child.
I was in my grandmother's house and an
uncle scared me by telling me there was a
bogeyman waiting for me on the second
floor. I can still remember that moment —
vividly. I've been afraid of the dark ever
since; not too crazy about that uncle, either.
I'm also nearsighted and that doesn't help;
it adds to my lack of security in the dark.

CHAPTER 7

She was the top woman star of the entire world in the fifties, with Gary Cooper and John Wayne running neck and neck for top male star. Her contract at 20th Century Fox brought her $250,000 a year and she was up to three academy award nominations. She had played fiery, tempestuous women in her last three pictures (*Demetrius and The Gladiators, Garden of Evil* and *Untamed)* — and she was now told she would have to begin her fourth picture. The studio was using her name at the box office for all it was worth. She paid off!

Clark Gable, through with his contract after twenty three years at MGM (the only studio contract he ever had), made a deal with Darryl Zanuck at 20th Century Fox for two films a year, for $400,000 guaranteed up front and 10% of the gross.

The first, *Soldier of Fortune* — obviously a title to throw the spotlight on him — would start in Hong Kong late in 1954. Gable wanted his young flame from MGM, Grace Kelly, to be cast as his co-star. At a press conference to publicize his new studio contract with Fox, he was quizzed about his first film and his new leading lady, Susan Hayward. Gable looked dumbstruck and muttered, 'Who's she?' The reporters thought it was a joke and kidded him along. But to Susan it was no laughing matter, she was furious.

Susan had tested for Scarlett O'Hara to appear opposite Gable's Rhett Butler decades ago when she was a fresh kid from Brooklyn and he was king of the movies. They almost met at a party given for him after he came out of the service. The whole town was throwing parties for him and he escorted singer Jan Clayton to one particular party, and was very attentive to her until Susan Hayward walked in — then his attention was gone. Gable was fascinated by the way Hayward looked 'sexily' at men. It wasn't sex, it was myopia. She was trying to find them without her glasses. Hayward didn't respond to Gable by going into a swoon. When Jan Clayton told her after the party that Gable stared at her all night she said, "He did? Why didn't somebody tell me?"

20th Century Fox told Susan she would have to go to Hong Kong for foreign location shooting. She couldn't legally take her sons out of the country without their father's and the court's permission and she didn't want to leave them in Barker's custody, as they never came back the same after their visits with him, and she feared further damage to her position as their mother and refused to go.

The chief of 20th Century Fox, Darryl F. Zanuck, who had guided Hayward's career to further prominence at Fox, was in his office in the executive building when a furious redhead stormed in, leaving behind her a secretary with mouth agape.

Zanuck started to rise.

"Stay right there Darryl!" she said.

Seated behind his mahogany desk in a tweed jacket and knitted tie, his moustache pressing an expensive cigar he sized up the situation as Hayward tore into him, pounding on his desk.

"I'm not leaving California, and I'm not going to do this picture."

"Now Susan," he said calmly, "This will be very good for you, after all this is Clark Gable and —"

"Screw Gable," she snapped back, "Get him Grace Kelly."

"Darryl I can't go — I won't!" she said, trying not to go into all the details.

"Susan," Zanuck said. "Now listen — you want to do *I'll Cry Tomorrow*, we all know — I've agreed to loan you to MGM — but first you'll have to wrap up this picture with Gable…"

And so they compromised.

When they eventually teamed up on the lot for shooting, she was very cool.

The scene came where Susan was to slap Gable across the face, after he had made an inopportune remark.

Gable grinned and told her not to feel shy; to let him have it — to make it look convincing. If not they would have to do another take.

She said she'd try her best. The director called for action — and got it; Susan hauled off and swung her right hand, landing a hit that sent Gable staggering off balance.

The making of this film was to run concurrently with the beginning of *I'll Cry Tomorrow* and towards the end of the shooting, a meeting was arranged between the producer of *I'll Cry Tomorrow* and her new director, Daniel Mann.

It was Daniel Mann's first meeting with Susan Hayward. He had only recently arrived in Hollywood from the New York theatre. Studio boss

Hall Wallis of Paramount Pictures had brought him out to direct Shirley Booth in *Come Back Little Sheba*, and the Italian actress Anna Magnani in *The Rose Tattoo*. Both pictures had brought considerable acclaim to the director and an Academy Award to each of the stars.

Larry Weingarten of Metro-Goldwyn-Mayer, the producer of *I'll Cry Tomorrow*, asked Mann to direct Susan Hayward in this film and

Susan and Clark Gable.

pre-production meetings were arranged. Weingarten, a mild mannered individual, was not cast in the usual mold of Hollywood producers. In fact, at a casual glance he could easily have been mistaken for an English professor from a nearby university.

Mann had never met a Hollywood movie star; Shirley Booth was from the stage and Anna Magnani was a star of the Italian screen. Hayward was a true product of the Hollywood system.

For their meeting, she wore a plain suit, blouse and gloves and a light make-up, not chic, but well groomed.

"There was an innate shyness, a self protectiveness about her, particularly in meeting new people and especially producers and directors. As soon as she felt you were honest with her," said Mann. "Her natural instincts as an outgoing lusty dame from Brooklyn came through.

"Susan was really keen on the role," he went on. "Very receptive about the meeting. There was nothing grand about her, but she certainly had all the professional concern about who she was going to be dealing with in a film of this nature.

"As I remember it our meeting was friendly; she was observing me, and I was observing her. She represented to me a lovely young talented lady who was going to have to go through a great big emotional role about somebody who became addicted to alcohol, the story of Lillian Roth."

Susan looked Mann over appraising, the individual who was going to be her director as she had director approval. She saw someone with an athletic build, dark hair and blue eyes, a serious, intelligent man whom, she must have decided, she could get along with.

She lit a cigarette and listened as Weingarten spoke to Mann and herself about general schedules and the target date for the completion of the movie. Following this Mann talked to Susan about the essence of the character of Lillian Roth, with all her strengths and weaknesses, the role that Susan would practically adopt as her own nature. Susan must have wondered how deep he was going to dig, how much he was going to probe. There would be areas where they would be on no man's land together and with her highly personalized acting, they would either have to meet or cancel each other out.

"Larry," Susan said to Weingarten during a break in Mann's talk, "It's imperative that whoever is going to direct this role — the role of a woman's life and her attempted suicide — had to be somebody I can accept; not simply accept legally but accept in a sense of working with extremely closely. I want to do this role right," she emphasized. "And I cannot accept someone I am not at ease with." Thus, she made her position clear to her new director.

Susan said very little else at the meeting in the executive's office. She never was a big talker but she didn't miss very much either. She had easily detected in Mann his sensitivity, and his air of self-assurance. He could be strong with her without pushing too hard, something she needed. Also,

Susan in I'll Cry Tomorrow.

had he not brought two middle aged actress's performances on screen to the critical acclaim of the industry and public's acceptance at the box office?

Shooting was to begin with the last scene of *I'll Cry Tomorrow*, the scene at the El Capitan theatre in Hollywood and Vine. In this scene, the regenerated torch-singer walks down the aisle to tell her story on the television show *This Is Your Life* to a television and studio audience of a combined total of some 40,000,000 people. The host of the television program, Ralph Edwards, introduces the honored guest to the audience. Susan, as Lillian Roth, meets the people who were responsible for saving her, after being helped on stage by members of Alcoholics Anonymous.

"We were going to open with that and all my instincts told me this is not the way to *start* the picture," Mann reflected. "This is a moment of climax of her coming back as a whole person again."

The house was full of people who had come to see the Ralph Edwards show. Edwards was on stage and Susan was waiting to make her entrance from the lobby through the doors of the theatre and down the center aisle.

A ramp was built from the back of the theatre over the top of the seats the full length of the theatre so that the camera could move with Susan. It would be on her as she walked down and would move with her and arc over to make the audience visible. They were ready for a rehearsal of the first scene.

Susan walked down the aisle with Mann looking through the lens. The elevation of the camera cut off the heads of the audience and all he could see was Susan's head and shoulders so he told the crew to put the camera down as low as it would go. The theatre had been contracted for and was loaded with lighting and other equipment for the shooting. There were hundreds of extras and Susan was being very patient as they launched into their first day. She was aware that the director had a shooting problem. In fact, it was obvious to her he was not at all happy with the shot. She heard him say it would not really do justice to the dramatic impact of her being aware of people staring at her and the moment — soon — that she was going to have to come down and face the truth; to be stripped emotionally naked and exposed to a world wide audience.

They rehearsed again and Mann asked that the camera be lowered even more to capture the expression on the audience's faces, only to make the discovery that it could not be lowered anymore. He turned to the assistant director and the MGM chiefs standing by.

"I am not going to do this shot," he said, "it doesn't make sense. My responsibility is to you, the studio, and the studio is synonymous with Susan, the audience, myself — and it just doesn't make sense."

He went into a huddle with the men surrounding him. Whilst directing each shot he would mentally fuse it into his image of the completed film and he was not prepared to compromise on this image. This had a tremendous impact on Susan who standing by watching and listening.

The executives were overwhelmed that Mann would take this position. It was unimaginable to them — even worse, it was his first picture at MGM.

"Danny you gotta do this!" said one of the studio executives.

"Look I'm not going to argue with you," he replied. "This is not a question of temperament or other nonsense. My first responsibility is to make this picture, and my making this picture means that this scene is the reaching of a climax — a lifetime of what she has gone through, and not to get the dramatic impact would be a terrible loss, and wouldn't really be right for me as a director and certainly not for Susan. No, no way! I'll go home. I have a nice backyard and I'll sit there and when you want me..." he broke off and walked away.

It was then that Susan realized that she had, as a director, a man who was going to be involved with only the best that could possibly be achieved, both cinematically and regarding the development of the character. Mann and Susan never discussed the decision, however, her attitude towards him was very much affected by it and she began to open up to him a little, feeling that she could trust him.

Ironically, when they got around to the scene again and decided to rebuild the ramp, there was a problem, which evidently disallowed them, as a movie company, to go into a theatre and film a TV show for a movie. They finally built the ramp on the MGM lot.

Another important moment came when Susan and Daniel Mann were to test each other. Cinematographer James Wong Howe was going over the script with Mann. The Oscar winning Howe was one of the greatest cameramen in the business, and was brilliant at underlying moods.

In preparing for her role, Susan had studied the mannerisms of seriously ill alcoholics and visited the cells of unfortunates in the Los Angeles County Jail. Through the bars of their cells, she has studied women with the "shakes."

In one scene, Susan had to play Lillian Roth at her absolute rock-bottom, lost in her alcoholic obsession as she sat in the bar with the winos, it would be very important now not only to photograph Susan's emotional involvement in that atmosphere but literally (if possible), to photograph the reflection of the place as registered in her face. She was to be completely lost, not aware of what she was doing, because she had been wandering around drunk for nobody knows how long.

"Danny, I'll tell you what; I want to make a test of Susan without make-up," Howe told Mann, "Susan has freckles, which are kind of a wholesome thing — but if I use a blue light the freckles will give us a texture to her skin and make her look really wasted."

Mann went to see Hayward, to talk about it.

"What! You want me to appear without any…Danny…" she said. "I-I don't know."

"Alright Susan, I am not asking you to appear unpleasant or ugly. I am asking you to appear as she did at this point in her life. Make-up can't create that. With no make-up and Jimmy's ability to get it, it will give us tremendous sympathy for Roth's appallingly wasted life at this moment."

She thought for a moment, "I've never done anything like that I've always tried to cover these things up, but I'll do it — O.K. I'll do it."

The scene in the barroom is where Lillian, now a chronic alcoholic, is living in almost complete forgetfulness. She makes drunks laugh by reciting a childhood job seeking speech — 'I'm Lillian Roth, I'm eight years old, I do imitations and dramatic parts' — and the winos finally discover that this *is* the lady they remembered. They laugh at her while Susan sits there laughing too; and as she's laughing big tears, like drops of blood, are pouring out of her eyes. It became one of the most unforgettable moments in the picture.

Susan changed a lot during this period, very much aided by the story of Lillian Roth's torment, and often went into long trances and became at times quite unreachable. She brooded and had frequent fits of severe nervousness and bouts of delirium tremens, similar to those that Lillian Roth must have experienced. The pain of her early years, which she was summoning for the role, sent her, in the early part of the filming especially, into desperate depressions. She could portray the lonely, desperate, frustrated singer so well because she had experienced similar emotions; despite the fact that many of her troubles were self made.

"It was one of the great moments in my whole career," Mann said about the barroom scene not simply because it was a classic moment of laughter and tears, but that she had the freedom and capacity to involve herself in a very personalized moment."

"Only an actress of great courage, talent and magic could have done it. It could have looked phony to be laughing and crying at the same time, big thing about Susan's talent is that none of this was representative.

What Susan did is what she experienced — that's why the audience experienced it."

As an actress and as an individual, Susan understood the story very thoroughly she was able to involve herself in these 'magic' moments, helping to make her the actress she was. In Susan's tragic life, there was a deep understanding of irony and pain. Mann picked up on this and was determined not to close her off or risk invading her with intimacies that might cause her to reject his direction.

A week later Susan Hayward tried to kill herself.

She was alone in the living room of her house in Sherman Oaks on that Monday night, April 25, 1955. She must have heard the grandfather clock strike midnight as she slammed the phone down on Jess Barker over another argument about the upbringing of their sons. Her thoughts circled hopelessly. The marriage had blown up the year before in a flare of headlines. She had seen him just four days ago — very reluctantly — and he had challenged her custody of the twins. She was driven to distraction by Barker's threats to take her boys away from her.

Sitting barefoot on the couch, dressed in pajamas, her head thrown back in exhaustion, a wave of depression must have swept over her. She could still hear his angry voice echoing in her ears. Divorce yes, but no end to the recriminations and quarrels. Timmie and Greg were sleeping upstairs, but they had never seemed so far away from her. Kept late at the studio for a conference, she had come home after their bedtime and crept up to look in on them, their two motionless forms outlined under the covers with only their heads visible. She couldn't just take them away someplace else, she was on the treadmill of her career and obligations she had built up did not allow her to break away from the only 'security' she had every known.

The house was so noisy during the day with the boys tearing about and Cleo the housekeeper trying to keep some kind of control. In the evenings Cleo's daughter, Willy Mae, joined her mother to help out with the boys when Susan worked late at the studio.*

At night, everything was deathly quiet. She had tried to go to sleep, but could not rest so she had gotten out of bed and gone downstairs to have a drink and a cigarette, and curl up on the couch. When she was found later that night, beside her lay the script of *I'll Cry Tomorrow*. She had probably been going over it before her suicide attempt.

Now, in her highly emotional and suggestible condition some of the thoughts in the script may have begun to work on her mind, so that her interpretation became even more personalized than usual, assuming a new significance.

Reading the scenes, she must have been aware of how the conflicts and fights with her own mother had much in common with the characters in the script. Susan's own mother was constantly badgering her about her drinking which had worsened considerably since her marriage to Barker and had continued to increase since the separation.

At some point, she took a large handful of sleeping pills, washed down with her usual bourbon, and decided at the last moment to call her mother.

Ellen Marrener, awakened by the ringing telephone in her home, picked up the receiver, angry and irritated at this interruption to her sleep but she quickly focused her attention as she heard her daughter's slurred speech, barely voicing the words, "Don't woo-ry Ma, you, you're taken care of."

Alarmed, she told her daughter she would call her right back and immediately phoned her son Wally, who remembered the call vividly.

"Wally, Susan just called me, she's talkin' kinda funny Wal, somethin' is goin' on out there. I'll call her and keep talkin' you get out there right away," his mother said.

Wally, following his mother's orders, jumped into his clothes, got into his car and in fifteen minutes was at Susan's home in the valley.

"When I arrived," he said, "the maid had heard the noise of her falling and had called the police. They hadn't arrived, neither had the ambulance and Susan's lying on the floor by the couch."

Shortly afterwards, speeding through the quiet suburban streets, a squad car screeched to a halt at the house on Longridge Avenue. Two police officers rushed across the patio and pounded on the door. They rushed past Wally as he opened it, and found Susan Hayward lying unconscious on the floor of her living room. The clock in the living room showed three o'clock. In Susan's bathroom cupboard upstairs, the detectives found two empty bottles of sleeping pills.

There are conflicting reports surrounding this incident — one of them had her mother calling the police department and saying, "My daughter is Susan Hayward. I'm afraid she's going to commit suicide." Another had Detective Wilkerson pounding on her front door yelling, "Susan, this is Wilkerson of the Detective bureau. Let us in!" — and getting only a 'yeah!' as reply, kicking in the patio door; there does appear to be validity in the patio-door incident as the L.A. Police Dept. used the Hayward suicide attempt case in a brief which was part of a move to reverse a Supreme Court ruling on illegal trespass. Chief William H. Parker contended that if his men had not broken down Miss Hayward's door, though it violated the law, she might have died.

"They just stood there," Wally said, "What are you gonna do," he cried out. "Just let her lie there until the ambulance gets here? Why don't you put her in your car! That might have been against the law," Wally went on, "but anyway the police put her in their car. They picked her up, one grabbin' her under the arms, the other by the legs with me holdin' her under the middle."

Reporters had just arrived at 3801 Longridge Avenue as Susan was being carried out of her house down the steps. The flashlights from the cameras lighted up the scene like a movie set. They yelled at the Detectives Wilkerson and Brondell for information. Wilkerson asked them to clear a way to the squad car and Brondell bit harder on his cigar and ignored them.

"Who are you?" they asked Wally.

"Who?" they said when they couldn't make out what his answer was.

"Her brother?"

"He don't look like her brother," they shouted as they scrambled over one another to get a closer shot of Susan — without make-up, her hair matted, pajamas dishelved and her face cold and expressionless.

"Once the police put her in the car," Wally continued. "I followed, and we got down to Ventura Blvd. about a half mile away and here comes the ambulance. Anyway, I followed the police car — I asked them if I go through a red light O.K.?" They said, 'Follow us.'"

The car raced to North Hollywood Receiving Hospital. In the emergency room, a team of doctors and nurses syringed out her stomach and she was prepared for transfer to Cedars of Lebanon Hospital.

Hovering between life and death, the woman who managed her career, home and family with computer-like efficiency had crashed.

Susan's mother sat at the kitchen table, on Longridge Ave. with her son Wally and her daughter Florence. Wally had returned from the hospital with the report that Susan's condition was critical. (Ellen Marrener and Florence were not very much in touch with Susan at this point and Wally had to keep them informed). They were having a drink to console themselves. The twins had been sent back to bed by their grandmother, "Mommie had a stomach ache and she was going to be fine," they were told. Nine-year-old Timmie crept downstairs and listened by the door.

He overheard his grandmother and his Aunt Florence arguing over what would happen to Susan's money and property if she didn't pull through. Grandmother was fearful of Jess Barker's claims to Susan's estate. Florence could have all her sister's clothes, furs, jewelry, and Wally would get what they worked out for him. Timmie never forgot what he overheard and the results of this conversation would considerably affect his feelings towards them in later years. During the divorce hearings, one of the children had reported hearing something his Grandmother said right after his father left home. In talking to his father just before he left he said he couldn't understand why Grandma should say, "She would kill you," and urge his mother to get rid of Daddy." No matter how these remarks were intended the effect of them on an eight year old must have been traumatic.

At Cedars of Lebanon, the chief medical resident was alerted to take charge as Susan was brought to her hospital room. She was given intravenous feeding so that drugs could be given to correct shock and during the pre-dawn hours, the nurse would check her pulse, respiration, blood pressure and the pupils of her eyes repeatedly.

At the root of her being, Susan must have wanted to live and some three hours after her arrival, she awakened from the coma.

A photo of the nearly dead Susan being carried from her home made the front page, with headlines bannering her suicide attempt. During her recovery in the hospital, an endless stream of 'Why-did-Susan-do-it?' articles appeared. Most of the articles assumed, at first that the strain of the divorce from Jess had caused her to overdose on barbiturates. Mystery lovers (including Howard Hughes, whom she had been dating) were later dragged into the conjectures. Jess himself, believing that he was the cause of the incident, told the newspapers that he had never stopped loving Susan; he wanted reconciliation and tried to visit her in the hospital, but he was the last person she wanted to see. Billy Graham shouted from his lectern, 'Movie stars are unhappy, miserable people' and went on to sermonize on Susan Hayward's attempt to kill herself. It all made hot newspaper copy.

The morning had come after all. Susan opened her eyes as daylight filled the hospital room. She was weak and her mind was in a daze as she laid there welcoming the sensation of being alive.

"She was kind of miserable you know," Wally said. "They stationed a guard at the door so you couldn't get in to see her. She said she didn't want anybody to see her. After two days my mother and myself were allowed in."

"She looked kinda sheepish, cause my mother was ready to ball her out, but I told my mother, "Now don't say anything to her — if she wants to tell us anything, let her do it."

Susan did tell them something, but it wasn't very much, she simply said that she was reading the script and forgot how many pills she had taken. She would neither admit nor deny that she had tried to take her own life.

On the third day in the hospital, Susan ordered a steak for lunch. She changed into a pink negligee and a filmy pick sleeveless jacket. Softly made up, her red hair brushed back shiny and loose, she was ready to meet the press, which had been waiting for her around the clock.

"Dr. Imerman says I can leave the hospital within the next day or two. I am very anxious to get back to my children and back to work. No, there's not the slightest possibility of a reconciliation — if Mr. Barker can discuss the future of our children in a rational manner I shall be willing to confer with him." — was all she would say about the whole affair. It sounded like a press release. So far as any other enquiries were able to determine, she never talked to anyone about that night. She did make one further statement, "There are some things that are between you and God only," she said, and putting her hand on a reporter's knee, continued, "Don't ever believe there isn't a God. There is. I know there is a God."

The following day, shortly after breakfast she put on a bright print dress and was ready to leave the hospital. An attendant brought a wheelchair into her room.

"What's that for?"

"Hospital rule, Miss Hayward."

"That's nonsense; I can walk alone — now!"

"The impact on me was terrifying," Daniel Mann said when he saw the morning paper, "Here was a human being whom I was concerned with on a very personal level and she had tried to take her own life. She would not see anybody at the studio, but she would see me. The studio sent a limousine over and I was driven out to her house in Sherman Oaks. This was a day or two later."

"When I arrived at the house there were reporters outside. I rang the bell and the door was opened about four inches wide by the housekeeper and when I announced who I was she said, "Yes, come in." It was all very magic and hocus pocus, like a bad mystery. She ushered me into the living room and I sat down."

"Miss Hayward will be down shortly," she said.

"The last I had seen of her was the picture in the newspapers as she was carried out inert. Now I heard footsteps on the staircase behind me and I turned around. There was Susan coming down the stairs, her hair all beautifully coiffured, and wearing an organdy dress and looking absolutely marvelous. As she entered the room, I made the faux pas of my life. She came bouncing in and said, "Hello Danny.""

"Susan, you look so alive!" I exclaimed.

"Oh!" she laughed.

"Oh, no, no, no, excuse me," I said, "I didn't mean to be facetious, but you look wonderful, marvelous."

"She laughed again and I embraced her."

A few days later Susan returned to work at MGM. The first scene to be filmed, on her first day back, was a big musical production number, built around the song 'Sing You Sinners', (insert photo of sing your sinners) in which she performed on a multi level set with a platoon of dancers.

Veteran costume designer Helen Rose, who had been assigned to do Susan's clothes on the picture, was one of the first people on the set to see her that day.

"Susan was being given the star treatment; a dressing room in the star building and a portable dressing room on the set. She was not at all fashion conscious but she was easy to work with — that is, for me she was. Danny was the one who got friendly with her. I was happy to be working with Danny Mann again; we had had a great rapport when we did *Butterfield 8* with Elizabeth Taylor."

"Susan was very lonely and very unfriendly and I knew she was going through some big personal problems. I remember when she came back following her suicide attempt. She was in a black mood that day and when I was alone with her in her dressing room, I told her off; 'Susan, when are you going to wake up and stop feeling sorry for yourself.' Her response to this was a sharply withdrawn silence but from that time on she seemed to perk up," the designer said.

Up to this point Susan had never sung professionally, but during the course of some routine pre-recording tests, MGM's musical chief Johnny Green was astonished by her signing voice. Green urged her to do her own singing rather than use a recording of Lillian Roth's voice for the soundtrack. He coached her privately. The first song was 'Red, Red, Robin, etc.'

"When they played it for the studio chief's they all agreed Susan could do her own soundtrack. She did her own singing though with the reservation that when they discovered that she really couldn't do it they would replace her with a professional, about the only recorded incident in which she insisted she couldn't do something.

Susan sat in her dressing room until she was called or. The knock on her door told her they were ready on the set. She looked into the dressing room mirror, checking make-up, hair and the low-cut, sleeveless beaded evening gown Helen Rose had designed to display her beautiful shoulders and arms. She put on her shoes and stepped out.

She came out looking absolutely radiant, although serious, and the set was 'electrified.' Something changed — became super-charged — in the atmosphere on the stage. Every one pivoted in her direction, not a word was said, but there was a powerful undercurrent of suspense. It was virtually impossible to go on as though nothing had happened, though there was a real attempt on everyone's part to ignore the facts of the shocking headlines just a few days ago. The entire crew was focused on her as she made her way, stepping over wires and in between lights and cameras. She climbed the ladder to the top of the set. (It was two floors of a building, with the fourth wall cut out and a camera boom ready to shoot by rising up to look into the house on either floor). She would begin on the top floor. It was one of the big MGM stages and there was a large assembly of technical staff with recording and other equipment, and legions of dancers and extras — all in the best tradition of MGM musicals.

Jimmy Wong Howe had the light he wanted, the dancers and the extras were posed for their cue, the boom camera advanced towards her, then — ACTION!

The music blared out and her tight serious look vanished as the energy of the performance, the lights, movement and action of the whole scene seemed to release her, "Brothers and sisters, startin' today, you can lose your blues whenever you choose by singing your troubles away," she belted out.

After the scene she ran, not walked, to her dressing room. She ran daintily like a ballet dancer. Her body small and playful, but her eyes were sad and serious again. She had returned, and now it was business as usual.

Susan never sat around to shoot the breeze with anyone. She followed an almost invariable pattern of returning to her dressing room between takes. One time during a break, she asked a chorus boy, in costume as a sailor for the number, "Got a cigarette?" As she sat down next to him, he gave her one and lit it for her. They called for the next take. "Thanks sailor," was all she said, as she took up her position, warmed up to a smile, and waited for her cue to go into her number again.

Once the musical numbers were shot, they went back into the heavy dramatic scenes. "I surprised Susan with this one," Mann said, "The boy-friend had passed on in the picture and there was a scene where she gets a drink from the nurse. I made an inquiry and found out that Susan liked bourbon so I said to the prop man get me the best bourbon in the world. I didn't tell Susan. I knew she would respond perfectly to it."

She always threw herself almost violently into her parts. She was an honest actress. When the director called for her, she was ready. She knew her lines. She did not always rise easily to the emotional peaks her roles required, she sometimes had to work up to them, feeling her way. Now she had to try to work her way out of this one — and there was no one around to direct her.

In preparing for bed, before going downstairs, she had evidently taken some of the sleeping pills her doctor had prescribed. They must not have had much effect, as there was evidence that she had been downstairs and awake for some considerable time before she was found on the floor of the living room.

She had never liked the nights alone and she kept some lights on all the time. As a child, staying at her grandmother's house, an uncle had terrified her by telling her there was a bogeyman waiting for her upstairs. She had always remembered that and had been afraid of the dark ever since. She never outgrew that bogeyman and her nearsightedness didn't help either, it only added to her fear of what she couldn't see and her lack of security.

She probably tried to distract herself by going over the script and coming across a particularly violent scene between Lillian Roth and her mother, she had underlined the words — "don't worry, Mom — you're taken care of."

"The shot is where the nurse sees that she can't sleep because she is in such pain and anguish and she decides she is going to give her a drink. She took the real bourbon and poured some of it into a glass. The shot follows the nurse handing her the glass, and I didn't tell Susan it was bourbon. She took hold of the drink and brought it to her lips. It grabbed her in the throat, but instead of stopping the act she finished the drink, put the glass down and dropped her shoulders — and you knew she was hooked."

"You son-of-a-bitch," she smiled slowly at Mann.

She started every morning by involving herself totally in her role and worked towards achieving the highest emotional key. She was appreciative of everybody on the set but very detached.

"She maintained a certain distance. It was not a conscious attempt to be different, she was concentrating on her work, which was very personal to her," was how Mann described the detachment, "nothing needed to be superimposed for effect."

Mann had young children and sometimes they would exchange small talk about them but that was about as personal as she got. Anything that was not strictly relative to the shooting was organized so that it would not interfere and Susan made one exception. She knew Daniel Mann's birthday and that he was crazy about the number nine so she sent him ninety-nine long stem roses, in a huge bowl. He was very touched by this gesture. Another small deviation to this rule was when Irene Pappas was in Hollywood at MGM. She was on a working visit from Greece and she asked Mann's permission to visit the set to watch Susan at work. She had been an admirer of hers and Susan was very popular in Greece. Mann agreed but kept the socializing between them distinctly minimal, as Susan preferred.

They worked until six o'clock every day but if they ran over to six thirty, she would never complain but she would say, "I'm coming in a half hour late tomorrow to make up for it." She was very accurate about her work hours, very professional.

Director Mann reflected on the suicide scene, "It was a very special scene because it had nothing to do with her playing alongside another actor. The circumstances were that she had left her mother (Mrs. Roth) and she was to go to the hotel and enter the room after registering."

Before all of these important takes, Mann would talk to Susan. He demanded that the stage be absolutely quiet, that everyone sit down.

"I would talk to Susan," he said, "and tell her the circumstances leading up to the point where she would make her entrance."

"She would become very upset and being crying and making other sounds — like animal noises — whilst I was talking to her. She would generate this terrible, painful emotion from deep inside herself, this searing conflict that was Susan, and she would begin to whimper and cry, and finally shout, 'ALL RIGHT!' Now I'd watch her start to walk onto the set. Then she would grab hold of me and I'd push her back and we'd shoot the scene. At the end of the day, I would really be involved in the most amazing kind of nervous energy her pain being the source of it. Somehow, she would generate it and use it in the scene. On some days she would start crying at nine o'clock in the morning and keep it going all day."

"Susan, this is a rehearsal darling, don't, don't, I would plead with her."

"No, Danny it's all right."

"She would go into rehearsal again and again with this great release of all that terrible pain this poor woman, Lillian Roth, had experienced. Now the actual suicide scene came and I sat down with her again. Everybody else was sent away."

"We're going to do the suicide scene and you know all about it. I can't tell you about suicide. Whatever that pain is you can't live with anymore, that's an area of yours alone. I'll leave it that to you. We're not going to pretend to deal with the actual experience; your life's worth — to live or not to live — is going through your mind. They way we're going to dramatize it, is not to try to understand or discuss it, but what I want you to do is to look 'now' and hear 'now' and see 'now,' all the things you are never going to be able to see, hear and touch again. This is your last time."

"Jimmy Wong Howe lit the set, the hotel room high up, which Lillian Roth has taken with the intention of jumping out of the window — and there was a silence, and Susan did one of those great scenes of which she was so capable as an actress."

When she touched the table it had all the moment of feeling 'she may never touch this again.' She looked at the walls — it wasn't just looking, it wasn't just seeing, it was measuring, remembering, a lifetime in a moment. She had an involvement with all these objects and lifeless as they were, they were going to be her last link with a life she was about to throw away, hoping perhaps that at the last moment even one of these lifeless objects would give off some kind of reaction to stop her and make her life seem necessary.

When the bellboy came in again, it was relating to him not only in thoughtfulness (a tip) but, 'I must see a moment of some recognition of me,' and as these moments built up so did the desperation and pain of decision, 'should I, shouldn't I, will I have enough courage — please God make it quick for me — let it happen,' and so she vacillated alternating between what little strength she had left and the weakness which was overcoming her, and all this vacillation finally heaped up in over powering, mind numbing confusion. Then not necessarily wishing to die, but finally giving up and being overtaken, perhaps by the thought that the anguish would at least end on death, or the hope, maybe, that one would survive in the end but the pain would all be gone, or would at least be recognized by others in the statement of the attempt, Susan, as Lillian Roth, finally got to the window ledge and looked down; when she saw far below her the traffic and the people; and as she actually sat on the ledge, she fainted, and by a stroke of good fortune instead of falling out she fell — in.

"I really believed that Susan got back on her feet from that experience in playing that role of Lillian Roth," Mann said, "that was the road back, so to speak, from personal problems, her mother, her marriage. She could have gone one way or another — like the suicide scene. I was with her and walked this path with all its pitfalls."

Susan became a firebrand right after finishing *I'll Cry Tomorrow*. The film would be a gripping experience for moviegoers, generate her fourth academy award nomination, and bring to her a new respect in the movie industry.

Then scandal and headlines struck Susan again when the police were called in for the third time in recent months. Small time actress, Jill

Jarmyn, dropped in unexpectedly early one morning at her fiancé Don Barry's apartment, 'for a cup of coffee.' Miss Jarmyn told the cops that she found Miss Hayward there wearing blue-and-white-polka-dot pajamas and a surprised look. Jarmyn called Susan 'a bitch' so Susan socked her, giving her a black eye. Jarmyn attempted to hit her back and Susan worked her over with a clothes brush and a stream of truck driver four-letter words. They wrestled around, smashing some furniture in the process, until Barry came out of the kitchen and pulled them apart. Jarmyn filed an assault and battery complaint against her attacker but later dropped it, saying, 'a public hearing on this situation would be bad for the motion picture industry.' An odd statement after the fact of her 'pose' for the press; a picture complete with black eye. More than likely, she was paid off to drop the charges.

When Susan was queried by the press as to what she was doing at Barry's place that time of the morning, she quipped, "He makes good coffee." Later, when Hayward learned about the engagement, she dropped Barry completely and never spoke to him again.

Though her position was clearly indefensible to Miss Jarmyn there is an illuminating unreleased item on Hayward's file at the 20th Century-Fox — "I'm a sucker for anyone who comes offering honey instead of vinegar. But if someone comes along with a chip on their shoulder I'm agin' 'em pronto. Life's too short to waste on phonies. The psychologists have been saying for years, 'get it off your chest.' It's the people who never blow up who wind up paying the piper or rather the psychiatrist. I am extremely touchy. Unless I'm approached in the proper manner I won't play."

One of her paramours, during this overwrought period described her as a "prowling animal," obsessed with sex. Susan's urgent need for a man caused her to feel, unrealistically, that her old friend Jeff Chandler, might be the one to end her sleepless nights, but nothing ever came of that. Susan had a serious sexual problem, which had begun years before. She was inherently frigid and could not achieve an orgasm.

She finally went to what she called her Hollywood psychosexual shrink for aid. He told her how brilliant she was — she had an IQ of almost 170, in spite of her lack of formal education — at which she stood up and leaned across his desk, "If I'm so smart," she said, "why am I paying you $500 an hour?" and walked out.

She gave up on that idea completely and her final solution was to become a virtual wildcat during her love making encounters, acting out the thrill of the orgasm as a substitute for experiencing it. Some men would respond to this, others could not and when a man couldn't Susan would become furious with him, although she was fully aware all along that the trouble was with her.

Yet in spite of everything that was heard or written about her there were important people in the film industry who still described her as an innocent. They even held that her innocence helped catapult her into stardom, giving her international star status. As one of her directors put it, "She had status, recognition and money but she would have given it all up in two minutes for some real love."

At five thirty on the afternoon of August 19, 1955, on Stage 19 of the MGM studios in Culver City, the shooting of the last scene of *I'll Cry Tomorrow* wound up with pickup shots of a sequence in which Susan — her hair matted, her face tear-streaked, and her clothes filthy with grime from the streets and wino bars — wrecked her mother's living room. While she went off to her dressing room to clean up and put her face back on, the rest of the cast gathered around the remains of a small nightclub layout on another part of the big stage. Food was stacked on a row of tables, and a couple of bartenders began operating behind a bar, which had been previously used in the filming *Occasion* to celebrate the close of the picture.

A four-piece orchestra began playing songs from the picture and about a hundred or so people were gathered around slapping each other on the back, congratulating each other, sampling the buffet and dancing.

Soon, Susan reappeared wearing dark glasses, a blouse and black toreador pants, all vestiges of her afternoon as a sodden drunk having vanished. Someone clapped for attention and Director Mann made a short speech thanking everybody for their efforts and cooperation, which was followed by a long round of applause.

"And now," he said. "Let's hear from Miss Hayward."

Susan stood up, "I've loved every minute of it," she said. "And I've never had to work harder, or felt such a wonderful sense of achievement. Bless you all — I love you dearly."

Some of the wardrobe women dabbed at their eyes, and other members of the crew were swallowing hard.

Susan slipped away early. She went back to her dressing room to pick up her belongings and walked out of Stage 19 alone; a small frail looking figure making her solitary trek across the parking lot, she stepped into her car and drove off without looking back.

What of her future? As far as her career was concerned, she had nothing to fear, but what about 'the great void' in her personal life. What kind of man would be attracted to a domineering, career-conscious actress, after all, the glamorous, introspective, redheaded Susan Hayward was not necessarily the most popular girl in Hollywood. She had lived through this crisis, but who would pick up the pieces if there were another.

Part of her, the celluloid Susan Hayward, was now placed and stored in neatly labeled cans in a biographical story that would be forever identified with her. In retrospect, her recent experiences would be mild compared to what she had yet to face.

For the moment, there was to be a reprieve from some of her frustrations and uncertainties. In December of that year, she was to meet a man unlike anyone she had ever met before, a gentleman from Georgia by the name of Eaton Floyd Chalkley.

* After the scene when Susan goes shopping on Rodeo Drive Cleo continues…"Pam she was 5 or 6 and goin' round tellin' all the kids Susan Hayward is my Auntie, these black kids in the neighborhood, you gotta be a nut, as black as you are, how can Susan Hayward be your Auntie.

"I was at Fox MGM Paramount, I been on all these sets and Jess took me in one day, what's she doin'? Bathsheba, he said, and I was out there all day watchin them kill each other then she'd go in her make up place and get made up again, do the same scenes over again, same, same, over and over. She wanted me to play the Negro part in *The President's Lady,* the maid, the black woman. I wouldn't take it, even her mother got on me about that, she said," Cleo why don't you accept it Susan wants you so much." I said, I don't think I can make it, but they needed a woman who could speak southern and I'm southern and my vocabulary is kinda southern. So she wanted me to do this part. I wish I had now, after I grew older. I must a been 'bout 33, at that time. I was afraid I would embarrass everybody and myself. And I didn't want to be embarrassed. You see uneducated people can be very shy, I was afraid I couldn't remember the lines.

OSCARS

---

*Awards are beautiful to win; everytime
you get a prize, it's a magnificent feeling. I
was very happy to get an Oscar — I'd lost
out four times before I finally won — but
it wasn't the highpoint. The big treat was
winning the New York Film Critics Award.
That's a tough one to win, not because they
know so much but because most of them are
such rats and they don't like to give anybody
a prize, especially anybody from Hollywood.*

CHAPTER 8

It was Washington in the early twenties — a frightening time to be young. The uncertainties of a post world war were being felt everywhere and America was going on a gaudy spree. Morality was undergoing a revolution and Calvin Coolidge prosperity embraced an era of zooming stocks, emancipated women, rum running and rebellious youth.

On the corner of 6th and B Street was the usual corner drug store. It was owned and operated by the most unusual Doc Geiger. He would oversee the crowd of boys, sometimes as many as twenty-five or more, who congregated there until around 8 o'clock each night before leaving to keep their dates. In Washington as in all cities at that time, there would be complaints about gangs loitering on street corners and disturbing the peace of neighborhoods. Many of the guys went around to Doc's protected territory, and when the police came to break up a mob near the store Doc's boys would leave by the back door. The cops, seeing the place empty, would then leave the area. After this had happened a few times Mrs. Geiger, a kind old lady who knew her husband enjoyed the company of the youths in the store, with their discussions about politics and one thing or another, called the 90th Precinct and strongly defending the boys — asked the cops to leave them alone; they wanted them there at the store.

Doc, a fallen away Catholic, repeatedly said, "None of my boys ever went bad."

One of his boys, Tom Farrell, was in the seminary and Doc promised that when Tom was ordained he would go to confession and make his peace with the Almighty.

Tom Farrell was one of the 'Renroc' team of four boys, who were as close as brothers. They were all good ballplayers, good athletes and they formed the team and called it 'Renroc' — which was corner spelt backwards — after Doc's place on the corner, as it was the most important influence in their lives at the time.

The eldest of the foursome was Vincent Flaherty. Vinnie, as he was known, stuttered badly all his life, but he went on to become an ace sportswriter in spite of his hardship with words. Tom Farrell was going to become a priest; Thomas Brew, who was also to enter the priesthood, was the lynchpin of the group, and Eaton Chalkley completed the foursome.

Virginia born (1909) Eaton Floyd Chalkley was the tallest of the four and at 17 was a robust, handsome youth who took good care of his appearance, prompting Thomas Brew's mother to remark to the boys, 'Why don't you all look more like Eaton?'

Thomas Brew, who was to become a lifelong friend and an important spiritual influence in Eaton Chalkley's development, accepted his scholarship for athletics to Georgetown University, the oldest Catholic college in Washington. Eaton, a year behind his friend Thomas was in his last year at Eastern High School in Washington.

Eaton and Thomas, the closest of the four friends, parted when Thomas switched to Mount St. Mary's College at Emmitsburg, Maryland in June 1934.

After graduation, Eaton went off to Xavier College in Cincinnati, Ohio and not long afterwards, he rejoined his friend, Thomas, at Mount St. Mary's. Now reunited, they became closer than ever.

Eaton's strict upbringing at home must have contributed considerably to what Thomas Brew was later to describe as an air of very assured self-passion. The Chalkley's attended St. Mark's Episcopal Church faithfully, where Eaton once had been an altar boy and had sung in the choir, and while he continued to practice his religious beliefs in the faith into which he was christened he was also taking another path at the Catholic College. It was whilst at Mt. St. Mary's, especially during the months of October and May (the months of the Blessed Mother) that Eaton, a non-catholic, was first in the morning to say the rosary in the grotto behind the college. He went to all the devotions in the chapel because there wasn't an Episcopal church nearby, and it was here that the interest and the seed for his conversion to Catholicism took place.

Thomas Brew graduated 18 months ahead of his friend, in 1932, at the lowest point in the depression. Over 13 million people were unemployed and the bottom dropped out of his father's work putting him among them. Thomas was the eldest of the Brew family and felt it was up to him to do something about their dire straights.

Although he had had ideas about entering the priesthood — which had become more specific during his last year in college — he found work as a teacher. During this period, he thought he might be making a mistake about his desired vocation in the priesthood and considered going to Law school at night whilst teaching days. The teaching was very badly underpaid and though he wasn't really interested in becoming a lawyer, he felt he needed some kind of professional training. Hopefully, he thought, the situation at home would stabilize itself when the others got older and he might then reconsider his vocation in the priesthood.

While Brew was teaching at Gonzaga High School, where he had once been a student, Eaton was preparing to leave Mt. St. Mary's.

At around this time, the Federal Bureau of Investigation had begun to expand from a rather small insignificant department to what it was later to become under the guidance of native Washingtonian J. Edgar Hoover. Hoover gave special consideration to boys living in Washington who wanted to work for him and Eaton Chalkley began as a clerk for the Department — June 1934 — making $1200 a year, a good salary for a young man of 21 during the depression. Eaton now wanted to advance to special agent and began attending law classes in the evenings, eventually working his way up during the late 30's.

It was then that Eaton and Thomas Brew decided to enter law school together, beginning in the same class.

During his early years with the FBI, Eaton struck up a friendship with a rather plain, quiet girl by the name of Dorothy Rowland. Always smiling and outgoing himself, for some reason he took to the inhibited and withdrawn girl. Dorothy was a catholic and once again, Eaton was drawn into the catholic religion by his association with her.

Vincent Flaherty was by this time a sports reporter for the Times Herald and he would soon write about Thomas Farrell's first mass in his sports column. Father Farrell was quite a football and baseball player, as were all of the 'graduates' of Doc Geiger's drugstore, and among other things, Flaherty mentioned "that Doc Geiger was at St. Joseph's for the first time in 40 years." True to his promise, when the day came in 1936 for Tom Farrell's lifetime vows into the priesthood, Doc Geiger sat in the front pew with Tom's closest friends, the old 'Renroc' team from the early twenties in Washington, Vincent Flaherty, Thomas Brew and Eaton Chalkley.

The next night the newly ordained Father Farrell went to Doc Geiger's place and, following Doc upstairs, heard his confession.

Several months later, with Tom Farrell now Father Tom of St. Mary's Govans and Vincent Flaherty having moved out West to a spot as a sports reporter for the Los Angeles Examiner, Thomas Brew and Eaton still probably the closest of the original team, confided in each other; Brew on his calling to the priesthood and Eaton on his plans to marry Dorothy Rowland, now that he was feeling more secure in his job with the F.B.I.

In November of 1936, Eaton and Dorothy were married in St. Patrick's Church in Washington by a priest from Mount St. Mary's. Because of their mixed faiths, they were married in the rectory. Thomas Brew was Eaton's best man.

Eight months after the wedding, Eaton and Thomas finished law school giving them both an L.L.B. degree from George Washington Law School in June 1937.

Four months out of law school in September of 1937 Thomas Brew entered the Jesuit Novitiate to begin his studies for the priesthood where he would remain for the next eight years and set his course for his calling in the priesthood.

Eaton was promoted to FBI agent and was sent to Indianapolis, Indiana on his first assignment. Dorothy Rowland Chalkley cried miserably as she left Washington, her home, and her family.

At around the same time that Eaton and Dorothy were leaving Washington, young Edythe Marrener, of Flatbush, was joyously packing to leave Brooklyn. She couldn't wait to "get out," hoping — swearing — that she would never return. She was leaving for Hollywood, California to test for the part of Scarlett O'Hara in *Gone With The Wind*.

While Eaton took to his new home and made fiends easily, Dorothy was homesick, lacking the self-confidence, to make in it — what was to her — the outside world. Later, when she learned she was pregnant she wanted to go home to be with her mother, to return to Washington and familiar surroundings.

But it was there in Indianapolis that their first child was born, to the unhappy mother, a son to be christened Joseph after the choir director of St. Mark's; the church that Eaton had attended in Washington.

When Eaton was transferred to Seattle by the FBI things got worse for Dorothy and the first cracks appeared within the marriage.

Eaton left the FBI in December 1940 and went to work in the legal department of General Motors at their headquarters in Detroit. He had finally converted to Catholicism having come into the Catholic Church of his own choosing after many years of exposure to it and many years of self-discovery. Once he moved into his new faith, he committed himself devoutly and forever.

Dorothy could find ample excuse to stay at home now with Joseph to take care of and another child expected. But after the birth of their daughter, she became more somber and withdrawn.

Eaton took his family back to the Washington area and they bought a home in Falls Church, Virginia. A large colonial house on a hilltop

Dorothy was back home and close to her family and she could no longer complain of being away. Now she was unhappy because Eaton was away on business trips. Even after the birth of a second daughter June, and with three children to care for she was not happy with her life. No matter what Eaton did, it was not right for her.

Eaton had developed an ulcer and in Chicago, it began to bleed profusely, to the danger point. He had to be given blood transfusions and in those transfusions, he was being given tainted blood.

In Hollywood, meantime, Susan Hayward's — the ex-Edythe Marrener — popularity zoomed to the top with a second Oscar nomination for My Foolish Heart. Her studio kept her busy and (as a replacement for Jeanne Crain) she was sent on location to Georgia for the filming of *I'll Climb The Highest Mountain.*

One of Georgia's most beloved characters in the 50's was restaurateur, Harvey Hester, who seemed to know just about everybody. Harvey owned the most famous restaurant in Georgia, a picturesque old place 20 miles out of Atlanta known as Aunt Fanny's, which was an unreconstructed slave quarters with brick floors and huge fireplaces, named after a famous old slave who had lived there. The film company went to Aunt Fanny's often and one day the director asked Harvey if — just for fun — he would take the role of a southern gentleman in the movie they were shooting. He agreed, and Hester and Susan hit it off beautifully right from the start and he became her "Uncle Harvey."

Following his divorce from Dorothy, "Eaton continued to work for General Motors, travelling to every state in the union on his investigative work. On his trips to Los Angeles, he customarily looked up his boyhood friend 'Vinnie' Flaherty. He preferred staying with him rather than going to a hotel, it was more like home. They often talked about the old neighborhood, the three schools they had attended together, and the other two members of the Renroc team, now Fathers Farrell and Brew.

During his travels, Eaton discovered Carrollton, Georgia. Fifty miles out of Atlanta, with a population of under 10,000, on the Little Tallapoosa River, it was fertile farm area. He liked it right from the start. Divorced and a confirmed bachelor, he decided to settle just outside the quiet, pleasant town. He was going on 42 years of age that May.

Eaton had met a man in Carrollton who owned a GM agency. He was getting ready to retire and was looking for a buyer. Eaton made his interest known to General Motors, clearly stating that this was the place for him. His reputation and the impact he made on the agency owner closed the deal. Eaton knew he had a good investment in the Cadillac agency but he also knew he was going into strange territory. He didn't know a solitary person in Georgia.

However, he also intended to go into private practice as a lawyer and he expected that that would involve some travel, which would allow him to keep in touch with his old friends around the country.

As it happened, Vincent Flaherty did know someone in Georgia; he knew Harvey Hester, and Eaton could not have wanted a better introduction into that part of the world. Hester was in Los Angeles visiting a friend and his visit there coincided with one of Eaton's visits. To introduce Eaton to Hester, Flaherty threw a cocktail party at his home in Westwood just before Christmas.

Eaton was with an attractive girl, his date for the evening, when Hester arrived with a familiar redhead on his arm, Susan Hayward, who he never failed to keep in touch with and always looked up when he was in the area.

The two were met by their host and Susan looking over Flaherty's shoulder, quickly noticed the tall stranger looking very assured and confident standing beside the tinseled Christmas tree, alone at the moment. She noticed him first because he was so tall. She was squinting a bit to focus in on him and Eaton Chalkley smiled at her across the room. Then people came between them and cut off their view and she lost him in the crowd.

Flaherty walked towards Susan a moment later to see if she wanted anything and out of the corner of her eye, she again saw the stranger who had smiled at her walk past them.

"Yeah, Vince," she murmured.

Flaherty caught on and talking Eaton's arm, said, "You haven't met have you?"

She looked up at him.

"Merry Christmas Miss Hayward," he said in his deep rich voice.

"Is that Dixie I hear?"

"Carrollton, Georgia," he laughed.

"Where's that!"

"About 50 miles out of Atlanta. It's a small place but it's growin'."

"Are you vacationing out here Mr. Chalkley," she said always one to get to the point.

"No, it's a business trip. I have a car agency in Carrollton, but my law practice takes most of my time. Anti-trust cases mostly."

"Does it bring you to the coast pretty often?"

"Why, yes!"

"Well, tell me more Mr. Chalkley."

She listened and gradually the other voices at the party faded out of focus leaving only his voice in her ears. Later when the group broke up, Flaherty suggested that the few remaining guests go over to Mocambo for Sunday night dinner.

At Mocambo, Susan was sitting out most of the evening, as Hester didn't dance. She and 'Uncle Harvey' were talking about the trip to New

Susan and Eaton

York for the World Series when they had gone to Yankee Stadium to watch the Dodgers in Susan's native Brooklyn, on one of the brief visits she allowed herself there. Her interest in baseball caught his interest in her, among others. Susan kept her eyes on Eaton as he danced with his date. Flaherty told Chalkley he should ask Susan for a dance.

"Why should she want to dance with me?" he asked.

"Just ask her, you'll see," said Flaherty.

Meanwhile he told Susan that Eaton wanted to dance with her, as he escorted Eaton's date to the dance floor. The moment the two were alone at the table, Susan said, "Well, shall we?"

Vincent Flaherty telephoned Father Brew to tell him about Eaton and Susan. He enjoyed playing Cupid in this romance.

Susan wasn't taking any chances and breaking all the rules in courtship, she went after him with all the energy of one of her movie characters.

Father Brew vividly recalls Susan saying right from the start, "This is the guy I want to get."

Producer Marty Rackin's wife, Helen, who had seen them together a number of times, said just about the same ting; "Eaton was quiet and reserved, he brought out the best in her and she brought out the best in him. He was a real southern gentleman, and Susie being in this kind of atmosphere, the movie industry — well, let's face it — these are not southern gentlemen. He was like a breath of fresh air to Susan. Maybe this is the kind of man she had in mind all her life. When she met him at this party, just before Christmas he was with another woman. But Susan looked at him and must have thought — 'this is for me' and went after him. She fell in love then and there."

Susan used Chalkley's friends as romantic go betweens to lure him time and again from his Georgian home in Carrollton to Hollywood, where she was completing *I'll Cry Tomorrow*, and she pursued him in the grand style.

When the picture was finished publicity man Stanley Musgrove was hired to campaign for an Oscar for her performance, as everyone knew she was going to be nominated for it. Musgrove had been recommended to her by Mike Connelly, who was on the Hollywood Reporter and was a writer on the script for *I'll Cry Tomorrow* with Gerald Frank.

Susan had recently moved into the house in Sherman Oaks following her divorce from Jess Barker, and the don 'Red' Barry headlines and the suicide attempt.

Musgrove told about his first meeting with her at 3801 Longridge Avenue and how startled he was to find the house practically empty.

"At first it was tough going dealing with her because I felt like I was up against a stone wall. Then all of a sudden, she was different and I told her so. She said, 'My doctor put me on something new and it makes me feel better!' — I asked her what it was. She said 'miltown,' which was new at that time. I told her I was going to get some dolls' and if ever you run out, I'll keep you on it.

"I leveled with her and she had a little humor about it. She had met Chalkley and she wanted him. He was a marvelous guy. A real dude. A real hunk, who had marvelous manners, a lovely sense of humor, and she set her cap for him. She was relentless about it."

Susan phoned Musgrove, "I want to see you, Stan. I want to give a party and I don't know how. I've never given one before. This place needs all kinds of fixin' up. And who is the right caterer?"

"I recommended the character actor Eric Blore's wife, Clara, a classy kind of woman," Musgrove said, "and Clara went over to the house, took a look around and nearly fainted. There was nothing to work with."

"Do you realize the only glasses in that house are Kraft cheese jars," she told Musgrove unbelievingly.

"It was true; everything had to be brought in. Furniture had to be rented. She only wanted to make an impression on Eaton, to show him she could entertain and do things in style so that when she got to his home in Carrollton she would be able to do it," Musgrove said.

Clara Blore did a miraculous job, transforming the place into an elegant setting for the party. She put gardenias in little urns in the powder rooms — that kind of thing — she ordered wonderful food and it was all first class. Susan made up her own guest list, which Musgrove thought peculiar. After reading it he asked her if she wanted any help with it, 'No!' she replied sharply.

Musgrove, at the party that night, recalled it this way: "Susan purposely invited only a handful of Hollywood people, like her agent Hugh French, and no name stars. She wanted to fill the house with what she thought were the intelligentsia, educated people, like doctors, dentists, psychiatrists and friend's of theirs, she figured this was the way to go. The way to impress Eaton."

The house was jammed with people and there was an evident strain among the guests. Nobody knew anyone else, but, as so often happens in Hollywood, everybody went anyway.

"Suddenly everybody seemed to get drunk and the whole party took off. They turned out to be the worst behaved bunch I've ever seen in my life. They got smashed and jumped into the pool with their clothes on. It had her crazy, she was about to pass out, until she saw that Eaton loved it."

Undaunted, Susan planned another party for Oscar night. It was planned as a winner's party. Clara Blore was called in again to make it work.

For her performance in *I'll Cry Tomorrow*, Susan got glowing reviews everywhere. Honors for her role continued to pile up. She and James Cagney were the recipient's of Best Actor — Best Actress Award from *Look* magazine in 1955. *Redbook, Motion Picture Exhibitor* and Englan's *Picturegoer* also named her best actress. She was a sure bet to win.

On the night of the Oscar presentations, looking radiantly happy and beautiful, Susan was seated between her 11-year-old sons. She was more hopeful than ever as her chance of getting the Award was now as great as it had ever been.

She came home from the theatre stunned; she couldn't believe she hadn't won. Louella Parsons was there waiting with a few close friends to console her. Stanley Musgrove brought actress Mary McCarthy, and Eaton waited, quietly watching her.

It was generally believed (though it was never mentioned publicly) that the academy was full of uptight members and that she had lost the Oscar because of the scandalous headlines, such was the climate of things in Hollywood in the mid 50's.

Anna Magnani won Best Actress Oscar as the neurotic Sicilian born seamstress in *The Rose Tattoo*, directed by Daniel Mann.

Susan was aware of Eaton standing alone in the background as she moved around the room to see everybody, hugging Louella, talking to everyone, behaving as though she had won and soon the whole thing took on a climate of real joy. Susan had lost the Oscar but she was winning what she wanted even more — Eaton.

Going up to Musgrove, she gave him a kiss and said, "You were supposed to get a $5,000 bonus if I got the Oscar, I am sorry you won't get it now."

Musgrove was taken aback, "Susan had been so unstable; been going to a shrink, had been in all this trouble, was bitter about losing the Oscar, yet she was so sweet about my not getting the $5,000 bonus."

Little was mentioned about the Italian actress Anna Magnani who won over Susan's performance until Mary McCarthy, after a few stiff drinks, went up to Susan (never one to kid around with about herself) and said, "Let's all go over to Joe's Little Italy and have some spaghetti." Everyone screamed laughing. Susan froze.

One evening, shortly after the Oscar party Mary McCarthy was having dinner with a friend at the Villa Nova, a popular Italian place on the strip. Susan, who loved Italian food, showed up with Eaton and they all met briefly.

Mary McCarthy, again feeling no pain, thanked Susan for the party 'the other night' but before she left them, she attempted another half-hearted job, "You know you should have won that Oscar Susan but you were drunk too much, you could tell in every scene that you'd been drinking." As McCarthy said, "The look that Susan gave — I just prayed that the floor would open up and dump me into hell."

Musgrove explained it this way, "I never heard Susan laugh. Susan was humorless, even Garbo had humor. Susan was the only one I've been around — and I've been around plenty. Some roared with laughter, I mean Ava Gardner, Myrna Loy, and Mae West, but Susan — nothing. That's why I think she was a little more cracked than the rest of them."

Whatever plans Eaton and Susan made for the future they kept to themselves. He went back to Carrollton and she stayed in Hollywood. Other men would have been overwhelmed by Susan, but Eaton held his own and was not overpowered. She was frustrated by his lack of commitment. She was in love with him and wanted to get married. She also wanted to get out of Hollywood, especially after getting a backhand swipe from the industry by their voting a foreign actress for the Oscar. She worked hard to get Eaton's approval, but felt rejected by him, and Hollywood.

With the twins in boarding school, she packed and left for Europe for the Cannes Film Festival.

On Saturday morning May 14, 1956, arriving at London airport she immediately landed in trouble. She was changing flights for a plane to France and under her mink coat; she hid a toy Yorkshire terrier. As she walked to the plane, quarantine officials spotted it and they politely explained the situation to her. She lost her temper, held the plane up and fought to keep the dog. She lost the argument and the dog.

Outfitted in a tight fitting pink sweater, Susan posed for French photographers in Cannes when she arrived for the festival. With her red hair flying wildly as she posed on the French Riviera she asked them where the men were, 'No actors," she emphasized. "I mean *men!*'

It can only be surmised what Eaton must have thought on reading this in the newspapers back in the United States.

In Cannes, she shared the spotlight briefly with Hollywood's and Europe's luminaries. Diana Dors, Kim Novak, Ginger Rogers and her old friend, Ingrid Bergman among others, all wearing their hair combed back neatly and primly as Hayward took the spotlight with her windswept mane winning the Festivals' 'Best Actress in the World' award — that May 23, 1956.

She triumphed with the equivalent of the Foreign Oscar sweepstakes picking up top honors at the Cork Festival in Ireland, and the Mar del Plata in South America. Out for a good time she also picked up a few admirers along the way. She cabled home the news of her victory and signed the cable — Susan Maganini. Susan had grown distrustful of Hollywood people after being shunted by them, and accepted by the world.

When she got back, she stayed for a while with her sons, and then took unexplained weekend trips alone. She dated a philosophy professor Dr. Frederick Mayer at the University of Redlands who fell in love with her. She switched partners and went from publisher Gordon White to disc jockey Bill Ballance, her agent Hugh French, followed by Brazilian millionaire Jorge Guinly. But with all of them, in the middle of the night she yearned for Eaton Chalkley.

Susan's agent at that time was Jack Gardean and he called her about doing a picture *Top Secret Affair* at Warner Bros. for producer Martin Rackin. It had been originally intended for Humphrey Bogart and Lauren Bacall, prior to Bogart's death.

Helen Rackin who often came on the set to be with her husband Marty, said about Susan: "She was basically not a Hollywood person. She was aloof and didn't go to many parties. I think she would have liked to have been a singer — she used to sing for friends. Anyhow, Eaton Chalkley was flying in regularly from Georgia to see her again. When Eaton came back, Susan was divinely happy and she looked marvelous, you could see that she was very much in love with him. Eaton was a big strapping guy, very tanned. He stayed at the Beverly Wilshire while she was filming *Top Secret Affair* — six to eight weeks. My husband called Susan 'hooligan' and they were very, buddy-buddy, got along great. Eaton sent her yellow roses during the picture. She loved them — kept them in her dressing room. When we went to lunch one day, with Kirk Douglas, I remember they were talking about how they hoped their children wouldn't go in the business. Susan wanted to give her sons a life away from Hollywood."

Because of her happiness at being reunited with Eaton, Susan was much better than expected in the sophisticated comedy. With the picture over, Susan planned Christmas for her sons and Eaton. It was her favorite holiday and she decorated the house in Sherman Oaks, giving every detail her personal attention.

Stanley Musgrove was invited out to Susan's for a Christmas party that year — 1956.

"By this time the house was first rate. It was incredible, the transformation, from the silver and the crystal to the linen, she did it for him. She even had a friend of hers, an editor of *House Beautiful,* come out and help her get the house ready. It was lovely, nothing lavish. For instance, the Christmas tree was all done up in ribbons and bows, it was just a lovely party. She really wanted this guy, she was madly in love with him, and she gave up practically everything to get him — he was the boss."

Susan, who always based her decisions on her hunches and emotions rather than reason, with her sons in Palos Verdes boarding school, left Hollywood in January 1957 and went to Carrollton for a dress rehearsal of what life would be like there; seeing Eaton's home, meeting his friends and driving with him around the quiet town.

Eaton had an instinctive nose of phoniness and since the movie, industry had more than its fair share he made it clear that he did not intend to live in Hollywood. If they were to be married, he wanted to live in Carrollton, where he had a home, a large piece of land and cattle and horses.

The rural beauty and peace of the countryside were the answer to a prayer to a woman who had been managing her own life, and fighting in the Hollywood jungle for a career since she was seventeen.

Back in Hollywood after her visit with Eaton, columnist Earl Wilson was warned about questions in an interview with Susan, with no mention to be made about Jess Barker. (Jess Barker had just been ruled the father of a daughter born out of wedlock to Yvonne Doughty he was ordered to pay $50.00 a month support. Miss Doughty screamed, 'I hate you. I hate you!' at Barker in court. Their daughter, born December 9, 1956 in an Encino Hospital, was named Margana Ruth Barker).

Wilson humorsly chided Susan about this before the interview, somberly she replied, "You ask me and we'll see."

Wilson: "Are you going to marry Don Barry, the cowboy star?"

Hayward hollered: "Who? It never entered my thoughts, it's a very distasteful subject and actually I think you're no gentleman to bring it up."

Wilson: (about Lillian Roth) "Didn't she have guts to write that book?"

Hayward: "She had guts to live it; I just hope the movie will make everybody more tolerant of people who are going through their own personal Gethsemane."

With that, Susan pushed a cigarette out in the ashtray, got up and left.

Susan was offered every script in Hollywood with her choice of leading men. She chose a role on location in Georgia — in real life — with the one man she hoped would star with her for the rest of her life.

Friday evening February 9, 1957, Marty and Helen Rackin were expecting Susan for dinner, to celebrate their move into their new house in Benedict Canyon. Edmund O'Brien, the actor, who had gone to school with Susan in Brooklyn, made a foursome. They held up dinner when Susan didn't show up at the expected time and waited and waited but still she didn't arrive. Getting no reply from her telephone number, they finally sat down to dinner. Then there was a knock on the door and a telegram arrived — "Sorry couldn't make dinner — married Eaton Chalkley." No one had to look around for small talk for the remainder of that evening.

Susan took out a marriage license under her maiden name, Edythe Marrener. Justice of the Peace Stanley Kimball performed the ceremony in Phoenix, Arizona and with Eaton firmly grasping her hand; she looked up at him and said, "I don't want to look back. From now on I'm going to look forward, always." Eaton would be 48 years old that May and Susan 40 in June. His boyhood chum Vincent Flaherty was his best man and Father Brew and Father Farrell were given the long awaited news by phone.

Ellen Marrener was surprised at the news when she heard it over the radio. When reporters phoned her home for a comment she declared, "I haven't talked to her in weeks. I don't know what she's up to."

"When I read in the papers they had flown to Phoenix and got married. I just wanted to yell and cheer. She got him!" cheered Stanley Musgrove.

There was a shadow over their happiness because in the eyes of the Catholic Church Eaton was still married to Dorothy Rowland. To the residents of the small town of Carrollton, Georgia, the worldwide publicity surrounding the marriage of the red headed movie star to the devout catholic Eaton Chalkley was all rather shocking — to be talked about in hushed tones. After all, Susan Hayward was a common law wife.

On April 4, 1957, Eaton went to the Superior Court of the State of California in Los Angeles, to sign an affidavit allowing him to take the Barker children back to his home in Georgia. They were now 14 years old and were to be enrolled at Georgia Military Academy. He also went ahead with plans to build a new and larger home on a 100-acre tract, which he owned in Carrollton. Susan, despairing of ever winning an Oscar or even finding another role to equal *I'll Cry Tomorrow*, just wanted to complete her contractual obligations and forget Hollywood. Behind the scenes, however, things were taking place, which were yet to lead to her much-coveted Oscar.

It began June 3, 1955 with a woman whose life was terminated for a crime for which she was sentenced to death. Barbara Graham was executed in the gas chamber in San Quentin prison, a short distance away from San Francisco. Public Relations man Graham Kislingbury, who was working for producer Louie De Rochemont of Cinerama, told De Rochemont about his college roommate Ed Montgomery who was an ace crime reporter with the *San Francisco Examiner*.

Ed Montgomery had won the Pulitzer Prize for 'best local reporting' work for the investigation for the bureau, then known as the Internal Revenue, in 1950, which lead to the Kefauver hearings. He was also the crime reporter on the Barbara Graham case. De Rochemont liked what he heard so Kislingbury put De Rochemont and Montgomery in touch with each other and Montgomery agreed to go to New York and do a working script about the Graham story. Soon afterwards, De Rochemont became interested in the Cinemiracle and dropped his option, leaving Montgomery with a script and no producer.

However, Kislingbury now heard that his former boss, producer Walter Wanger, was in San Francisco with his actress wife Joan Bennett who was to appear at the Alcazar theatre in *Janus*. He called them at their hotel and they made a luncheon date for the next day in the Redwood Room of the Clift Hotel.

Wanger, who had been a pillar of Hollywood and six times president of the Motion Picture Academy, had lost a fortune with his picture, *Joan of Arc*. Ingrid Bergman, the star of the film, had fallen from public grace and was deadwood at the box office then over her scandalous affair with the Italian film producer Roberto Rossellini. Wanger had to vacate a tiny office he had been reduced to taking in Hollywood. Washed up and broke, in a fit of rage probably fuelled by his despondency he shot agent Jennings Lang in the groin over Long's attentions to his wife, Joan Bennett. He was sentenced to 90 days in jail.

Over lunch, Kislingbury told Wanger about the Montgomery script and offered it to Wanger.

"I've got nothing better to do," said the former producer. "Why not?"

Ed Montgomery joined them later and from the letters of Barbara Graham, the court transcriptions and his articles about the case they completed the script, The Barbara Graham Story — retitled *I Want To Live* — from a line in one of Miss Graham's letters.

Walter Wanger, as an independent producer, had given Susan some good breaks and she felt she owed him a favor now that the chips were down. She had been looking for a chance to return something to him.

She was no longer under exclusive studio contract so he had a copy of the script mailed to her in Georgia.

It was eighteen months since she made her last film and Susan, never a lover of city life, felt released from 'the cage' now that she could fully indulge herself in outdoor activities.

When the script arrived, it was put in Eaton's office; she would get around to it in due course — she really had no great desire to return to Hollywood, away from Eaton, and she had agreed to read the script purely as a favor to Wanger. One day, Eaton found it tossed among his papers, read it and talked it over with Susan.

Even in Carrollton, Georgia, Hollywood was only a telephone call away. Susan always said, "I hate to pick up the telephone. It's always bad news!" Eaton picked up the phone call from Wanger and she encouraged by Eaton, set up a meeting in Hollywood with him.

Wanger and Ed Montgomery were waiting in a Hollywood restaurant when the Chalkley's walked in. Over a three-hour luncheon, they mapped out the story of the B-girl, accused of murder, railroaded to a conviction and executed in a gas chamber. During the discussion Susan watched for Eaton's reactions to the various facets of the story and what its require-ments would be in production, time, etc. and having satisfied herself, by a private code of silent communication with Eaton (which they often used in company), that he was in agreement she agreed to do the role. Now for the first tine, protected by her husband's business acumen, she would also get 37½% of the movie profits. A gentlemen's agreement was reached without the aid of agents, contracts and lawyers.

In March 24, 1958, Susan went back to work on the Samuel Gold-wyn lot for Walter Wanger. She had a mobile trailer for her dressing room and during the difficult months of shooting ahead Eaton would be unfailing support. The long stemmed yellow roses from Eaton would be ever-present on her dressing room table, a constant reminder of his love and encouragement.

At one end of the trailer was a reception room and she would often invite Ed Montgomery — who was the consultant on the film — in there to sit and talk. Striving for authenticity, she questioned him on every possible detail to help in conveying the character of the doomed woman. Susan was fascinated by the contradictory traits of personal-ity in the controversial woman, who had had an extraordinary effect on everyone she met.

"There was nothing flim-flam about Susan Hayward," Montgomery said. "It was all business. Eaton would sit off to one side on the set, quietly observing never interfering and Susan would ease up and smile when she looked his way."

"Eaton was a good listener, he asked questions and he listened. He didn't talk a lot, he didn't have too much to say but when he said something, it usually made sense," Montgomery remembered, "it wasn't just idle chatter. He wasn't running around the place letting everybody know he was Susan Hayward's husband. He took an interest in my family. On one occasion, my wife and our three children came down to visit me. Susan did a rare thing, mainly because Eaton shared it with us. She took time to show us around the studio, and around the set, explaining things."

No one ever talked to her when she was walking onto the set. They were warned not to talk when she came out of her dressing room and started toward the set because she had established a mood and was ready for the scene.

Eaton walked on the set on the morning of Monday, April 15, 1958 and asked the director Robert Wise to halt the shooting.

Mrs. Ellen Marrener, Susan's seventy-year-old mother, was in Mount Sinai Hospital with a heart attack and Eaton brought Susan the news that her mother had died. She lit a cigarette and stared indifferently toward an empty spot on the sound stage, silently angry with Eaton for stopping the scene. She felt nothing. The only one of the Marrener's who meant anything to her now was her brother Wally. Susan and her sister Florence were no longer on speaking terms.

Following the funeral, her mother's ashes remained in a box with a vault number attached, stored on a shelf in the crematorium funeral parlor. Ellen Marrener wasn't officially buried until several years later.

"Yes, my mother was cremated," Wally said. "I had a deed to a place back in Brooklyn, where my father is. There was a place for my mother's ashes, but I decided to keep her ashes out here in the Chapel of the Pines."

Stanley Musgrove, who was working on the picture as assistant to Robert Wise, spoke of one of his visits to the set around this time, "When Susan's mother died during the making of *I Want To Live* — to her it was like closing a door. She was *not* inconsolable. I can tell you that."

Director Wise went to San Quentin and witnessed an actual execution. Susan went too, though it is not certain that she witnessed the execution with Wise but she did sit in the chair in the gas chamber. Robert Wise said she was wonderful professionally but he found it impossible to relate to her personally. The only time he felt any warmth or real contact with her as a human being instead of as his star actress was when they were shooting in downtown Los Angeles one night. Some ragamuffins were leaning against the fence, watching.

Susan stared at them and said to Wise, "See those kids over there?"

He looked over; "Yes", he said.

"Those are like Park Avenue kids compared to the gang I grew up with," she said reflectively.

That was the only time she was ever less than totally professional in her conversations with him.

Wise said of her that, "She had a chemical combination that could excite and hold audiences as surely as Garbo and a few others. She was one of the few actresses who could hold up a movie all by herself."

On completion of the picture Musgrove, as publicity director, had to plan ads, publicity, tours and so forth and was told by Wise to check with Susan, just to be sure, that she was clear (Susan was also working at 20th Century Fox on *Woman Obsessed* directed by Henry Hathaway).

The producers of the Figaro Production of *I Want To Live* paid Barbara Graham's five-year-old son and her husband a total of $500 for any damages that they may suffer as a result of the movie based on her life. A deplorable compromise.

Stanley Musgrove recognized the additional motivation Eaton had given her and told her, "You're going to win (the Oscar) this time." She never said, 'I know it,' but felt good about it," he said.

"What will you say when you win?" he asked her.

"I know what I would like to say," she replied. "There is one person I would like to thank above all others — Me!"

With Eaton by her side, Susan went out on tour to sell the picture. Ed Montgomery, who was portrayed by Simon Oakland in the film, on tour with them commented, "We were on tour at Thanksgiving and we stopped off at their place in Georgia. This was the new house. They were in the process of moving from their last place. It was on a rise over-looking a lake. The twins were there — although you wouldn't know they were twins. One was tall and redheaded, the other short and of a different stature. Susan was very friendly; her husband was a very independent individual. Susan was going to cook the Thanksgiving dinner and the day before Thanksgiving, we went into Carrollton to do some shopping. Everywhere we went it was 'Mrs. Chalkley;' she was just Eaton Chalkley's wife."

Frankly, she wasn't the best cook in the world and she knew it.

"You know, I haven't done enough of this," she said, "but I'm learning."

Eaton laughed as he watched her and went on dicing the celery to go into the stuffing.

"I'm glad you're here, Eaton I wouldn't have remembered to put that in," she quipped.

"On Thanksgiving morning I can remember the twins being out in the field with a horse, Gregory was stroking the horse's neck and mane, and the back of his ears. Timothy was standing alongside, not touching the horse — just watching."

Montgomery continued, "Eaton brought over a dinner set and extra chairs from the other house. They apologized for the fact that their dining room furniture hadn't arrived, so this was sort of a makeshift affair. We all pitched in and did the dishes afterwards.

Eaton did the washing, I did the drying and the boys helped a bit. Susan sat on the kitchen stool, over to one side, smoking a cigarette. Eaton told her she had done a good job, put out a good Thanksgiving dinner — to relax and let the men work.

"'Thank heaven, it's over,' she said smiling.

"After dinner, we went to the cabin by the lake. She liked to pump the piano player there and change the piano rolls. She would sing and Eaton would sing along."

After Thanksgiving, they continued the promotion tour, in all travelling to over 12 cities as the picture was being released around the country.

"She had a certain shyness about her," Montgomery said, "I don't think it was because she 'thought I'm above all this,' but she didn't like to give autographs and the fans could think up the darndest things to ask her. That used to annoy her and then she didn't sign."

Susan, commenting on the fan syndrome: "I don't think there are as many fans around now as there used to be; maybe for rock musicians, but not for actor's and that's good. People are more sophisticated; they can accept a performer for what he does and idolize him. I could never understand youngsters putting actors on a pedestal. It should be men and women who really contribute something to humanity. The man who makes a really fine law or does something for humanity in medicine — they're the ones who should have fans. Even as a child, I don't remember idolizing an actor. It seemed so — misplaced."

Eaton tried to be with Susan in as many cities as his business would allow, she always wanted him with her, and they were on the phone all the time if they were not together. Eaton never missed Sunday mass or Holy Days of obligation wherever he happened to be.

"We went to Chicago, Philadelphia, and Boston, and Eaton and I had gone ahead to New York. When Walter Wanger and Susan arrived at La Guardia airport, we met their plane. Eaton had a surprise for Susan and handed her a huge box at the airport. She couldn't wait and opened it right there. It was a mink coat. She put it on and wouldn't take if off."

"Susan hardly drank at this time," Ed Montgomery went on. "Often at around 10:30 at night in the Chalkley's hotel suite, Eaton would call room service and order drinks for Wanger, me and himself. Susan usually 'didn't care for one.'"

The Chalkleys went abroad to France, Germany and Italy to promote the movie. She, in turn, was honored by a Golden Globe Award; the David di Donatello, Sicily; the Silver Bear from Berlin; Golden Gaucho, Argentina and more, when the time came to choose the most outstanding performance by an actress in these foreign countries, making her an international favorite.

Back in the States, after the promotional tour, they would occasionally go to Santa Anita racetrack to place some bets and to see Susan's brother, Wally.

"Hey Wal can you get us a table at the racetrack?" Susan would ask her brother.

"This would be on a Friday or Saturday, it would be a big day. I'd say 'I'll do my best' 'cause I'd have to go through channels but being there so long they'd say 'for you Wally?' and I'd say, 'it's not for me, it's for my sister.' 'For you and your sister, anything.'"

"When I would visit them at their table she'd say, 'Here Wal, here's twenty bucks go bet it for us and we'll split.' So I made her a little money. But I'd tell her she'd have to take care of the maître d' and the waiters, and she said, 'Don't tell me all about that. Eaton takes care of all that.' 'OK!' I said, 'but remind him will you, 'cause you're puttin' me on the spot.'"

One day, while they were driving home from Santa Anita after a not-so-lucky day at the races, they heard on the radio that Susan had been nominated for the Oscar.

On April 6, 1959, Eaton Chalkley's big hand was folded reassuringly over his wife's, as they sat in the Pantages Theatre the night of the Academy Awards.

Susan's heart was beating very fast as she watched Kim Novak and James Cagney up there on the dais as they opened the white envelope which contained the name of the winner for Best Actress of 1958.

The applause almost deafened the next words as the name of the winner, Susan Hayward, was given over the microphone. Susan kissed her husband and like a long-coiled spring suddenly released she springed from her seat. She gathered the folds of her black satin dress lifted them slightly and ran prettily like a ballet dancer to the stage — in those twelve seconds that it took to arrive there were twelve long years of grueling work.

The night of the awards Walter Wanger gave Susan a gold religious medal — on one side is the figure of St. Gemesius and the words *"please guide my destiny"* on the other side is engraved — *"To Susan — Best Actress and Best Friend — WW"*

Susan on Oscar night 1958 with David Niven.

She thanked Walter Wanger, the man who had helped her get her First Best Actress Nomination and had given her the part that got her her Fifth Nomination — and the Oscar.

All of Carrollton Georgia was watching on their television sets — and on a portable TV set in a school classroom, Susan's two sons, given special permission to stay up, watched the Oscar telecast.

Stanley Musgrove thought it odd that she didn't thank her director Robert Wise — as usually those best performances are heavily credited to the director.

Henry Hathaway had this to say, "Of course when she made *I Want To Live* and the other one about the drunk (*I'll Cry Tomorrow*), being mean was part of that picture. She came on as Fuck You! That's her nature, that's why she was so good in them. No, she never said that — I never heard her swear — to tell you the truth."

The police had to extricate Susan and Eaton from the Pantages Theatre and carve a pathway for them through the crowd as they arrived to enter the Beverly Hilton Ballroom where the Academy's annual dinner dance was being held. Seated inside at a table on the perimeter of the dance floor with Joan and Walter Wanger and Bob and Dolores Hope, the table was bombarded with a barrage of camera flashes from the surrounding photographers. Eaton tried to duck out of range and let Susan take the spotlight. He joked with them saying, "I didn't win anything."

Susan chimed in, "If it hadn't been for him, I wouldn't have either."

A photographer asked her to pose for a photo kissing the Oscar statue, "I don't kiss anyone but my husband," she quipped.

Strangers jammed the dance floor to congratulate her and to get autographs but Susan only wanted to get away as soon as she could and Eaton wanted to run, too.

This time she had a home to go to and someone she loved to go with her.

Of all the reporters' questions, the one she answered most easily was, "What was she going to do next?" She turned wearily to Eaton and said, "We're just anxious to get home."

"He" stood on the table in their Beverly Hills Hotel suite, slim, golden and small to have created such a fuss that was heard around the world surrounded by a forest of red roses tagged with congratulatory cards.

Susan stared at him, "I've wanted him for so long — "

"I know," Eaton said his arm around her.

"But we still have a plane to make. We're going back home tonight."

With her, Oscar cradled in her hands, Susan walked across the room and opened the lid of her suitcase, and packed Oscar inside.

"He'll look wonderful over our fireplace," she said.

Just before they left the suite, she took his bouquet of yellow roses in one arm and grabbing Eaton by the other, said, "I'm ready — let's go home."

CAPITAL PUNISHMENT

I'm in favor of it. I can only judge by my own feeling and I take it very personally. If somebody hurt anyone who was close to me or whom I loved and they weren't put to death for it, I would kill them myself. I am not a bleeding heart; I am not inclined to say "oh well they can be rehabilitated." If someone commits a crime — he should be punished for that crime, whether he's sane or insane. I don't believe in just letting people commit crimes and then go unpunished.*

* It's interesting to note Miss Hayward won an Academy Award for her performance in *I Want to Live!*, one of the movies' most potent anticapital punishment statements.

MORALITY

Morality today (1972) is so much looser at the seams. People of my generation were brought up in a much more strict fashion— there were certain things you simply did not do. All this sexual freedom the kids have today can hurt later on, especially the women. You've got to be able to respect yourself and if you just sleep around with anybody, how can you have respect? They might not think it's important now but there's going to come a time when it's going to hurt inside.

CHAPTER 9

Fifty miles from Carrollton, Georgia, in the Catholic Church in Cedartown, Father Charles Duke addressed his congregation from the pulpit at Sunday morning mass. Many of them were from Carrollton where, on the following morning, Mr. and Mrs. Eaton Chalkley were expected home.

When they returned, Father Duke told them, their relationship toward Eaton Chalkley would have to change. Chalkley was the first Catholic to go into business in Carrollton and in the beginning; he was regarded with wonder, a certain amount of suspicion and some definite prejudice. His charm and friendliness, however, worked very much in his favor and their doubts about him soon disappeared. There were many 'closet' Catholics there at that time, in this heavily Protestant and Southern Baptist area, but Eaton was proud of his chosen faith. He joined the Rotary International Organization and suggested that they have a catholic priest come in to say grace once in awhile, and he was the reason why people down there who either through fear or timidity, had given up going to church now came out of the 'woodwork' to attend.

Although Cedartown was regarded as the parish and Carrollton the Mission, Carrollton in fact, had the larger parish taking into account the Georgetown University students and their families.

Father Duke somberly told his congregation that Chalkley was setting a bad example that he had done wrong.

His marriage to this woman was not celebrated in the church and it was a matter of deep sincere regret. He may have gotten a civil divorce from his catholic wife but in the eyes of the church, he was still married to her. She was an adulteress.

"These people will always be welcome in the church," he said. "But they were not to get extraordinary attention."

The congregation filed out silently after the service.

The next day Eaton Chalkley arrived in town bringing with him his world famous redheaded movie star wife and Carrollton went crazy. They were met at Atlanta airport by a delegation headed by Mayor Stewart

Martin, and then a two and a half mile long motorcade drove the 50 miles to Carrollton, where another throng of local people were waiting to greet them.

The red carpet was rolled out and they were met with a parade, four bands, the keys to the city, a special edition of the local newspaper and with banners flying everywhere.

Susan couldn't make out what the banners said, because she didn't have her glasses on, but she knew what they meant.

Among the cheering crowd, Father Duke watched for a few moments then withdrew, and his friendship with Eaton Chalkley was over — forever. The loss of his friend left Eaton with a deep sense of unworthiness, and may also have eventually contributed to leaving a mark on his health.

Now, fallen from the church, deprived of the sacraments and unable to receive communion he was left only with the privilege of his devotions, which he practiced assiduously.

To Susan, it was such a perfect marriage. Nothing was missing — everything and everyone was so wonderful.

The Chalkleys came home to their new air conditioned modern ranch style house, faced with granite from the famous Stone Mountain nearby and roofed with crushed Georgia marble. It was situated in a pine grove that overlooked a man-made 15-acre lake on their 450 acres of land and was complete with a guesthouse.

The twins were attending the Chadwick School in Rolling Hills, California, completing their school semester, after which Susan intended to move them out to Georgia permanently. Again, she appealed to Superior Court in Los Angeles to get permission to take them out of the state, removing them from their Hollywood — Bel Air environment. Susan spoke of the advantages to the children of growing up in the atmosphere of a small town, living a normal life. Their father would, of course, be allowed proper visitation rights.

"The boys will share a paneled bedroom when they come home on weekends from the Military Academy. We have a playhouse on the grounds where we entertain neighbors and friends and have barbecues and parties. On Sundays, the family drives in to church. Whatever mistakes I have made as a mother, I want to put them behind me."

To anyone who had doubts, Susan explained, "I like being just plain Mrs. Chalkley. I love my husband and I want to be his full-time wife. I want to be with him all the time. This is the way I want to live."

A different point of view was being voiced out West; "They always come back," said one Hollywood cynic. "She's too much of a fighter to stop fighting, too much of an actress to stop acting, too accustomed to Hollywood excitement to retire."

When Susan first came to town, she decided to go to the First Baptist Church on Dixie Street but when she arrived at the church there were crowds of people outside, watching for her to make an entrance. The curious among the crowd thought she looked odd; slender, thin legs, with freckles on her arms, face, and that red hair — very Irish looking for a Baptist out of Brooklyn. She turned around and walked away and never went back.

The boys were finally allowed to leave California and shortly after their arrival, they were enrolled in the Georgia Military Academy, and while Eaton was attending to the farm and his various other business interests Susan began to organize the house.

It had black Georgia slate floors, walls of tongue-and-groove logs, painted white, and a huge fireplace in the living room connected with the one in the master bedroom on the other side of the wall. She would interrupt Eaton from time to time to ask his advice about certain things, such as whether they should have one or two sofas in the living room near the fireplace, and so on. She hired two black servants, Katie, a small, round, 'Mammy' type and a tall attractive, light-skinned young woman, Curlee.

Used to sleeping until noon when she was not working, Susan now insisted on getting up every morning to fix Eaton's breakfast. She tried her hand at cooking and baking and did the gardening. Meanwhile she had to juggle movie commitments to complete works in progress, which took her away from her home for weeks at a time.

Woman Obsessed was in release and Walter Wanger wanted her for *Cleopatra* but 20th Century Fox wanted Elizabeth Taylor. She was offered some of the prize roles of that decade but listened with total disinterest, as they would only be breaks in her newfound happiness. Because of his waning career, she did accept a plea for help from her old friend from Flatbush, Jeff Chandler, to make *Thunder In The Sun*. It meant going on location to Lone Pine, near San Diego, for some time and being separated from Eaton, which was distressing to her. She could never bring herself to say goodbye to him and would make a salute on leaving, 'I'll see you in the funnie papers,' * she would say, as she left; then she would keep looking back until he was no longer in sight.

* Referring to *Peanuts* by Charles Schultz; Sunday, May 21, 1972.

Her love for him made any parting almost impossible but, as Eaton agreed, Jeff Chandler needed her support to get another foothold in his career.

Late one night at the lodge in Lone Pine, a telephone call from Carrollton woke her up. She heard that Eaton, suddenly taken ill at home, had been rushed to the hospital. The news of her husband's collapse after

Curlee Mae — Susan and Eaton's maid.

midnight on July 24th, 1958, only 18 months after their marriage, sent her racing in a studio car to Los Angeles Airport to make an emergency flight to Atlanta at 1:20 A.M. When she arrived at the hospital in Atlanta, Eaton was being treated for a kidney ailment. He calmed her fears and insisted that she return to Lone Pine and not hold up production. Very unwillingly, she left with a promise she would be back as soon as possible to take care of him. "I'll see you in the funnie papers," she said, more cheerfully than she felt, as she left. His yellow roses arrived as usual the next day.

Bob Sidney, her 'pal' from *The Conqueror* movie answered Susan's call for some advice on a Flamenco dance she was called upon to do in *Thunder In The Sun*. It was about the only memorable moment in the entire picture.

Susan now had to meet her commitments for Fox's *Marriage-Go-Round*, and MGM's *Ada* with Dean Martin before she could settle down again at the ranch with Eaton. She wanted to quit the movies, but Eaton felt that she had this gift, this talent, and she should use it, and she was guided by him in this as in practically everything else.

None of the films she made at this time were of any importance to the public, to the critics, and least of all to Susan. She was much more concerned with playing the country wife, and she entered this role with the same determination that she came to be known for in her more memorable screen characters.

She just simply wanted to be with Eaton, almost trying to make up for the years without him. She hated location shooting which took her away from him.

At twilight one evening, she heard the faint sound of a car approaching along the winding road through the pinewoods. It grew louder, then stopped and she heard the familiar rumble of the garage door closing. Then came the click of a key in the front door and the voice that said, "I'm home!" She greeted him with a hug and kisses then went into the kitchen to prepare dinner. When she came into the living room, she noticed the kindling in the hearth had already caught alight, and Eaton was stretched out across the couch. He had turned on the television and she heard the announcer give the title of the feature film to be shown that evening *Adam Had Four Sons*, starring Ingrid Bergman.

"That's an old one," Susan called out. "I was in it too," she added, looking at Eaton.

Then the announcer said, "I wonder if Susan Chalkley is watching tonight?"

"Is she watching?" Eaton asked, as she sat down beside him.

"Only if you want to. I can run out and put on the steak — during the commercial."

She got up and walked back to the kitchen. She wasn't Susan Hayward — all that was past — as Susan often said to Eaton, "It's all yesterday's spaghetti." She was now Susan Chalkley!

Eaton promised her that when she was free, they would take a trip to Greece and Italy and when they were finally able to leave it was as the leaves were turning, heralding the arrival of fall.

"When Eaton and Susan first went to Rome on a trip, it so happened that Father McGuire was stationed in Rome at the headquarters of the Jesuits," said Father Brew. "I got in touch with him and told him they were coming and to do what he could for them. He would get them into places they would not be able to get into on their own. That was the beginning of their friendship. I first met Father McGuire at Gonzaga High School, I was the teacher there and he was student in my class."

In Rome, Eaton introduced Susan to the Reverend Daniel J. McGuire who was serving as American secretary to the Jesuit headquarters at the Vatican. It was Eaton's heartfelt desire that Susan would move toward his religion and her introduction to the Vatican would be another step in that direction for her.

While on a stop over in England, Susan signed to do *I Thank A Fool*, when her friend Ingrid Bergman had to bow out of the film, which was to have reunited Bergman with Cary Grant. When they returned from Europe in October, there were a pile of scripts awaiting her. (One of them, *Back Street*, sent by producer Ross Hunter would give her a sympathetic role.)

For now, with the holidays approaching, she was becoming very excited about her first real Christmas in her Georgian home amidst the pine trees. A firm believer in astrology, Susan believed that the stars were right and things were falling into their allotted placed. Best of all, she knew where she belonged.

Father Morrow, a young priest in Cedartown, recalled that particular Christmas Eve; "The first time I saw her was in our older church in Carrollton. This had been an Episcopal church, the oldest structure in town, but the Catholics had bought it when the Episcopalians moved out when they outgrew it. The building leaned in both directions and could only hold about 60 people. When they kneeled on the kneelers, they would sink to the floor. Eaton had arrived with Susan, she had furs on and I recognized her from the movies. When the midnight mass was over they left and I didn't get to greet them. Harvey Hester was with them too."

"Two or three days later when I was in town a pick up truck came along and the driver was a lady wearing a scarf over her hair, slacks, and a jacket. She was blowing the horn and yelling 'Hey, Father!' She pulled the truck over to where I was and started to chat right away. I wondered who she was, for the first minute or two, then I realized that it was Susan, and she was saying how badly she and Eaton felt that there had been no introductions, and she made up for it."

Eaton wanted to go to Mass every morning, not just on Sundays. Cedartown near Rome, Georgia, was almost 50 miles away, a 2-hour drive from Carrollton. The church in Carrollton, opened only on Sundays, was too small now and Eaton felt a new church would be desirable. Father Morrow, in agreement with him, urged the Bishop that Carrollton needed its own church; Eaton had started the parish interest in the Catholic faith and would now donate the land. Susan and he would provide funds for building the church on 14 acres of land across the lane from their home, and they would seek a resident pastor.

Bishop Hyland called Father Morrow that December of 1960 and asked him to become pastor of the churches in Cedartown and Carrollton, and to 'oversee' the construction of the new church.

One day Father Morrow drove by the Chalkley home and found Eaton, dressed as usual in shirt and tie, in the gatekeeper's little red house which he had converted into an office. From there you looked out over the fields, and down below was a road that led about a half mile to the house — a rather grand stone house where they lived. "I thanked them for their donation. I was working with the architect and Eaton was very interested in the plans. He would explain to Susan what was happening. The name of the church was to be Our Lady of Perpetual Help. Susan said, 'Father we are never going to leave here. We chose the highest piece of land to build the church on, so we could see it from the house.'"

"The building of the church brought me close to them and I started to go out in public with them," Father Morrow said, "I could easily see their beautiful personalities and I was able to ignore who Susan was as far as the rest of the world was concerned. I subscribed to Worldwide Marriage Encounter — 'don't be afraid to hold your honey's hand' — but because of my Irish background and being raised in staid Connecticut I was not used to it. In restaurants, they both looked at the same menu, sometimes holding hands while looking at it. The looks back and forth whether of disappointment or affection — you could see it always. All she needed was security.

"She would say to a waiter on walking into a restaurant, 'No, we don't want that table we want *that* table,' though she would be unrecognized. She had 'that voice' and in dealing with the plumbers or anyone on the farm, she had 'that voice' — you're not getting her money until the work is done right. There was no softness in dealing with people like that. He was the same way if you were not doing your job. Susan was always afraid of somebody taking advantage of her."

"They went often to Aunt Fanny's Cabin, owned by Harvey Hester. He wasn't pleasant to look at — extremely stout — but he had a smile and a personality, a sort of old shoe kind of guy."

Near the completion of the church, Father Brew came down to stay with them, and to place the outdoor Stations of the Cross, on the church grounds.

"I lived at the gatehouse when I went down to visit them, which was as often as I could, Eaton would say, 'I'm just a half-ass Catholic, but I'm going to keep my foot in the door, no matter what.' The worst language Eaton ever used was a 'hell' or 'damn.' Susan made a real effort to eliminate that kind of talk. She could talk like the best of ladies, and most of the time when she was with Eaton, she did."

Father Brew was right, for all the nine years that Susan was married to Eaton, living with him in Carrollton; she played the role of a sweet, well-bred small town wife and believed in it. For Susan did love Eaton and the daily use of her acquired play-acting skills was the only method she had of subordinating her feverish temperament to the requirements of Eaton's refined lifestyle. She learned how to be just folks. She gave to charities and went to church picnics, waiting in line for her turn at the buffet table. And made friends of his friends (like Mary Williams).

The telephone operator at the Wedgewood Motel outside Carrollton had the following story to tell: Susan used to race through a small town called Ranburne, Alabama, on her way to Carrollton, Georgia. The speed limit was such that you more or less had to creep through Ranburne.

One time, when the cops pulled her over to the side, she got out slammed the door and shook her fist at them in fury. "If you stop me one more time," she shouted, "I'm going to buy this goddamn town and build a bridge over it." Then she sped off, refusing a ticket and cursing like hell.

Mary Williams was one of the few Catholics in Carrollton when Eaton Chalkley first moved into town. Mary always said, about Susan, 'She was as Irish as Patti's pig and she didn't have that red hair for nuthin'."

"I moved to Carrollton in 1947 when my Paw saw the sign to buy this place, 'comin down from Savannah to see his mother. The property dated back to 1880 when they raised cotton on the land," Mary told strangers.

When Eaton first brought Susan to Carrollton (before the house was built on their land) they rented barn space for their two horses from Mrs. Williams, who had a home on fifty acres of land, and they would go horseback riding on the property. Mary Williams was in her 50's at that time, a mischievous little lady who loved to dance — especially the tango. Trim and nice looking, with grey hair, she lived in a brick house, built by her husband, which was completely pine paneled throughout the first floor. It had a disordered comfortable atmosphere and in the living room was a huge brick fireplace. The large kitchen with its built in preserve cabinets had windows over looking a garden patch, which you passed when you came through the side door.

Susan became very fond of Mary Williams and they spent hours drinking coffee and smoking cigarettes at her kitchen table. She would enjoy 'Miss Mary's' antics, especially when she did a tango while drying the dishes in her kitchen — much to her black kitten's wonderment. Susan treated that kitchen like her personal domain and there is a sign there written in a bold hand that reads: THIS IS THE KITCHEN OF MISS SUSAN I AM THE BOSS IF YOU DON'T BELIVE IT START SOMETHING.

Seated one day at the large round kitchen table, holding a cigarette Susan said to Mary, 'I guess you heard I make the boys work. I worked hard and God willing I stay alive long enough to raise them. But if I shouldn't those boys have got to know they have to work for a living. I am not going to give them everything they want so they can go around and waste it and be bums.' (During the summer, Greg worked as a mechanic in car dealerships and Timmie worked in one of the department stores as a salesman.)

Content and happy, Susan gained weight and let her hair get a shade darker. She saved store coupons and when she had enough for something she wanted she would pick up her friends, Mary Williams and Ann Moran, and take them to the stamp redemption center. Ann teased her about this one day. "Susie, you saving stamps and pasting them in books, you got to be kidding."

"Well, I need things too!" she answered with a pout.

Father Morrow, who was the first pastor at the Church of Our Lady of Perpetual Help and became a very close friend of the Chalkley's, remarked about the times he spent with them: "Eaton wanted to stay on the farm, he told me that. Susan liked to fish, so occasionally they went to Florida. They bought their own boats and stayed at Pier 66, where they also docked, before they bought a house on Nermi Drive in Ft. Lauderdale. They had a flat boat for fishing on the lake near the house, but the serious fishing was done in Florida where they had three boats. One was a party boat, one was for racing — this boat they took to Bermuda — and the third was for fishing. The boats berthed in Ft. Lauderdale where they usually stayed."

When Susan knew it was time to go back to work she followed a strict regimen. "If she knew she was going to make a movie a masseur would come out from Atlanta. She would get more circumspect about what she would eat. She knew I liked brownies and often she would bake them for me. Susan told me, 'Eaton won't eat many of these, but my will power is not strong.' I knew if a movie were coming around I wouldn't be offered any brownies."

Father Morrow would have to do without brownies for months to come as Susan (and often Eaton) left periodically for picture assignments. He would phone the house and Curlee, answering would say, 'They flew to California Father — you know how it is."

At that time, Susan started filming two pictures to be released the following year; Ross Hunter's *Back Street* and *The Marriage Go-Round*, which was Susan's last picture under her old Fox contract and would wind up a ten year association. Asked if she had any regrets about leaving the old home lot, she replied, "Not the slightest. Let's face it — what have I done here in the last five years? One, *Soldier of Fortune*, in which I played a mishmash; and two, *Woman Obsessed* about which I have no comment. The picture I'm doing is all right, but the studio has nothing planned for me. They used to plan things when Darryl Zanuck was in charge. But since he left — nothing. It's the old question of being a stepchild everyone takes for granted."

Susan's independent air was, of course, largely due to her happy marriage to Eaton and her life in Georgia.

"I love the life down there. If you want to fish or hunt you don't have to drive a hundred miles, it's right there. And it's faster to drive to Atlanta 50 miles away, than it is from the Beverly Hills Hotel to the Los Angeles Airport 15 miles away. But I also like the way of living; it's much easier and more relaxed. We have a lot of good friends down there; none of them in show business. I like it that way."

Actress Vera Miles, who was in *Back Street* with John Gavin and Susan, told Stanley Musgrove that while working with Susan she tried to get to know her.

She had met her through Musgrove some years before. After Susan had finished a particularly difficult scene — doing it sensationally — Vera, trying to lighten the mood, humorously told her, "It must be terrible to be such a lousy actress.' If looks could kill, Susan gave her one that would have done so on the spot. Vera later told Musgrove that there was just nothing she could say, and if she had said anything, it would have made it worse. As she explained, it was just her way of saying, 'how great you are.'

Susan defended the picture after it was released by saying, "These days, unless you have incest and a couple of rapes, the critics are not impressed. *Back Street* is a love story. It's a simple old-fashioned love. And I think audiences have liked it. You didn't feel dirty when you came out of the theatre."

In June of that year (1961), her long time friend and trusted Hollywood ally Jeff Chandler, died in the hospital of blood poisoning. Susan was deeply affected by this loss and fighting mad with the hospital. She claimed that they had killed him by their incompetence in mistreating his condition and considered suing the hospital for malpractice, but it never went any further than that. Her distrust in doctors and hospitals was compounded by this latest tragedy. The muscular handsome star with premature steel grey hair was dead at 44.

Susan had one more picture to do before she could return to Carrollton. She was reunited with her *I'll Cry Tomorrow* director, Daniel Mann, at MGM to do *Ada*, with Dean Martin.

On Susan's birthday June 30, 1961, Marty Rackin gave her a party. It was at agent Jay Bernstein's home on Doheny Drive. Her old beau Bill Holden showed up to wish her well, and the guests all were happy to see Eaton with her; he visited her often on the set and whether or not he was there his long stem yellow roses came faithfully each day.

That month an article appeared in an issue of *Confidential* magazine provoked by her sister Florence entitled, 'My Sister Susan Hayward Has Millions, But I'm On Relief.' Pictures of the sisters stared from the magazine cover.

She was very upset by the newspaper accounts and spoke to Ann Moran about it, "What would you do Ann?" she asked her plain speaking friend. "Let her go to work," Ann told her. "Yes," Susan agreed. "Let her go out and get it the way I got it — work for it."

Over for lunch one day, Father Morrow mentioned other articles recently prompted by Florence Marrener's pleas for help. "I had heard about these magazines and newspaper stories, they weren't complimentary. They said things about their marriage and her previous marriage. I asked them why they didn't do something about it in court. I said if somebody lied about me like that, I'd take them to court. They both said the publishers would love the publicity and they had concluded that there would be no point to it. You would sue someone this month and someone else six months later."

The knowledge of all this, however, did not help Eaton with his strong religious beliefs. He felt badly about all the adverse publicity since he had married a movie star, and thought of how it may have affected his children.

Eaton was in touch with his family and was always concerned about them.

"Eaton's son Joe was a high strung nervous kid," said Father Brew. "He was a nice kid, but he wasn't the best student. He couldn't stick to the books but he eventually made it. He graduated from St. Joseph's Academy, in Bardstown, Kentucky. His mother came to the graduation and, of course Eaton, and I was between them at dinner. Eaton had high hopes for the boy, but one thing — Joe could not reconcile himself to this new set up, he never accepted Susan."

There were many activities in preparation for the new church. Ann Moran, "the best baker south of the Mason Dixon Line," and chairperson for these functions recalled one of them.

"We had what we call a rubbish sale, and Eaton gave us some clothes to sell and Susan did the same. Anyway, I baked him a banana cake in return. On Sunday morning, he came in and gave me a check, saying, 'Ann that was the best banana cake I ever ate.' I gave the check to Father Morrow. He looked at it and when I explained he looked at the check again and said, 'that's the most expensive banana cake I ever saw.' I though the check was for five dollars — it was for fifty."

"Susie and I became friends through Eaton," Ann continued. "She would come over for a social gathering once in awhile and she suggested I turn the banana cake into the Pillsbury contest. So I put it in one year and nothing happened. She said I should try again, and to put her name on it, 'Just say, I love your banana cake, Maybe it will help.'"

Father Morrow, talking to Ann one day graphically described Susan's appetite during this period. "Honest Ann," he said. "I saw that woman eat a half of a cake at one sitting. But she did give me a little piece."

In Griffin's, Carrollton's only department store, the town electrician stopped a neighbor, "I just came from Susan Chalkley's house and you know what she was doing, she was freezing vegetables. Well, I never expected a movie star to freeze her own vegetables."

In answer to a reply that 'she is just like you and me,' the electrician could only say, "Well, she sure surprised me."

"She did do her own freezing," Ann verified. "And she used to do her own cooking too. One time I called her up and said, "Susie, do you think Eaton would like some city chicken?'

"What's city chicken?"

"Ask Eaton."

"Oh, my God yes," he said. "That's mock chicken."

"You get a wooden skewer, put pork and veal on it," Ann explained. "You dip it in egg and roll it in cracker meal and brown it — ."

"Well — I was cooking Eaton some curry."

"Alright then I'll give it to him tomorrow," Ann told her.

"Oh, no, the curry goes off — the city chicken comes in," Susan insisted.

"With her, anything he wanted he got."

Thinking back, Ann went on, "She would go into town with a babushka tied around her hair — she did her own hair. She'd wear a hat and sunglasses and off she'd go. Nobody had to deliver anything; she went after it. I spotted her in Bohanas's store one time and I walked in and said, "Susie, you stranded?"

"Yeah! Eaton's down the way."

"Do you want me to take you home?"

"No, when he gets through he'll pick me up."

"The heck with that, no sense waiting here. I'll give you a lift," Ann offered.

"I couldn't do that to Eaton, he'll come and get me sooner or later," she said patiently.

In town, nobody stared at her but they would look back after she went by. They would turn around and say, 'Hey, there goes Susan Hayward!'

"I know they see me," said Susan, "and they are surprised to see me but they leave me alone. We can go and come as we please. I can be myself in Georgia."

At first, the students from Carrollton College and West Georgia College rang their bell constantly, asking for her autograph, until they locked the gate that led to the main house down the road.

One of the storekeepers near Adamison Square in town described what happened when Eaton drove Susan into town: "The pick up truck would pull up and Eaton would lift Susan off the truck and raise her high over his head. She would laugh and he'd kiss her, then he would let her down and she would dash into J. Carl's Cleaners while he went off somewhere else. She would take up a position outside, along the street, and wait for him to come and get her."

"She followed him around like a puppy. So he wouldn't run off I guess. No matter where he moved she'd have to be with him," said the counter girl in McGee's Bakery off the Square.

Susan could often be seen standing among the cattle — no milk cows, only steak cows — with her hands on her hips just watching Eaton in the fields doing his daily chores, ready to assist in anything if he needed her — even to putting up a concrete fence post for the farm.

When the front gate was locked, Susan told Ann to drive around the back to the neighbors and drive up from there to her back door. Ann drove around to the back of the Chalkley house with her young daughter Judy one afternoon to pick up a puppy — one of her Dalmatians had had puppies and she gave Judy one and kept one for herself. Hers had one blue eye and one brown, "she just loved it." They walked in through the kitchen and called out to Susan who was upstairs.

"Her bedroom was huge and it overlooked the lake," said Ann as she remembered. The king-size white and gold bed. The master bedroom done in white and yellow. The white walls and rugs. The golden yellow chairs and chaise lounge. And the gold bedspread. "She was straightening up her dressing table, on which were huge bottles of colognes and perfumes."

"I noticed the two bathrooms off the bedroom and I asked her about them. She said, 'Well Ann, you know, when Eaton gets in there he's worse than a woman. I always have to hurry up and get out. So I just put another one in.' Her dressing room was about the size of the kitchen. Susan had many dresses from her movies hanging there."

She invited Ann and a few friends to a private screening of *Gone With The Wind* in the tiny Carroll theatre in town because Eaton wanted to see the film with her.

Susan was very contented with her life in Carrollton and told the cynics back in Hollywood who bet she wouldn't be.

"We have hills and streams, foxes, raccoons and possums right on our own land. The crickets serenade us at night. There are all kinds of things to do. We ride over our land throughout the seasons. The countryside is so green, the air is so clear. There is a deeper satisfaction in being told you're wonderful by the man you love than having a big raise in salary."

Susan never affected a honeysuckle and magnolia accent but her Brooklynese, Hollywood cultivated, Southern assimilated speech confused on old-time shopkeeper.

"Are you from England?" he questioned her.

"No, I'm from a place called Brooklyn," she told him.

"Where's that?"

"That's up North."

"Oh, I see. Well I knew you weren't anywhere's around here."

Christmas in Carrollton was always one of Susan's happiest times. The change of seasons brought with it cold weather and sometimes snow,

warm kitchens and a fire in the living room. The snow-covered countryside brought a lot of joy to Susan as she and Eaton scurried around
buying presents and searching out a pine tree for the decorations, which
she added to each year. Eaton was always very happy when Father Brew
could be with them. Susan must have been pleased for Eaton but one
wonders if she might not have been somewhat jealous of her husband's
uncommonly close relationship with Thomas Brew — a relationship that
in many ways closed her off. In particular, over Father Brew's deep interest for Eaton's health, which Susan must certainly have considered her
own special concern.

All in all though, with Greg and Timmie, Mary Williams, Ann Moran,
Harvey Hester and some of their other special friends it was always a true
family Christmas. They had more to celebrate than ever before with the
completion of Our Lady of Perpetual Help Church.

The entrance to the church was black slate and the inside was done in
earth tones, with beamed ceilings and paintings in the Eastern European
style. The Second Vatican Council called upon simplified churches, so as
not to be distracted by a lot of statues, giving attention to the altar and the
pulpit. The dark woods, white and gold background with gold candlesticks
on a simple white and gold altar conformed to the design requested.

About the only time Susan went to Mass with Eaton was on Christmas
Eve. The church was appropriately decorated for the holy season and Ann
Moran handed out the hymn books for the choral singing.

Susan, on being offered one, said, 'I can't sing!' Ann shoved a book at
her anyway, 'just make some noise then…' she said.

Father Brew said the Christmas Eve Mass, and afterwards Susan and
Eaton would invite their friends over.

Ann Moran — asked every time — remembered: "We always went in
on Christmas Eve for a holiday drink, right after the midnight Mass. They
had a gorgeous tree with golden angels, red ribbons, and silver bells. The
fireplace was ablaze, casting a golden glow on her Oscar on the mantle
and there were huge silver trays of food and silver coffee urns filled and
placed around. I said to her, 'Susie, they are gorgeous; just beautiful silver.'"

"Ann, if every you need them or anything for a church affair come over
and get them," she offered.

"I always baked her a special Christmas fruit cake which she was wild
about — we had such a lovely time those evenings," Ann said thoughtfully.

A shadow fell over their happiness, however, which no one spoke about
that night. Father Duke was invited to the dedication of the church and
later to Christmas Eve Mass and a visit with the Chalkley's and their

friends. He refused to come, saying, 'it would be like patting Eaton on the back for what he had done." Soon afterwards, Father Duke asked for a transfer from the area and left Carrollton and his one time close friend forever.

Father Morrow, who on this occasion could not make the Christmas Eve party, arrived the next day for a Christmas lunch. He recalled that visit.

"I arrived at the ranch and there was Harvey Hester. Eaton used to egg me on to get Susan to Mass more often, and 'Uncle' Harvey as well. He called them pagans, jokingly, but without smiling. I said, 'Harvey I missed you last night at the Mass.' They all started laughing. It seemed Harvey had spent the night in the pokey. He would go around with bottles of liquor as Christmas gifts and have a drink with everybody. He was heading out of Carrollton for another party by way of Buchanan. I guess he was weaving and he ended up in the pokey. He couldn't get anybody to get him out until finally he got hold of Eaton who arranged it for him."

"It was nice having you with us last night," Father Morrow said to Susan.

"Well, the day will come when I will be there every Sunday but not until I can receive communion," she emphasized.

The Chalkley's were leaving Carrollton again, this time for the United Kingdom, early in 1962, taking Curlee the maid with them. Susan was to begin shooting *I Thank A Fool*. Most of the location scenes were to be filmed in the tiny fishing village of Crookhaven in County Cork, Ireland — the same part of the country where Susan's grandmother Katie Harrigan had been born.

Her next film in England was the prophetic *Stolen Hours*, a remake of the earlier Bette Davis hit *Dark Victory*. In the movie, Susan has her hair shaved off for a brain tumor operation and then has to wear a wig. A portend of a true-life part she would, in time, be destined to live next time off-camera.

While not working on the Shepperton Studio set, where the non-location shooting was done, Susan spent quiet hours in her dressing room knitting Eaton a sweater. She always had his picture in a silver frame on her dressing room table — next to which were the ever present yellow roses. It was her favorite photograph of him, one of many they had taken on their travels. She fell in love with the Cornwall coast of England while filming some of the concluding scenes for the picture, and they considered buying property there.

The New York Times reviewer later wrote of her performance, "Susan Hayward is never allowed to go off the deep end. Her first fears of the unknown malady that afflict her are honest and real. As to her refusal to face up to the seriousness of her condition and her terror stricken resistance to medical help, especially impressive is her reaction and that of the people around her when she discovers that she has only a few months to live — there is no hand wringing martyred posturing of playing to the grandstand…"

Susan found some brocaded material of gold and white, which was later used on the chapel wall of the church. Whenever she traveled abroad, she and Eaton would visit as many churches as possible and Susan would always point out the statues of the saints. When they came back Susan spoke to Father Morrow about this, 'Father you have to put statues in the church, I want to buy them.'

Father Morrow explained how it would hurt the simplicity of the décor and Eaton agreed.

"Well Father," Susan promised. "You won't be Pastor here always and someday I'll get my statues in."

Helen Rackin talked about Susan's next movie, "My husband was head of production at Paramount Studios and they were going to make *Where Love Has Gone*, and he got in touch with Jack Gordean, Susan's agent, and told him about a great part in the picture for Susan. Mary Rackin phoned Susan and discussed the story based on Harold Robbin's novel, which seemed to be a left-handed account of the Lana Turner — Johnny Stompanato murder case of 1958.

"My husband was a great salesman, before she knew it he had talked her into saying she would do it. She read the script, but a week before starting she had second thoughts about it and called Marty."

"Marty, I don't know if I want to do this," she said.

"Suddenly she decided it wasn't right for her and she wanted to get out of it. That's where Eaton came in, he said, 'Listen Susan you did promise Marty you would do it, it would put him in a bad spot.' Then he said to my husband, 'Marty, Susan will do it.' I must say Eaton is the one who talked her into doing it.

"Eaton and Susan came out and stayed at the Beverly Wilshire Hotel. My husband had cast Bette Davis as the mother. Knowing what I knew about Bette Davis, I didn't think that she and Susan would get along. And they didn't."

"Bette Davis was a pain in the ass on that picture and Susan was patient with her but in the end she even drove Susan mad. I asked Marty why he didn't get Barbara Stanwyck for the part of Susan's mother? And he replied that 'Bette Davis was 'hot' right now.' I think he realized he had made a mistake because had he used Barbara Stanwyck, she would have been far superior."

At the press conference for the historic signing of the contracts for the film Davis and Hayward were photographed together. Susan had just completed the remake of Davis's *Dark Victory* (*Stolen Hours*) and Davis said, "some pictures should never have been re-made."

The script called for the stars to hate each other, which seemed to be less of an acting chore than a reality.

"She's a bitch!" Susan confided to a close friend. "— but a real pro!"

Bette Davis answered a question about Hayward to her interviewer saying, that she remembered with sadness Susan's unkind treatment of her during the shooting. She admitted she admired Susan's performances immensely up until the point that she had to work with her.

"Where indeed has love gone," Miss Davis pondered.

Hayward countered that Davis wanted to rewrite the script, naturally throwing more scenes her way, and wanted the death scene, which was originally intended for her, to last for pages.

A witness to it all said, "They were jealous of each other. Susan was frightened of Bette, who came on too strong, and reacted with obstinacy. Bette had just made a terrific re-emergence with *Baby Jane* and Susan was afraid of her walking away with the picture. The old fighting spirit returned to Hayward and eventually she stormed the front office demanding they shoot the film the way the script was written when she had signed for it, or she wouldn't continue.'

Eaton kept her under control and the picture was completed. He promised to take her home as soon as possible. Before they left town Marty and Helen Rackin invited 'Hooligan' over to their house for dinner.

"She loved steak, very rare, it had to be bloody. She told Marty she liked several of the outfits in the movie. Mary said, 'Look, Hooligan, they're a gift from me.'"

"No," she said. "I never want anything for nothing, what ever I want I pay for." She made a check out right there and then, Helen recollected.

A few days later back in her home in Carrollton, Susan, who had not seen her sister since 1958 when her mother had died, was shocked to read about her again in the headlines;

'SISTER OF FILM STAR FIGHTS FOR HER BABY' told the story of Florence having to appear in court to retain the custody of her two children. A son, 17, in a foster home and a baby girl in General Hospital. Susan's older sister confessed she was on welfare and destitute. The papers mentioned that she bore a striking resemblance to her actress sister.

The reports showed that Susan had helped her many times in the past but that she had not given any assistance recently. Susan's attorney said his client had 'no comment,' this having been a long drawn out situation and Miss Hayward and her husband preferred not to discuss it.

Eaton could not help thinking of his own family, under the circumstances.

Joe Chalkley, who never accepted his father's marriage to Susan Hayward, wanted — in some way — to prove himself. He tried several things — but mostly he wanted to fly, and his father made it possible for him to get his license.

Father Brew had never forgotten the outcome: "I was in Detroit on retreat. I got this call from Eaton. Joe had been killed in a plane crash — a storm someplace out of Louisville, Kentucky. I expressed my sympathy. I couldn't say anything definite to him at this point, about my joining him as I was out there attending a seminar. I did go to the funeral and Eaton met me at the airport. He had not expected me to be able to attend. I shall always remember what he said, 'This is more that I hoped for.' We went from Louisville to Atlanta and then to Washington. Again, it was this in-between thing which I was caught up in. Susan wanted to go, but Eaton insisted that she not go. The three of us, Harvey, Eaton and myself went to Washington alone, on a dreary September day in 1964."

Alone, at home in Carrollton, Susan came face to face with the reality of her husband's ties to his family and his religion and her unaccepted position as his lawful wife. Eaton's marriage to her was not a true one according to his church. Now, for a man of his conscience, fallen from the church unable to receive the sacraments Eaton's guilt gravely darkened with his son's sudden and tragic death — leaving her the outsider.

She did everything she could in acting the part of a catholic wife, as well as she knew how.

One wonders whether Eaton might subconsciously have held himself responsible for his son's death. The building of a church may have been partly for the community, but as much to amend for his religious indiscretion in marrying out of his faith. Susan, knowing all this, would have accepted any faith he was attached to — out of love for him.

How idyllic her life seemed, but underneath it all were serious problems. Eaton was deeply disturbed over his religion. Susan did everything she could to lessen his guilt and to make the marriage appear morally and socially correct. That was part of the reason she worked so hard to become part of the local scene.

In fact, Eaton sensing her dilemma once asked, "Where does the acting stop?"

Susan tried to take his mind off the tragedy by taking him close to the sea in Florida. For the next two years, she absolutely refused to leave him no matter how great the challenge of a movie role. They settled into the house at 220 Nermi Drive in Ft. Lauderdale where she wanted him to rest and regain his failing health and she was determined she would make it happen.

THE STAGE

The stage is the hardest work in the world. Doing the same performance night after night after night sent me right up the wall! I've had only one experience with the stage, in Las Vegas a few years ago doing Mame, *but that was enough. It was a challenge for me and I did the best I could at the time, but I was terribly glad when I lost my voice and had to quit the show. I learned my craft entirely in front of the movie camera and I must say I much prefer making movies, where every day is a different experience. And, too, I have no great feeling or awe about 'the theatah;' I don't consider myself an 'artiste.' I'm just a working woman, that's all, and I'd much rather work where there's a little variety.*

CHAPTER 10

Susan's agent Jack Gordeane phoned her. He wanted her to come to Hollywood to discuss a part in her old friend Joseph L. Mankiewicz's next film *The Honey Pot* to be filmed in Venice. Susan, knowing how much Eaton loved to go to Rome, and Venice, readily agreed to it, believing that this change would be just the ticket.

She told reporters: "My specific reason was Joe Mankiewicz. He's brilliant and what 's more, he has heart. Nowadays I simply won't do a picture unless I know the director and his work." She added humorously, "I was getting restless anyway. It's good for me to work, its good discipline. I was getting lazy and a little fat. My husband realized this about me — "

While in Hollywood, she met up with the Marty Rackin's again; about this time, Helen said, "There was a big change in Eaton. He had gotten very, very, thin. He laughingly said that on the boat, he had tripped and had hurt his leg and it was giving him trouble. My husband said, "My God Eaton, you've lost a lot of weight.' Susan cut in defensively, 'He looks marvelous!' I think she felt that Eaton was seriously ill and you know she just didn't want to face it."

Father Brew said that Eaton's illness had originally started with an ulcer in Chicago. This went back to his first marriage. The bleeding was quite profuse, to a point of danger and they had to give him blood transfusions, and in those transfusions, he was getting tainted blood. It showed up as Hepatitis in the last three years of his life. His spells got progressively worse.

"You could see the color of his infection. This big, strong guy was wasting away; it was his good health that kept him alive as long as it did."

Eaton, not wishing for Susan to go to Italy alone and — perhaps — having a premonition of his approaching end, summoned up from some hidden reservoir the strength to join her on this trip. Before they left for Italy, he wanted to see as many of his old neighborhood friends as possible, it was as though he were tying together any loose ends of his life and saying his farewells.

"There was a reunion in Washington at the Carlton Hotel with as many of the old gang there as could be reached on short notice," said Father Brew, "everyone there was shocked by Eaton's appearance, this yellowish tinge to his skin. He did not look like himself. He was but a shadow of what everybody remembered. He knew his time was running out and he wanted this reunion with his old friends."

A bittersweet happiness warmed by memories of earlier visits journeyed with them as they arrived in Rome that September of 1965. The last time they had seen Rome, Eaton had found a renewal of spiritual solace in visiting the many churches. Now, Susan prayed fervently that he would find, in addition, a renewal of his former strength.

She hoped she could make it so, far away from all that could remind him of the death of his only son. As they disembarked from the plane in Rome that fall, Susan was very watchful of Eaton, though careful not to betray the fear for him within herself.

While shooting during the day, Susan constantly checked up on her husband at the hotel. She noticed his old enthusiasm returning, as he gave her that familiar smile when she left for the studio, and when she returned.

"I'll be right back, sailor," she would say, and salute him a goodbye. When she arrived at the studio, she found his yellow roses in her dressing room.

Actress Edie Adams working on the picture in Rome said sadly, "We all had a bad time. It was just a hard luck picture. Cinematographer Gianni di Venanzo died suddenly during the shooting. The movie was plagued with so many misfortunes. It read beautifully, a clever satire. We worked eight months on it, from August 1965 to March 1966. I got everyone to take hepatitis shots at my house; everyone took them — but Susan. She said, "I'm lettin' no doctor near me!"

"She was a small gutsy lady, she let nobody near her — we all kept away. She trusted only Joe Mankiewicz."

"I arranged for gamma globulin shots for the cast as well. Susan was under some kind of strain. I would have liked to have gotten close to her — to get to know her but she wouldn't join in with the cast on any social level. She seemed — bitter," was all that Edie Adams could finally say, to sum up her impression.

Eaton's condition worsened. He came down with the recurring liver ailment. He sought medical treatment in Rome but had to return to the

United States for more extensive care. Susan arranged to take her husband back to be hospitalized in Fort Lauderdale at Holy Cross Hospital, the first week in December.

By one of life's fortuitous coincidences the chaplain at Holy Cross was a priest from Mount St. Mary's who knew of Eaton Chalkley, but had never met him. He also knew of Eaton's invalid marriage to Susan Hayward, and through this, his removal from the practice of the sacraments, except when there is danger of death. The hospital chaplain absolved the dying man, heard his confession, anointed him and administered Holy Communion. Eaton Chalkley was at peace with himself at last. The albatross had dropped from around his neck.

Father Brew hastened to the bedside of his friend at Holy Cross Hospital, "I want to speak with Tom alone, please — " Eaton asked Susan to step out of the room. Hurt and confused by his request she left them to themselves. They talked privately. He also told his friend that he had made his confession, received communion and that he was happy to be back in the church.

"When he came home from the hospital, he had to have nurses around the clock." Father Brew said. "Then he insisted that she go back to work on the picture that she had contracted for. He said to her, 'you agreed to do it, do it. I'll be alright.'"

A helpless and desolate Susan flew halfway across the continent of Europe, leaving Eaton in the care of nurses, and doctors and Father Brew, to spend the unhappiest Christmas of her life.

"The next few weeks were rather difficult," Father Brew said, "She was calling every day, asking how he was. What can you tell a person on the telephone? He wasn't getting any better and it came to a point where the doctor said, 'you have to tell her.' So she came home."

From that moment on, Susan never left his side. That January, Father Morrow called from Carrollton.

"I would call periodically and ask how he was. Susan asked me to come down, 'You've been talking about coming and if you want to see him again...'"

Father Morrow left Carrollton for Lauderdale and the Chalkley home on Nermi Drive.

"I took a cab to the house and when I arrived she was waiting outside in front of the driveway. 'He's excited about your coming, but he's sleeping, suppose we wait awhile, let him get as much sleep as he can. He'll wake up after awhile," she said, as she led the way around the house to the canal. "I'll take you out to the boat."

She wanted everything very quiet for him. Then we went back inside because she said, "I don't want to leave him too long."

"She was very gentle with him. She was doing the nursing. Walking back and forth." "Father, you know he's receiving communion now and it had made him so happy."

"What about you?" I asked.

"I started the instructions, but I am more concerned about easing him through this. Then I'll look after myself."

"We went on in, this time, he was awake."

He had the rosary in his hand. I made a comment about it and Susan said, "Oh, he's constantly got those in his hands."

"Eaton and I had a nice visit, but Susan was either running for the water or running for the medicine. When we got a few moments to ourselves, she voiced something that was troubling her. She knew that Eaton wanted to be buried on the church grounds. From the first day that we ever talked about a church going up there, they also said there should be a cemetery.

The church wanted to avoid getting all tangled up as it could be a big business, running a cemetery. When I mentioned it to the Archbishop he wasn't keen on it."

"During the conversation, I interrupted Susan and asked her if I could use the phone. I didn't tell her but I called the Arch Bishop and told him Eaton Chalkley is back receiving the sacraments. He was entitled to a full Catholic funeral and would like to be buried at the Church of Our Lady. Susan would like him to be buried at the church. Why can't we?"

After a long pause, the Archbishop answered Father Morrow; "When you get back you announce that the parish is going to have a cemetery, so the announcement will precede the one that Eaton Chalkley is going to be buried there."

Father Brew, who had to leave, returned to his dying friend as soon as possible, "In the interval when he was home I would go say mass and bring Holy Communion back to him (from the church nearby)." In his waking moments, Eaton prayed with Father Brew, while holding on to a crucifix.

"That crucifix did not come from Pope John XXIII (as has been reported) it came from a priest of whom Susan and Eaton were very fond. It came from Father Samuel Robb — it was his crucifix, one that all Jesuits receive when they make their vows. Father Robb had died and the crucifix was given to me. I took it to Eaton and he kept it right beside him until he died."

Susan picked up the crucifix, she knew its background and where it came from.

"May I have it?" she whispered.

"Yes," said Father Brew.

She was to keep the crucifix with her always right up until her death, clutching it as she died.

She was there at the end. She held his hand. His last words were of his concern about her — not materially but spiritually. He was concerned about her soul.

Susan called Father Brew with the expected sad news of Eaton's death. She wanted to take her husband's body back to Washington so that his old friends would have the opportunity to pay their last respects. More importantly, she wanted to make it easier for Eaton first wife, Dorothy Roland, and his family by her to attend. Susan's one and only meeting with Eaton's first wife was to be at the funeral. The following night she took Eaton back to Carrollton for his burial.

The winter sun was filtering thinly through the windows in the chapel of Our Lady of Perpetual Help. Dressed somberly in black, Susan stood erect, looking straight ahead during the service conducted by Father Brew. Her diminutive figure now seemed an even more pitiful defense against the world of which Eaton had been her fortress and protector. This was one role for which no amount of preparation could have been made. Susan, though she covered it well was shocked and bereft.

The small gathering moved outside in silence to the open grave, where Eaton's boyhood friend Father Brew intoned a final blessing as the coffin was lowered into the ground.

"She was very composed," Ann Moran remembered, "They invited everyone there to go back to the house. Harvey Hester had the people from his restaurant bring food over to the Chalkley house."

Mary Williams walked Susan back from the church and was the last one to leave the house, leaving Susan by herself. After everyone had gone, Father Brew, who had returned to the gatehouse, left to return to the church for some private moments of prayer.

It was dusk when he stepped out of the church. Below him across the way, he heard the pitiful wailing sounds of a woman crying. He could see a form stretched out across the recently filled grave. Susan Chalkley was clutching at the earth and sobbing uncontrollably.

On that cold January night, she was wearing only the simple black dress that she had worn for the funeral service as she lay face down stretched across the grave.

Father Brew walked over to the prostrate and forlorn figure and helped her gently up from the ground.

"I want to be with Eaton," she cried, "I want to be with Eaton." Thomas Brew put his arms around her and held her, silently.

Susan Hayward, the widow Chalkley, boarded a plane for Venice a few days after the funeral of her husband. She was returning to complete the filming of *The Honey Pot,* and for the first time in almost ten years, there were no yellow roses from Eaton to greet her in her dressing room.

"My husband wouldn't be very proud of me if I hadn't finished what I'd already started, she said stoically, in response to suggestions that she could probably have arranged a release from her contract.

She returned to the set locked in the prison of her grief. Her co-star Rex Harrison must have sympathized with her remembering his own sorrow when his wife Kay Kendall died. Director Joe Mankiewicz offered what help he could but was unable to communicate with her beyond the perfunctory necessities of moving the shooting along.

"I came in on page 20 and got murdered on page 45," she later said about the assignment. She might have been talking about the way she felt about her own life now that she was without the one person who had given it meaning. When she was through with her scenes, she returned to Carrollton, Georgia.

The loneliest woman in the world now stood often and seemingly endlessly at the graveside of her departed husband, until finally in deep mourning, she would retreat, and close the door behind her inside the house she had once shared with Eaton.

Unable to sleep at night she sought refuge from her private agony in Mary William's home, staying with her for the first few days, sleeping in the upstairs bedroom. She then asked her friend if she would come back with her to the ranch and stay with her there for a while. Susan drank heavily now, trying to find an escape from her loss and relax herself enough to bring on some badly needed sleep. She had much to think about but uppermost in her mind was her determination to convert to Catholicism. Only as a catholic could she be buried in the consecrated ground next to her husband and that, she determined, was to be.

Susan spoke to Father Morrow about the possibility of conversion during her first visit with him since Eaton's death. "You try to see what the reasons are behind it," he said, and questioned her at length about her intentions. She became impatient with him, "I always wanted to,' she said, 'but the church wouldn't let me."

"You know what it will mean," he cautioned her. "You will have to be very circumspect about whom you might marry in the future."

Susan must have thought he was out of his mind to ever suggest she might marry again.

"Never, never, will there be another man. I could never meet a man like Eaton Chalkley," she cried.

Father Morrow urged her to follow the instructions. "It will take awhile," he said. Susan was upset by any suggestion of delay.

Susan knew Father Brew would be firm in his attitude toward her conversion, and that there was no way in which he would speed up the procedure for her.

"Susan went enough times to Mass with Eaton to get some idea of the Mass and its meaning," he said. "I think being with Eaton and seeing his principles and ideals had a lot to do with her interest in Catholicism. When she told me she was going to do it, I didn't get overly enthusiastic about it because I thought she was going too fast. I wanted to be sure it was a calm reason judgment, rather than an emotional reaction. Also, I wanted to be sure she got a good knowledge of the catholic faith (in) assuming a few obligations that she did not have before — something you don't jump into feet first and then ask afterwards, what have I gotten into?"

"I wanted to be sure she had an understanding of the church's laws on marriage lest the whole thing comes up again, but she was determined and she had this date fixed in her mind — June 30th."

Alone at night in the house, Susan would look over towards the church and its recently consecrated graveyard with its one grave and her own words came back to her, "Father we are never going to leave here. We chose the highest piece of land to build on, so we could see it from the house."

Six months after Eaton's death, Susan travelled incognito to Pennsylvania. She was preparing to be received into the catholic faith in the church of Saints Peter and Paul in the Pittsburg suburb of East Liberty and she was going to meet with Father McGuire, with whom she had been in contact.

Susan had told Father McGuire that she had come to a decision in her hours of grief that she could only find solace and comfort in Catholicism, and had asked for his help. She flew up to Pittsburgh on the Wednesday night of June 29th, 1966 and went directly to the church, arriving at 7:30 p.m. The next day, Thursday June 30th, the day of her 49th birthday, she returned to the noon Mass and stood before the altar in Saints Peters and Paul Church and was baptized into the Catholic faith by Father McGuire.

"What I feared might happen did!" said Father Brew. "Father McGuire happened to be Pastor of the church up there in Pittsburgh and he could arrange everything very quietly, the way she wanted it. The church was called St. Peter and Paul and her birthday coincided with the feast of St. Peter and Paul.

"I felt her knowledge was a bit on the superficial side," Father Brew commented, "I first met Father McGuire at Gonzaga High School where I was teaching and he was a student in my class. He is a very pleasant, kind, thoughtful person."

Father Morrow, observing Susan's six hour crash course in Catholicism said, "She went up to Pittsburgh and found a Jesuit up there who gave her a quick study — she found a guy who would do it for her — he was not a man of the Parish."

Of her conversion Susan said, "I became deeply interested in Catholicism when I went to Rome with my husband in 1958. My husband introduced me to the Reverend Daniel J. McGuire, who was serving as American secretary in the Jesuit headquarters at the Vatican.

"From that time on, I began to move toward this beautiful and moving religious faith with deliberate and determined steps. The more I attended Mass, the more I became convinced that someday I would convert."

Susan was baptized just before the noon Mass on that Thursday receiving her first Holy Communion. Several persons attending Mass recognized her and gathered around her after the service. The press was alerted, but Susan, distraught over having lost an earring that Eaton had given her, said little about her conversion.

She left Pittsburgh shortly afterwards and few to Fort Lauderdale where she was greeted and congratulated by her two sons, now both grown young men attending Auburn University.

Now a catholic, Susan probably hoped that her new religion would bring her the peace of mind that Eaton had once given to her and would have wanted her to have.

Back in Georgia, she asked Mary Williams to "walk behind me when I go up to receive communion for the first time at Our Lady of Perpetual Help on Sunday."

She still could not bear to be alone in the house and Mary Williams spent a great deal of time there with her.

"The maids didn't spend the nights, so I stayed with her. One time I was in the living room and I could hear her talking on the telephone from the bedroom. Some feller called her from Atlanta, I don't know what it was about, but she really let him have it. I said, 'Lord, I feel sorry for you poor fella' on the other end of the line — she was really sounding off."

"The next day I got up early and I told the colored woman if Susan wants to know where I am, tell her I'm in the yard (all 450 acres of it). I stayed with her cause she didn't want to be by herself."

Three months later Susan sold the farm.

"There are certain times in your life when you have to jump in the stream and swim," she said, "and there are other times when you jump out of the stream and watch it go by — until the time comes to jump in again."

She decided to move permanently to Ft. Lauderdale. Rather than run away from the past completely Susan felt sure she would be happier there where she had spent so many good times with Eaton. Much as she loved the ranch in Carrollton, it was not the place for her — alone.

"A woman can't manage a cattle ranch alone," she said, "at least not this woman. The cows scare me." Then she added, "You need a man like Eaton to run things on a ranch and know what should be done."

It was a difficult decision to sell that vast acreage of field and stream. "I loved our life out there, so had the boys, we enjoyed every minute of it."

Father Marrow thought back on this time, recalling that Susan had sold the house for only $250,000, including all the furnishings, and her comment on its sale, "I don't want anything to remind me."

Susan had changed a great deal by this time. She remarked that nothing has ever been smooth sailing for her, "Nothing but the wonderful ten years of total happiness with Eaton. When you say ten years, it sounds like a long time. When you live it and are truly happy, it is only a moment."

Susan was trying to pick up the pieces of her life in her own way and turned down all offers of work and any kind of interview saying that she "craved anonymity."

For the next eight months, Susan sat and stared at the water. She smoked five packs of cigarettes a day, rarely leaving the house on Nermi Drive. She drank Jack Daniels and Johnnie Walker Black Label and Beefeater martinis in huge brandy snifters and talked about her life with Eaton to Curlee, who listened patiently, and went along with her ramblings.

She continued to refuse all requests for interviews and seldom spoke to anyone on the phone with the exception of her brother and a few close friends.

Eventually, through an influential connection, a young man with the Heart Association managed to catch her interest. His southern drawl and polite, charming manners coupled with a racy sense of humor made an impression on her. She talked to him often and accepted invitations for benefits and charity affairs on behalf of the Heart Fund. Ron Nelson, the public relations man with the outfit, took up with the lonely star, becoming an escort and a personal friend. Susan learned to relax, joke and drink with him, and through it all she felt no pressures as he made no advances. It was a strictly platonic and easygoing friendship. She slowly came out of her shell and then joined him in a whirlwind of social activity, usually revolving around frequent cocktail hours. Dressed in her favorite uniform of white slacks and a navy blue shirt, with her hair tucked under a floppy white hat and wearing the inevitable sunglasses, she either went out on her boat or sat on the deck behind the house with her new buddy, Ron Nelson.

In May of 1967, 16 months after Eaton's death, there would be a break in the routine of sun and fishing, and drinking. She was offered a movie role, a cameo part, in *Valley of the Dolls*, at $50,000 for two weeks work at her old studio, 20th Century Fox, when Judy Garland was released from her commitment for the role.

Ken Dumaine, an actor on the Hollywood scene for years, worked on the picture and talked about why Garland was let go. "I remember when I went over to Fox to do Valley of the Dolls they knew right away Judy was having problems because she recorded the big number 'I'll Plant My Own Tree' and a few days later they had her back to redo a few bars that were not too good in the playback. They told her that Friday that they were shooting the number the following Monday and she said, 'Oh, we must have a playback before we can do it.' She didn't even remember having just done it. Each morning that she was due at the studio, they had a driver go over to her apartment to call for her. He would arrive there at 6:30 a.m. to pick Judy up at 7 a.m. and he'd wait throughout the morning, sometimes up to 12 noon, before he could even get to her and bring her back to the studio. Suddenly, Mark Robson, who was directing the picture said we can't put up with this. So they called Susan in. She had no time to prepare for it. She jumped in at the last minute and started working on the number."

"Nowadays I simply won't do a picture unless I know the director and his work," Susan said, "Mark Robson is directing it (*Valley of the Dolls*) and I first worked with him 24 years ago. We did *My Foolish Heart* together. Another reason is that the part's short, and good, and the salary's terrific."

Susan expressed regret at Judy Garland's leaving the film and she insisted that Garland be paid in full before she would sign for it. She got the part away from Jane Wyman and Bette Davis. She said of Garland, "She's such a talent, such a fine actress. I guess I don't understand these things though. I've enjoyed every minute of my career. It isn't art to me, its work, and darn good work, but it's never been my life. There are other things vastly more important to me."

Now that Susan was back in the news, she began to open up and talk to interviewers about her return to the cameras, seemingly enjoying all the attention she was getting again. She told one Ft. Lauderdale reporter: "I was getting restless. It's good for me to work, it's good discipline. I was getting lazy and a little fat." As for her life in Lauderdale, the so — called Venice of the North, "I never really like the city. When I was a kid in Brooklyn, I used to hate taking subways. I think finally settling here was what I was looking for, the clear air and most of all the fishing."

For the moment Susan put aside her rods and reels, said goodbye to her stuffed marlin and other prize catches, and with Curlee following behind she left Florida for Hollywood.

Stanley Musgrove met up again with Susan at the Fox studios while she was there for her two week stint for *Valley of the Dolls*.

"I realized she was slightly mad. She was very sweet, too much so."

"I'm just in agony, still, over Eaton's death," he told her.

"Oh, I'm not. I just have joy, for the time we had together. I don't resent it. I am not bereaved. I don't think of it that way. I just think of him with joy for the wonderful times we had together. A lot of people didn't have the times we had."

"Susan," Musgrove asked her, "What do you do?"

"I go fishing all the time," she enthused, and repeated things she had told other people, how she loved fishing and, "Just before coming to Hollywood, I caught a 7 foot 1 inch sailfish." She had two boats — "and I'm the captain of both."

"She had skin that if she were out in the sun for three minutes it would burst, and she told these incredible stories. She would have looked so awful, freckled and everything if she had done all the fishing she said she did. There was a kind of madness about her. Also, she wasn't very good in her work, the picture stunk. But something was off kilter there. She never got into the role. I think the tumor had begun. Maybe a combination there — he died and the brain tumor started."

Susan wrote from her Beverly Wilshire Hotel suite one Sunday to her new friend Ron Nelson, thanking him for a gift he had sent.

Dear Ron,
The book is just charming. Thank you!
Worked this past Friday, and very happily too.
Of course it was like old home week when I went

on the set. Know most of the 'crew' from years
back and they all like me — and I like them.
Hope to be back in time for your birthday — but
also want the musical number to be as good as
possible so might ask for more rehearsal time.

Will keep you posted, my friend.
Best — Susan

Choreographer Bob Sidney was assigned to do the solo dance number for the film.

"Judy was doing the part of Helen Lawson. And poor Judy, it was very sad. I was introduced to her. I auditioned the 'I'll Plant My Own Tree' number that Susan finally did. I had it laid out for Judy and we already had it arranged, we had the chart done in Judy's key. We had had five days of her locking herself in her trailer and not coming out 'til 6 p.m. The first time I sang the song for her, I had to get under the table. She did the most outlandish things. Then I had to do it for her and Roger Eden. I had to audition it, I don't sing. Judy liked it; she liked the excitement of it.

"She would lock herself in her dressing room. They had people there just to see she had no booze. Lorna (her daughter) was a teenager then. She came running out of the room one day saying 'Mommie was strange, Mommie was taking something.' They had to dismiss her, nobody could handle her.

"Susan was called in and they paid her plenty because she had to come up from Florida, she had to give up her little fishing fleet. She came on the set a real pro. She arrived absolutely letter perfect. Everybody was impressed. Patty Duke was there and she was flip and all that, but the minute she met Susan she knew she was a strong lady, and it was no nonsense. None of the four letter words, Susan was a stickler for that. She never held up anyone. I can never remember them holding the camera for her — if they said let's go, she was there. She would let out an ungodly yell to clear her throat sometimes," Sidney screamed to illustrate.

"What the hell is that," I shrieked.

"You try it, it's good for you, you need it for your voice," she told him referring to Sidney's raspy, throat register.

"She was a big star when she left to go live in Ft. Lauderdale. She realized she had paid her dues and she wanted some personal happiness.

Wherever she met this Charlton Chalk, whatever the hell his name is —
he had to be a strong man. Susan would not respect a weak man; I asked
her if he was as strong as she was."

"You really are a problem," she smiled.

"She was delighted that I was on the picture. The first thing she said
to me was, 'When do we do the exercises?' Every damn day I used to get
black and blue because she never stopped.

"She's the only actress I know who never had any comment about
any other actress. When we did *Valley* [*of the Dolls*] and we were alone
she could have asked me about Judy Garland. She never once discussed
it, she never gossiped about her. Yes, she did make sure that Judy got
paid."

Sidney was waiting in her dressing room one day, "I had to know so
I asked her to tell the truth. 'Didn't you dunk Barker in the pool?'" He
was referring to the headlines before the divorce with Jess Barker where
the newspapers, in explicit detail, wrote of Susan's being thrown into the
pool at their home and Barker shoving her underwater.

"What do you mean?" Susan said defensively.

"I believe you did the dunking, you are stronger than he was," Sidney
suggested.

"I could do it!" she boasted.

"What do you do down there in Florida?" Sidney teased her.

"I look at the water. I have my fishing fleet."

"Oh, come on, what kind of fishing fleet, what kind of crap is that?" he
kidded her, "Really, don't you miss it here?"

"Miss what? This is a place to work. I'll always come back to work if
the price is right. I don't have many friends here anymore. I love living
down there."

Sidney was concerned about the scene in which Patty Duke pulls the
wig off Helen Lawson, played by Susan, and exposed a head of white
hair underneath. Susan insisted her hair be bleached white for that scene.

"Don't let them do your hair," he advised her.

"It won't work; you don't know what you're talking about. When you
change color, it isn't that bad. Don't worry I'm not paying for it!"

"Oh wear a wig Susan."

She explained to him how she had to be conscious in the whole scene
that when they pulled the wig off she would be exposed as the aging star
with the white hair. If she wore a wig underneath the top wig, it wouldn't
have felt the same to her and she would have affected her reaction. It
wouldn't have been honest.

Sidney watched her limber up for the dance routine, dressed in slacks and a tied up blouse and when she saw him looking, she tied a shirt around her waist.

"A little bit of a belly there?" he said.

"I didn't ask for your anatomical opinion," she answered him while exercising a good hour and a half.

Privately she asked him what he really thought about her condition.

"I remembered Susan in *Adam Had Four Sons*; she played such a bitch in it. I loved her so and when I got he chance to work with her I was delighted." Actor Ken Dumaine recalled first working with Hayward in *My Foolish Heart*, as a sailor in a scene at Grand Central Station, and then he did some standing scenes in *I'll Cry Tomorrow*. The last time, "I saw her was when she took over for Garland. I was one of the audience as she was doing this number for the camera.

"She had that great facility for lip syncing, and even though it was Margaret Whiting's soundtrack you could have sworn that she, Susan, was actually singing.

"I had seen Susan Hayward in public a time or two. She was not too friendly, she sort of played Miss Movie Star. She would arrive at a place and it was an — 'Out of my way — let me through', kind of attitude as she walked in and right through the crowd."

As for the role of Helen Lawson in Valley of the Dolls Susan remarked, "She's not exactly a person you'd take home to mother. She's a woman with a backbone of steel."

The critics singled out her brief appearance in the film as, 'like watching a Sarah Bernhardt' compared to the amateur histrionics of the rest of the cast.

After two weeks in Hollywood, Susan was back home in Ft. Lauderdale. "I wouldn't want to live in Hollywood all the time. It's like coming to a brilliant, creative, dream world. I like the simpler kind of life."

The simpler life that Susan returned to was another bout with the bottle, boredom, restlessness and more frequent forays into the local social scene on the arm of Ron Nelson. She was the prize catch of the community — the local legend living in their midst.

The twins were now 22 years old, with Gregory studying veterinary medicine at Auburn University and Timothy in the Armed Forces.

Susan phoned her brother in Hollywood at all hours of the night and sometimes she would phone Father Brew, or anyone who could talk to her about Eaton. In public, she would ramble on about fishing.

"I adore fishing in Florida — deep-sea fishing. You know — Hemingway, the big stuff. I love having a boat and being on the ocean. I'm out there every day. There are two fish I haven't caught yet and still must. I want a black marlin and a swordfish — they're very difficult to get, I've caught the other ones; I have them mounted and hanging like trophies all over my house."

Whatever she was doing, whether it was fishing or partying, flirting with the idea of meeting someone new, nothing worked. She didn't seem particularly happy with her freedom.

"I'm an independent," she said. "Very. Too much so. I always have been except when I was married to my second husband. You can't be totally independent when you have another human being to consider especially if you like the person and in my case, I adored him. I enjoyed that period of being — or rather, making believe — I was helpless. I could have stayed that way for the rest of my life but things didn't work out that way."

Back in Hollywood, Susan's brother Wally married for the first and only time. "I was working part of the time for Crown Management and they had this circus comin' to town. Carol (his future wife) was workin' in this gas station on Beverly Blvd. I knew the people there and one of the attendants said, 'Hey, look who's leading the parade.' Well, that was me in a jeep leading the route downtown. Behind me were the elephants."

Wally met Carol that day and as he said, "I kept this to myself — I'm like Susan that way — it was a kind of quiet thing. We took off and went to the Justice of the Peace. Later when Susan met Carol they hit it off right away."

Wally talked about Susan's behavior at this time. He was fearful that she might try to end her life because if ever she would have thought of such a thing it would have been after Eaton died, "because she loved him so much."

"What she did do," Wally said, "was get on the juice. She used to call from Florida and my wife would answer the phone and Susan would say, 'You takin' care of my brother? You feedin' him right? You doin' this for him or that for him?' So I would say to Carol, "Maybe you better get off the phone and I'll talk to her." And she would talk for a couple of hours — just to have somebody to talk to. She tried to get us to Carrollton at first and then when she moved to Florida, she wanted us to move down there. She said she could get me a job at the racetrack. But I knew at that time down there the racetracks were way underpaid. Out in California we were getting' the highest pay of any racetrack in the United States. So we never did go."

Father Brew had his own fishing tale to tell: "When Susan called me one time I told her my sister Ann was going down to Ft. Lauderdale to visit a friend. She said, 'tell her to call me.' Ann did and Susan said, 'You have to come out on the boat and we'll go fishing tomorrow.' So on my sister's line came this swordfish. I can't picture her reeling it in. Susan congratulated her and put a flag up. She had the swordfish mounted and sent it to my sister. It must have cost $300."

There were bigger fish in Florida who angled for a chance to catch her interest. Ed Lahey, for one, had his own special reasons.

Susan was asked to make a speech September 16, 1967, in Jacksonville, to all Republican leaders for Ed Lahey. There were rumors about her and the politician resulting from her help with his campaign for Governor of Florida. She told Father Morrow about being involved in his campaign, saying how much she enjoyed the contest. Father Morrow also read where she was dating other men (including Tom Shelton and Claude Kirk) and he mentioned it to her.

"Yes," she said. "But like I told you before there never will be another Eaton."

After all that build up, she withdrew, both from Ed Lahey and politics. Her experience with these politicians led her to say, "I've had enough of this! Dealing with these people!" When Susan felt she was being used, for whatever reasons, she walked out.

When Susan flew back to Carrollton, on rare visits, she saw her old friends Mary Williams and Ann Moran.

Ann and her daughter Judy took over a banana cake to Mary William's house for Susan. After they had caught up with the local happenings Susan rather apologetically asked Judy, "Did you hear Mrs. Chalkley is going out with another man?"

"Yes, Mrs. Chalkley," said the 12 year old.

"You know Mrs. Chalkley has to go out with a man once in awhile to these Oscar shows and these big things."

Judy shrugged her shoulders, "Oh that's all right, Mrs. Chalkley."

"You know if Mrs. Chalkley ever married a man he is going to have to be exactly like Mr. Chalkley, is that OK with you?"

"Sure that's OK!"

With tears in her eyes, Susan hugged her.

Susan heard jazz organist Jack Frost play one day in Lauderdale and thought he was great. She sent one of his records to her agent Jack Gordeane with instructions to get it over to Joey Bishop. "You tell Joey, Jack would be wonderful on his show." Bishop said fine only if Susan would make an appearance and introduce Jack. Susan went with Frost and his wife to Hollywood.

Backstage at the 'Joey Bishop Show' there was an aura of excitement Accustomed as the crew was to celebrities, there was something special about Susan Hayward, the lady from Florida. You didn't see her often in Hollywood — "she didn't do the town" — or make the personal appearances, even when she lived there. She moved through the backstage bedlam of the TV show creating a wake of curiosity.

Susan talked to TV host Bishop about her seafaring life in Ft. Lauderdale, and catching her first white marlin. She talked about the boats moored right behind her house — one for everyday use another for Sundays. She barely spoke of her past life other than saying it was a dream come true.

"I've learned to live again and I've learned to live alone." Her 23-year-old son Timothy was now at Fort Bennington, Georgia in intensive training for the Green Berets. Redheaded, freckled face Gregory was still studying veterinary medicine at Auburn University.

Susan was projecting a carefree image, attempting to conceal the deep-rooted emptiness that was invading her.

Her bogeyman had returned and was taking over. Then she was rescued by the offer of work from her old friend Marty Rackin. Rackin believed he had just the right vehicle to attract Susan to get her out of her lethargy.

He knew she couldn't even look at anything she and Eaton had been involved in, including the movie business (with the exception of a small part in *Valley of the Dolls*, which she did as a favor for Mark Robson). He realized too that after selling out all their holdings in Georgia, she had buried herself in her home in Florida. She had also tried big game fishing, safaris in Africa, motorcycle riding — but nothing erased the memory of her life with Eaton. She was living artificially, in a hazy cloud of alcohol.

Helen Rackin, speaking about her late husband said, "Marty got involved with Caesar's Palace and they were looking for somebody to play Mame. Mame is a gutsy dame and he thought it would be great for Susan because that's what Susan was."

Marty Rackin told his fellow investors that Susan was a 'buddy' of his and he called her at home in Florida from Las Vegas.

"Hey, Hooligan, how long you gonna sit there with the old folks in Sun City? How about coming to Vegas to do *Mame* for me on the stage at Caesar's Palace," Rackin goaded her.

Helen recalled Susan's reply to her husband, "Gee Marty, I don't know. This is what I'll do. I'll go to New York and see *Mame* and see if I can do it." Susan flew into New York to see Angela Lansbury in the stage hit and loved her and the play.

"My husband conned her into coming out here (to California) — urging her — 'Come on out here and we'll fly to Vegas and talk to the men there.'"

A month later Susan was in Vegas and that September 1968, she would begin rehearsals for *Mame*. First, she decided to make another visit to Carrollton. Susan was staying at Mary Williams' home when Ann Moran paid her a visit.

"Ann what do you think of me doing *Mame*?"

"Why not, all those other gals that can't carry a tune did it. I heard you sing, you got a rough voice, but you'd make a beautiful Auntie Mame."

Susan laughed and told them, "You know — I think I'm gonna do it!" They all cheered her, wishing her luck!

The director of *Mame*, John Bowab, had worked with practically every Mame who ever appeared in the role on stage. However, this was to prove a very new and extraordinary experience.

He began: "Susan was the only lady in a major company who did not audition for the role, everybody auditioned, from Ann Miller to Judy Garland. Caesar's has star approval, however. It was the only time we cast a lady without auditioning her. She was written into the contract by Caesar's Palace. They wanted her and they wanted her badly. Hers was the name they thought would be the big drawing card, and so did we. Except she was a lady who had never set foot on a stage. We knew she sang, how well we didn't know.

"It was big news and caused a lot of excitement. When she was finally introduced to us we were all really stunned. Susan had absolutely no figure at all. The body that all of us knew and loved, the great walk and the look and everything was gone. Her figure looked like an avocado or a round pear. The lady was dissipated, bloated."

Susan had flown up from Florida to New York to get into a rehearsal set up at The Broadway Arts rehearsal studio and to meet the cast. Her understudy Betty McGuire also playing another featured role in the production never forgot that meeting.

"We all were just waiting with bated breath for Susan Hayward to walk in. Now I had an image, we always have an image of somebody we've seen up on the screen. I thought she was taller and in walks this pint — sized lady. She's what — like 5'2" very plain, she had a kerchief on, a sweater over an aquamarine slacks outfit. No make-up with these wonderful freckles. It blew my mind. I went, "Oh my God anybody who was willing to walk in that ready, that prepared with the image of 'here comes the star' is some lady.

"We were all in awe. She had a wonderful black lady with her who had been her maid for years. Everybody just stood up and applauded and everything and she said, "Hey, wait a minute, hold the applause until you can see whether I can do it or not.'"

The highly acclaimed and awarded choreographer Oona White said, "When I first came to New York to meet with her and give her some exercises she looked like humpty-dumpty. She had no waist at all. It was a long pull. I sent a dancer with her back to Florida to make sure she did these exercises. She asked for it actually, she said, 'I can't do it alone. If I have to go back I know I'll just dissipate.' Her legs looked like matchsticks; I had to build up her legs. When I saw her standing at the dancers bar I thought, "Oh my God this is going to be a job getting her back in shape."

Diana Baffer, the young, pretty, dance captain, was introduced to her on that first day at the studio and had her own impression: "This little tiny thing looked more frightened that I was. I was with her a week in New York then they decided they wanted to send me down to Fort Lauderdale for a couple of weeks. I stayed with her in her house working with her every day for a long time. I adored her. Unfortunately, she was in such bad physical shape she never did build up the stamina that she needed for the part of *Mame*. She had little spindly legs and she was heavy around the torso. She had what I would call the typical drinker's body. Poor little thing it took her a couple of days in rehearsal just to do a knee bend. She was over 50 and it was an impossible thing to ask her to try one of the hardest parts in musical comedy.

"She did so many things that were so sweet. She had a terrific house-keeper, Curlee, the black woman. Boy was she close to her. Curlee took care of her more than anybody did."

Susan and the young woman had dinner together each night and over a glass of wine, Susan opened up and began to confide in her. Susan confessed that she had lost her will to live. That after she had met Eaton Chalkley she realized that everything she had done in her life to that point just didn't seem nearly as important. She just couldn't believe that he was taken away from her at such a young age.

Diana would listen to her talk about her religion and other things she seemed to believe in, "She asked my astrological sign and she wasn't a bit surprised to learn that I am a Leo. Her son Gregory was in vet school when I was there and she thought the world of him. She spoke very highly of him, how bright he was, what a great child he was."

When Susan introduced Diana to her other son Timothy she insisted Diana go out with him, "I only went out with him one evening. He was into a lot of pot smoking; there was no doubt about it. Susan said she was going to bed early so I went out with him and his friends. I was introduced to them by him as 'his old lady's dancing teacher.'

"I had mentioned that I liked steamed clams once and on my last night in Ft. Lauderdale she had, my God, like a bushel full of clams delivered. I ate until I just couldn't eat anymore."

Director John Bowab remembered that, "Oona White had a wonderful regimen of exercises and it was Diana's job to implement them. Susan phoned and said she wanted to be back up North with us. She didn't feel she was under the right kind of discipline, which was a stunner for us and we were thrilled.

"It was with pride that she could see the waist coming back, the bust like getting firmer but the thing she took the greatest pride in were her legs, which were pencil thin. The face was wonderful, the hair was long — which became a problem. To see her in a rehearsal studio, which was all mirrored, when Oona or one of us would come around she'd say 'Look what's happening' and point to the muscles in her legs — they were still thin but now they had shape and texture and resiliency to them. That seemed to generate the most excitement to her. Any of those ladies who have had a big drinking problem for some reason lose their texture, their muscle tone. The exercises she did were incredibly difficult, I wouldn't do them," said the director. "She worked at it, I mean an 8 hour day — at the same time she was doing her vocals every day with the coach."

"While Susan was rehearsing for the Vegas company, Jane Morgan was rehearsing to take over the New York company and Janis Paige was doing an understudy rehearsal. We had all three ladies on stage one Saturday at the Winter Garden Theatre. I'll never forget Susan was sitting on the floor; she was changing her shoes. Jane Morgan was on one side and Janis Paige on the other. Jane did a back flip with a couple of boys and Susan's face went absolutely green."

"What's that?" she asked unbelievingly, thinking it was something she would have to do while thinking they were holding back to give her a little at a time. Luckily, it was not part of the act.

While in New York in training for her singing and dancing stage debut for the scheduled Christmas holiday opening, she replied to a letter from Ron Nelson:

November 21, 1968

Dear Ron —
It's colder than a well diggers ass here in Fun City — and in a few moments I'll be in the Epsom salt tub.

Your letter was here at lunch time — when I returned to the apartment for a diet Pepsi before starting the four hour dance and exercise grind. Before Pepsi is always vocal exercises and singing time. On Mondays — Wednesdays and Fridays — after dance — Masseuse time — then there are always ten thousands incidentals!

I really collapsed with laughter at your version of the upcoming Harness Ball bit — I would say without hesitation that the lady will fill the bill amply — fore and aft!

Oona White.

*The work here — as you can well imagine — is at this point at which
we separate the men from the boys — I screamed with pain and wailed
that I was not a man or a boy but a poor weak female — and got a loud
round of applause — but no sympathy.*

*I'd just as soon have brought in Chinese dinner for Thanksgiving
but made the mistake of asking a few people over. I intend to kick them
out after they eat.*

*I am enjoying it though — in spite of my foolish gripes, it seems to
bring out the fighting Irish in me which has been too long buried under
the veneer of being a lady.*

*One of the loveliest things is discovering so much in common with
super active people — there is a deep simpatico that extends between us.*

*I'm pleased to hear that some of the Ft. Lauderdale crowd will come
to Vegas but regret that my job will make me unavailable for any kind
of social life — beyond ten minutes after the last show.*

*Give Kelly and Helen and the Seropians and the Erdmans my dear-
est love. Received a nice letter from Nixon. Miss everybody — but have
too much to do to really be homesick.*

Be good — be happy,

Your affectionate friend,
Susan

They had scheduled a Benefit Performance at the Winter Garden with
Susan doing *Mame* for the first time in front of an audience. She was
excited and frightened at the same time, but because of union complications, it was cancelled.

John Bowab recalled that promised event, "The interest in New York
was maniacal. When people heard that a run through was going to be
done 4,000 people would have killed me for tickets, they all begged to
come."

Weeks later Susan and Oona White flew out to Las Vegas for the
highly publicized opening. On the plane Oona said to her, "You've been
such a good girl I'm going to let you have one brandy after dinner." It was
Susan's reward for not drinking while in training in New York.

Vegas' Caesar's Palace, a $25 million caravansary, blossoming in the
cool desert with white hot fury on 34 acres, 1500 employees in Greco
Roman costumes, a $125,000 chandelier with 10,000 crystals. $200,000
worth of Italian statues for starters, attracted a multitude of people from
all over the globe. Now with Susan Hayward playing in the Greco-Roman

room, crowds would line up for hours to try to make one of her two evening shows.

Susan and Oona went right to Caesar's Palace but before they could get to their rooms, they were ushered into the dining room, and seated. Frank Sinatra who was appearing there introduced Susan and as Oona said, "the whole room fell apart." Now that the fiery redhead had come out of her cocoon, she was going full blast.

The first week in Vegas was a repeat of what she had done in New York. Dress rehearsals continued right up to Christmas day. During a break in rehearsals, Susan and the cast were invited by the hotel to have dinner in a private dining room. Then it was back to the show. Ann Moran sent up a five pound fruitcake from Carrollton to her, which she shared with the cast.

Scheduled to open the following night, on the afternoon of December 26, 1968, *Mame* was previewed for an invited audience of Air Force Personnel. When Susan made her entrance sliding down a banister blowing a bugle and singing, 'It's Today,' the men went wild. It could have been a scene from *With A Song In My Heart* when, Susan as Jane Froman, entertained servicemen on the U.S.O. tours.

Opening night, the room, which seated 1,300, was packed, with movie stars, who had flow up from L.A., the press, hotel management and any VIP that could use his influence to acquire a seat. The curtain rose on the smallest, most glamorous *Mame* in theatrical history, to great applause.

Director Bowab watched it all anxiously, "It didn't go as well as we wanted it to. The show was difficult to cut — it was a 90-minute version. She was too vulnerable, too soft, you wanted to reach out and protect her. With the other Mames you felt — well screw it — so what if there was a stock market crash she'd go on to something else — with Susan the audience wanted to go up there and take care of her.

"Susan, who did not wear a body mike, or use stage microphones felt that she had to fill the room and belted out every number. She felt more at ease with the ballads and when she sat down with the little boy, her nephew Patrick, and sang, 'If He Walked Into My Life,' she did it with a tenderness that was heartbreaking. The emotional rendering of the lyrics got in her way. The part of *Mame* calls for a player who can be cold, bitchy, and flippant. Ironically, for an actress who gained her reputation for tough portrayals on the screen, came across as femininely dependant. Every gesture, every line and lyric was listened to with extraordinary attention. I am sure many were wondering if she were going to make it. As one critic put it 'when Susan Hayward grabbed both thighs hard and with moist eyes and pouty lips told us that we need a little Christmas right this very minute, she was Barbara Graham pleading for her very life."

They also said she lacked stage authority, her timing was bad but still they found her a curiously affecting Mame and for certain, one the likes of which would not be seen again. The audience was in effect helping her through the performance cheering every gesture.

Stanley Eichelbaum of the San Francisco Examiner remarked, "I'm glad it's Las Vegas and not New York or Los Angeles. It's like a charity turnout for Princess Margaret — they even applaud her costumes."

Susan who had never faced a live audience in her 30 years of performing — determined to beat this latest challenge — won the first round.

In her dressing room after her opening night performance, the press bombarded her with questions, which she responded to with her usual direct honesty.

"You mean it didn't show?" she said when someone asked her if she were nervous, doing a little pirouette through forests of flowers and finding a free wall to lean against. "I'll tell you truthfully, I was really scared stiff the first 15 minutes on that stage."

"It's fun. It's not exactly easy — twice a night. But is anything worthwhile easy? After 30 years, I'm finally in the theatre! Still I'll be glad when it's over — I'll have new muscles." Then she swept everyone aside, "Okay fellas, that's it," she said. "I still have another show to do. But if you're ever down around Ft. Lauderdale and spot my boat, the 'Oh Susannah,' give a holler."

She and Curlee had taken a house in the desert, where Susan slept 'till noon to recover from the two shows the night before. Then she would spend the rest of the day indoors, taking her hot Epsom salt baths, reading and on occasion seeing a few people, such as Ron Nelson who made frequent trips to Vegas and, her new press agent, Jay Bernstein and some of the company members.

Betty McGuire was the only person in the musical history of *Mame* who understudied for Mame, Vera and, playing the role of Sally Kato, did all three. McGuire knew the rigors of performing and was amazed at Susan's labors. Susan was practically never off stage.

She stripped down for costume changes as her dressers pulled her in, between scenes, and pushed her right again on stage. There was no intermission break for *Mame*, it went right into the second act nonstop. Susan having to do all the dance numbers from the Mame cakewalk to the jitterbug, the songs, the comedy and the dramatic interludes. As her energy gave way, she would fall into the arms of the two dressers as they literally lifted her up under the armpits, dressed her, wiped off the drenching perspiration and toss her back in front of the footlights. They told her, "you'll have to project more." To the screen actress, who misunderstood the meaning, she shouted more to fill up the enormous room. In spite of all this, Susan began being Mame rather than Mame taking over Susan. When she was not on stage, she stayed in her dressing room to recharge her energy. However, she found some relaxation playing the slot machines. Before the first show and after the second show Susan disguised in dark glasses, kerchief covering her red hair wearing slacks and sweater stood by the one arm bandit and yanked it for all it was worth. Standing beside her, Curlee holding a cup of money watched intently as Susan fought with the machine to win. The hardened Las Vegas types surrounding her never noticed her; she was just another small time gambler in the crowd.

Ruth Gilette, who played Mother Burnside, fretted over her wearing her emeralds, coming to work. "She used to wear her jewels and everybody was worried to death about it," Ruth said, "She and her maid would get out of the car in the parking lot and walk into the hotel and she would be wearing her emeralds. We'd say, 'Honey, you must not do that somebody is going to hit you over the head.'"

"No darling," she would smile. "I don't think so. I don't want them in a safe deposit box — I wanna use 'em."

There was only one stage level dressing room, which, of course, the star had. The cast had to run up steps to reach theirs. Susan became concerned for the older Ruth Gilette who had to dash up and down three times a performance. She insisted that her friend share her dressing room for her changes — no one else even thought of the ordeal it must have been for the portly woman.

Susan spoke to Ruth about her late husband, how much in love she was with him and that she did the show to get over all that she missed being with him. Ruth and a few special people in the company that she became friendly with often went back to her house after the show. Now that the excitement of opening night had passed and the routine of fourteen shows a week began to be a grinding reality, she started to become restless and bored. There were surprises from time to time that picked up her spirits.

Her son Timmie had just married and as Susan had been unable to attend the wedding, he brought his bride to Caesar's on New Year's Eve. They watched his mother do her first show and at the end when Susan was taking her curtain calls, a spotlight was thrown on the newlyweds. Susan introduced them to the delighted audience and asked them to come up on stage.

Rackin had shuttled between Hollywood and Vegas, trying to find ways to keep her going. They looked for every conceivable way to save her energy. As the weeks passed, the situation grew hopeless. Hayward was a box office bonanza and Caesar's was in a panic.

"She developed Vegas throat," John Bowab explained. "There is something about the air in Vegas that affects singers vocally, she got it but kept pushing to overcome it."

The examining doctors warned her that she should either have throat surgery or quit the show. She had developed nodes, little tumors, on her vocal chords. Within the past year, she had had a hysterectomy because of a benign tumor, now for a second time Susan had shown herself prone to growth formations.

Marty Rackin went into long conferences with the management of Caesar's. Something had to be done, and quickly.

Ron Nelson, who was practically in absentia from his job at the Heart Fund in Ft. Lauderdale, stood by Susan in this crises. One night while she was resting in her rented home in the desert, he went sightseeing near The Strip. He spotted a crowd of gawkers standing in front of a store window. Curious, he made his way up behind them. In the window was artist Ralph Cowan, painting a life sized portrait of Susan in her closing costume from *Mame*; a white gown with a white fox collar trim. The figure in the painting was like a Barbie doll with a cut out of a Susan Hayward face pasted on, except for the exaggerated pert nose and heart shaped mouth. She stood on huge rocks against a turbulent brooding sky, the artist's interpretation of Susan's private life; the moon (her astrological sign) casting its light on restless waters. Every day he painted in the window before an every increasing, curious audience. As the painting neared completion, the artificially technicolored little doll, staring off into space became an unbelievable caricature of Susan Hayward.

Nelson, at the sight of the oil painted monstrosity, hastened back to tell Susan, thinking it would be just the kind of joke she needed to "crack her up," it was so Las Vegas phony.

"You've got to see it. It's so funny you won't believe it!" he howled. In disbelief, she questioned Ron further about the painting. She also found out that the artist had been given permission by Caesar's Palace to attend numerous performances of *Mame* to study his subject. "How dare they permit that," she exploded.

She refused at first to even look at the outrage but her curiosity got the best of her and the following night after the show, in her usual disguise outfit, she went with Ron to inspect it.

She stood unnoticed among the crowd of people staring up at the cartoon Hayward on its easel resisting the impulse to throw a brick through the window. "Just look at that candy box crap," she said just a bit too loudly as Ron pulled her away before a scene developed.

Curlee would shake her head in sympathy saying, "Ain't it exhausin'?" In truth it was more than exhausting it was slowly taking its toll on her health — dangerously so.

Her feet started to give out long before her voice. The producers were on the alert for any last minute problems. She was in no condition to continue to perform one night and they told Betty McGuire to standby to take over for her. Betty saw her in her dressing room trying to force her tiny feet, which had swollen up to five times their size into boots for the big Mame number. Betty finished the show that night and continued for the next few performances until the swelling subsided.

Susan watched Betty perform from the control booth. She marveled at how the stage trained McGuire did the part with such ease. With years of experience behind her the musical comedy performer, as Irish as Susan herself, with her red hair, freckles and big blue eyes, breezed through the show. One of the reviewers catching her performance gave her a wonderful write up.

Susan came into Betty's dressing room with the review crumpled up in her fist, and threw it at the dressing table. "Here, put this in your scrapbook. They loved you and hated me!" and walked out.

Susan remained distant and aloof to her understudy and Betty, awestruck by the superstar, kept her distance. With Susan back in the role, Betty then had to go on for the actress who played Vera Charles. Previously, during the Bosom Buddy number the other actress tried to upstage Susan. That night Susan missed a cue and tripped, falling on top of Betty.

Betty pulled herself together and in return did the same thing to Susan making it seem like part of the act. The audience caught on, howled with laughter and applauded as Susan and Betty broke up laughing as they untangled themselves.

"She called me into her dressing room after the show," Betty said, she said how much fun she had on stage that night. That broke it. She knew that I was out to help her not hurt her."

From that time on Susan trusted her and warmed up considerably, even asking her advice.

"How the hell do you keep that energy going? And where does that voice come from? What is that?"

"You must remember Susan that I'm a stage lady — that's what I'd be asking you if I were in front of a camera. That's what I've been trained for, it's years and years of training."

After that Betty began to give Susan breathing exercises and explained what stage projection meant. It was too late into the show for this kind of help and Susan resorted to a body mike to preserve what strength she had left in her voice.

During these times together, Susan would often speak about Eaton saying she really thought that for the first time in her life she had someone who wanted her just for herself. She felt used up and Betty remembered specifically her saying, "You don't know how bloody the nails became, climbing my way up."

But there was one man who cared and looked out for her and that was Marty Rackin. "He was down there faster than you can say scissors when something was going wrong or when Susan wanted to know anything," Betty said.

The sold out houses, the applause and the compliments coming from all directions had rejuvenated her and she was feeling in top form for a time. After the discipline of her months in New York and the rigors of performing every night began to fade, she became moody without a man like Eaton around to help her get through this taxing job. She went back to drinking and started to smoke heavily again. Feeling trapped in her desert home she grew frustrated and nervous. She was fighting an uphill battle.

She became distrustful of her understudy Betty McGuire. As an actress from Hollywood used to people stabbing at you from right to left she looked at McGuire as a threat — the understudy who can't wait to get on. Another time she found a dislike in the precocious child actor who played Patrick. Then it was the actress who played Vera. An unknown member of the cast who played the homely Agnes Gooch was the then unknown Loretta Swit, who later gained fame as the character Hot Lips in the television series *M*A*S*H*. Swit ingratiated herself with Susan and joined the select group surrounding her along with warm and motherly Ruth Gilette and hairdresser Charles La France who comprised the trio of her close friends.

Director Bowab conspired with La France to cut Susan's long hair. Her perspiration problems left her hair damp and limp after a short time on stage. Without telling her — to even it out — he clipped away until it was shortened to the right length.

The ever-faithful Curlee stood by to comfort and calm her during any darkening moods. She would stand in the wings each night. To relieve the monotony she would sing along while watching Susan perform. But when it came to 'If He Walked Into My Life,' she just knew that Susan was singing about Eaton Chalkley.

After 17 weeks and 96 performances, Susan faced the press. In a hoarse whisper and with tears in her eyes she said; "My doctors insisted I leave *Mame* and do nothing but rest my voice for several months. I love the show and the cast, and I hate to walk out on Caesar's Palace. What really breaks my heart is I've never copped out on any role or anybody in my 30 years as a performer."

Betty McGuire wept for her. Others choked up. She planned a big farewell party for the cast, "I want to go out in style and say thank you in style."

The party was held in one of the most stylish rooms in the hotel, with its white leather covered circular dining booths; two orchestras playing all the tunes from *Mame*; waiters pouring champagne; and a splendid dinner waiting to be served. All the guests at the private party were waiting for the star to make her entrance.

The doors to the room opened and there stood the 'hostess' dressed in a sequin-sprayed beige and lavender gown and her lavish display of emeralds. When the conductor struck the overture from *Mame*, Susan Hayward walked into the room on cue, every inch the star. Graciously, she greeted her guests and wasted no time in being served from the bar.

Unannounced, and at the management's invitation, the next Mame, Celeste Holm, suddenly appeared, dressed in simply street clothes. Photographers covering the event engineered a situation between the outgoing star and her incoming replacement by pushing them together to pose for publicity shots. Members of the cast who had worked with Miss Holm during the National Tour told stories of how temperamental and difficult she had been. Susan, resenting her presence, marched off to the powder room. As if searching for a weapon, she took her lipstick from her handbag and scrawled in big red letters across the mirror:
CELESTE WHO?????????
Then she had the audacity to sign it:
SUSAN HAYWARD

The entire cast made trips back and forth to the ladies room when word spread of Susan's angry graffiti to Miss Holm.

Celeste Holm came to the party, intending to stay only long enough 'for a visit' as requested by the hotel. She was brought over to Susan who was now seated next to Ron in one of the white leather circular booths, to be introduced. Betty McGuire, the on going Mame at that time, was seated to the far left, making an uncomfortable study of the three Mames.

According to an eyewitness Susan turned to speak to Celeste Holm confidentially, "I want you to know that these are great people you're working with."

Miss Holm listened perplexed, and smiled.

"I don't think you heard me right," Hayward said menacingly, "and if I hear of you abusing them, so help me, I'll come back here and kick your ass all the way back to Toledo, Ohio."

Every eye in the room turned toward them. When the publicity man said he had enough shots, Miss Holm excused herself and walked out.

Elated Susan got up and joined the merry group, ordering another drink. She signaled to those around her to begin dancing and was just about to take Ron onto the dance floor when he spotted artist Ralph Cowan coming through the door.

Ron quickly warned her that the gatecrasher was heading her way. She motioned for him to stand aside. She had taken care of Celeste "Who?" — now she would demolish Ralph "Who?"

Cowan introduced himself and proceeded to go into a long dissertation about his admiration for her ending with, "I'm such a devoted fan of yours, Miss Hayward. I've seen every movie you ever made…"

"Uh-huh," Susan said shaking her head.

"You're my favorite actress…and…"

"Uh-huh."

Cowan then made his pitch and told her of the thousands of dollars he had spent in paint, canvas and time to do the immortal portrait of her and for his labors of love, he was willing to sacrifice it — but only to her — at the give away price of $10,000.

"Really," she said in amazement then lowering her voice she yelled for the guards. "I want this man thrown out! How dare he crash my party — get him out of here!"

Everyone looking on loved it. Good old Susan she hadn't let them down. She stood with hands on her hips, giving them a scene they would never forget — just like in her movies.

As Cowan was being escorted out by the security guards to the exit, Susan tossed off a closing line in appraisal of his efforts.

"I saw your candy box crap, your little Susan Hayward doll that looks like if you wind it up it will cry tomorrow. Throw the bum out!" she ordered and lit up a cigarette.

The party was taking on a decided atmosphere of melodrama — starring the Hollywood redhead at her sharpest, meanest and most emasculating.

Curlee stood alone in the background quietly observing the scenes, and when Ron asked her to join in and have a drink, she simply and politely made it clear that she was just there to look after Susan.

Susan now took off her emeralds finding them an uncomfortable weight around her throat and gave them to Curlee. Curlee stood like a sentinel. She had important things on her mind and would break the news to Susan at the right moment the next day.

Marty Rackin bragged about his 'Hooligan,' "She lasted 17 weeks, 16 more than I expected, and she packed the room every night. Then she came down with desert throat and went back to Florida. I thought we had lost her."

Back in Ft. Lauderdale Curlee broke the news to her mistress; she was going back to Carrollton to marry the Reverend Frank Crowder. Crowder, a man much older than Curlee and in poor health, has proposed to her a long time ago, but out of loyalty and devotion to Eaton and Susan, she had stayed on long after Mr. Chalkley died. It was now time to return to Georgia and marry him.

Susan was now experiencing severe headaches, bad coordination, and even worse depression, when she came back to the house on Nermi Drive, which she had shared with Eaton. She could bear the memories it contained no longer and put it up for sale, still trying desperately to escape the past. Now, with Curlee leaving, another link with her past life was to be broken. She would truly be alone.

She had to make a change in her life whatever the risk.

She said later — after she had moved; "I don't keep scrapbooks. I have no interest in the past; why hang on to a dim memory of it? My husband once collected prints of my films to give me as a gift and I appreciated the thoughtfulness but I never showed them; they just took up space. When I gave up my house in Florida, I gave them all to a neighbor who I knew was interested in films and taking photographs. You see, things like that — holding on to the past — would just bog me down. Not everyone, perhaps, but me, yes."

Susan bought a condominium on the 9th floor of the Four Seasons building about a mile away from Nermi Drive, from which she could look down on the crisscrossing waterways. Not long afterwards, a surprise housewarming gift arrived at her new home. Caesar's Palace had shipped, by Air Express, a painting of herself as Mame by artist Ralph Cowan. She called Ron Nelson and told him to get over as fast as he could. She asked him to bring along a pair of garden shears, "I'm going to cut it up into little pieces and throw it into the canal," she said, inviting him to the ceremony.

When Ron arrived, they had their quota of drinks to get in the mood for their ceremony of vandalism. They began laughing hysterically, recalling that night of the farewell party and Cowan's comically aided departure.

They laughed even harder at Caesar's paying him $10,000 for it, as a gift to her. Eventually Ron convinced her it was so campy, he must have it for a place of honor in his apartment, to be illuminated and seen by his guests as they first entered his foyer. Somehow, this appealed to her and she made him a gift of the huge painting, with the promise that he burn it if he ever wanted to get rid of it. It still hangs in his apartment.

Susan looked marvelous as she approached her 52nd birthday in June of 1969. After the workout of *Mame*, she was trim and looking better than she had in years. Men tried to date her, hoping to use Ron Nelson's friendship as a means of reaching her. Apathetically, she dismissed any overtures. She would not let go of Eaton. She seemed imprisoned in a state of sad reflection almost preferring it to any change, ever after three years of grieving. She could not find love. She couldn't even find herself. She was still living for a man who was gone — kept alive only by his hold on her memory. She was so insecure; she felt that men only wanted her for her money or to use her for their own ambitions.

She sought no sexual liaisons, it was not in her true nature to be promiscuous and without a sincere, honest emotion; she withdrew from any momentary sexual encounters. Left by her sons for marriages of their own, with families to raise and lives of their own, she depended more on her friendship with Ron Nelson. The bond between them grew stronger, and he matched Susan drink for drink. It was a way to get through the long days and endless nights.

Ron was readily available to Susan for her sudden whims of coursing recklessly through the waterways of Ft. Lauderdale. If he complained of becoming seasick, she would laugh it off and tease him, "Poor Captain Tuna, the chicken of the sea."

She had with her on deck of the 'Oh Susannah' the mechanical bird in the gilded cage that William Holden had bought for her in Paris in 1942, and as they roared through the canals she sang along with its tweetering of 'Let's All Sing Like The Birdies Sing, Tweet, Tweet, Tweet, Tweet' as the 'Susanna's' tall antennas and fishing lines scraped the roofs of the bridges as she raced the boat under them.

She was warned many times by the Coast Guard to temper her maneuvers and be more cautious about ripping through the waters. They warned the other boats to beware, "the 'Oh Susannah' was loose on the waterways." Still, the resident celebrity got away with it every time.

Ron badgered her to attend parties with him. He needed her to support his activities with the Heart Fund. Her appearance insured a successful event. She in turn relied upon him to escort her to exclusive gatherings that she could not refuse. President Richard Nixon sent Susan an engraved invitation to the White House, which also included Nelson's name. Ron sitting next to Susan in a White House dining room overheard Richard Nixon confess to Hayward, 'You know, you have always been my favorite actress.'

Their play could sometimes take a serious turn. Susan and Ron were leaving a supermarket one afternoon when she caught sight of a Cadillac speeding away from a parked car it had just side-swiped. She jumped into her car and with Ron at the wheel yelled at him to catch up with the other driver. They managed to get near enough to the Cadillac for Susan to jot down the license number on a scrap of paper — next to it she wrote in capital letters CULPRIT. They returned to the parking lot and took down the number of the damaged car and next to this; she wrote VICTIM and left it on the sideswiped car's windshield. She called the police and reported it, also getting the victim's telephone number. When she called, the grateful woman wanted to thank her with a gift of some sort and asked to whom she was speaking. Susan said that didn't matter, but in her sailor's slang to 'help another person in trouble,' told the woman — "Throw someone a lifeline sometime."

If only someone could have thrown Susan one. She needed desperately at this time, as she sat and drank in her splendid penthouse apartment at the Four Seasons.

Ron took her to one particularly smart party and during the evening, they disagreed about something that left her very angry and she put him down in front of his friends. Insulted and extremely embarrassed by this time he remained silent for the remainder of the evening. The next day, as if nothing happened, she called him about going out on the boat. "No, I don't think I can make it this afternoon," he told her, making up some feeble excuse.

"What do you mean Ronsy-Ponsy," she said calling him by her pet name, trying to humor him.

"I just think it might be a good idea if we just didn't see each other for awhile."

"OK, have it your way," she said trying to hide her annoyance.

She called him again a few days later and he was very cool and excused himself, saying he had much work to do. This made her angry and hurt and she called him back and said he must come over; she had to see him, to tell him something. Still she did not apologize for the incident the other evening. She called again, in tears this time, and he could no longer resist

Four Season Apartments, where Susan lived from 1966 through 1971

and went right over to see her. After too many drinks, an argument flared up and she repeated the attack on his manhood that she had made at the party. He got up saying he had had enough and made as though to leave.

"You leave and I'll set this place on fire," she screamed at him, waving a lighted cigarette around.

He was used to her threats and left. As soon as he entered his apartment the phone rang, "I set fire to the apartment," she told him, "just wait a minute…"

"Susannah you're crazy."

"Oh yeah, well listen to this…" she held the phone out and crashing sounds came over the line. What he actually heard was the sound of firemen chopping down the door. She was almost certainly drunk. When she came back on the line, she said she had to go and tie her silk bed sheets into a rope and let herself down the balcony of the floor below.

He rushed out of his house over to the Four Seasons. He found her in the apartment below her penthouse, in the shower washing off the black soot.

The firemen, wearing gas masks, had broken into her apartment and found her on the balcony. They had given her oxygen to prevent any damage to her lungs, and put out the flames in the living room with hand extinguishers, and then escorted Susan to the apartment of Mrs. Carson, below. Mrs. Carson let Ron in when he arrived.

Susan's apartment was repaired and refurbished and several months later, on April 15th, she fell and broke her arm, while she said, she was waxing the floor. She had been drunk as she poured the wax and promptly slipped on it. Shortly after that, she broke her foot and moved around the apartment in a wheelchair. She was becoming self-destructive. She was also lonelier than she had ever been in Hollywood. She could have gone back to work, but she found this retirement community an excuse for not wanting to take any particular action. Bored and restless, she drank far too much and was plagued with persistent headaches, which she attributed to too much drinking.

She needed help, but refused any offers or suggestion of it, and though she seemed helpless to help herself, she just waited for someone who didn't come. She wanted something to happen — and it did.

Marty Rackin called her again "Hello, Hooligan," he began. He was making a picture in Mexico called *The Revengers*. There was a great cameo part for her, opposite her old buddy, Bill Holden.

Helen Rackin remembered her reaction, "He sent her a script and she called him, 'listen Marty, you've always been a good friend. I'll do it for nothing. I don't want any money.' He then said he would give her the minimum anyway and she flew out here. My husband was already in Mexico and Susan and I flew down to join him. It was in mid 1971 and Susan said she had to lose five pounds and went on hard-boiled eggs and liver twice a week. She did her own hair color and make-up and made no demands. It only took a week."

She was back in front of the cameras again, being watched over by Holden and Rackin. It was a lot better than sitting on the balcony of her apartment smoking a cigarette and holding a drink. She was glad to be back working again. After her scenes were completed, she returned to Hollywood, looking for offers.

She returned to the Hollywood limelight the night of the Motion Picture Relief Fund's big affair. It was an all-star benefit and it was also the night that Frank Sinatra announced his retirement, starting rumors that he was dying of cancer.

Afterwards, John Bowab and Oona White were sitting outside the Dorothy Chandler Pavilion waiting for their car and Susan spotted them and called out.

"She came running across over to us," Bowab recalled, "not at all like her. Hugging and kissing Oona — so very effervescent. It really threw us because we had heard all these stories about her. She looked breathtaking, prettier than when she did *Mame*. She was wearing green chiffon. They took a lot of pictures of her — photographers were snapping away like crazy. "Susan was in a bubbly mood, just radiant — that was the last time we saw her."

She was just happy to be back. She signed with Norman Brokaw of the William Morris Agency and was making the rounds with her new publicity agent, Jay Bernstein.

Norman Brokaw spoke of his meeting with Susan at this time, "She sat opposite me on the couch in my office and I couldn't believe it. She looked so young. I have always represented big stars like Barbara Stanwyck and Loretta Young, but this one looked as if the clock had stopped for her twenty years ago."

Brokaw, who knew of her temper and enormous talent, carefully brought up the fact that television was the big thing now. He had in fact put together a 90-minute movie-for-television written for Barbara Stanwyck. He said he would like to find another property of the same quality for her.

A few days later, Barbara Stanwyck was rushed to the hospital to have a kidney removed. Suddenly the property Brokaw had mentioned to Susan became available for her. It took him less than 30 seconds to convince CBS and Metromedia to continue *Heat of Anger*, the Stanwyck vehicle, with Susan in the lead.

Hollywood designer Nolan Miller was asked to take the script to Susan's home in Ft. Lauderdale. He took along his sketch pad, a case of fabric samples and a close friendship with the ailing Barbara Stanwyck, as well as an understanding of the role.

As he said, "Susan Hayward knew how close I was to Barbara Stanwyck. I was doing the TV movie with her. We'd been shooting two days when she got ill she was taken to the hospital and they didn't think she was going to live. They had to remove a kidney. For several days, it was will she live or die. The studio decided there was no way they could shelve the project, they'd gone too far and they couldn't hold it up. The doctor said if Missy (his name for Barbara Stanwyck) could ever work again, it would be at least a year, maybe two. So they decided to replace her and offered it to Susan. She said yes, she told me, because she had such a thing about Stanwyck. They were both from Brooklyn. As a young girl, Stanwyck used to support her family and the family would cash her checks at the local butcher at the corner. Susan used to hear a lot about Barbara Stanwyck and she identified with her. They were both very strong, very definite about likes and dislikes, fiercely loyal to people they love."

When Susan came to Hollywood, she patterned herself after her. She used to say she loved the way Stanwyck walked, like a cat, and she wanted to walk like that too. She wanted to wear the clothes Nolan had designed for Stanwyck but they were of such a different size it wasn't possible.

"I came back to work," said Susan, "because the grief finally was all wrung out of me and I had finished my job in raising the boys. They were both graduated from college, they both got married, and Gregory had already made me a grandmother. Besides, I looked around Fort Lauderdale and realized I was a freak in that society. I suddenly had an overwhelming desire to get back to Hollywood, where I could be a freak among freaks."

TELEVISION

I love television, especially the Movies-for-TV. That's 'where it's at' right now. I like the pace. You have to be there and ready, and deliver. Of course, once it's over, you collapse, but it's exciting.

CHAPTER 11

In the fall of 1971, Susan Hayward Chalkley sold her Four Seasons condominium, shipped her furniture to Los Angeles and rented a luxurious house above Sunset Blvd. She was 54 years old and returning to work in front of the cameras as a star actress.

She talked about the work itself on her return, to shoot *Heat of Anger*, "I feel like a pianist who hasn't touched a piano in years. You wonder if you can still play, and you're terrified, but then you hit the first note and it all comes back to you. It was easier I guess because I found myself in the midst of old friends. My co-stars are Leo J. Cobb and Fritz Weaver. The director is Don Taylor, who played the part of one of my husbands in *I'll Cry Tomorrow*. I knew the producer and writer from my Paramount and 20th Century Fox days; even many of the electricians and grips were familiar faces from movie productions I'd done. The only thing unfamiliar was the pace. I was frantic when I had to learn ten pages of dialogue every day, instead of the three we used to do in films, but I soon found out I was able to handle it. Fortunately my brain was in good shape."

Susan had to meet the press again for pre-publicity on her return to work in Hollywood. Her old time adversaries, including Hedda Hopper, were almost all gone, and Louella Parsons, her trusted friend, was in a sanitarium (and was to die in 1972).

Sitting in the Polo Lounge of the Beverly Hills Hotel in a navy and white pantsuit, wearing the familiar dark glasses and lighting up cigarette after cigarette, she fenced with a reporter. Her life long disdain for interviews and her grudging response to questions was evident over lunch. Her answers were either short or totally scrupulous.

The reporter complained that he hadn't been able to get a single good quote. "Then make them up." Hayward said in her familiar style, "You would have, anyway."

She spoke to others about her return to work and her future plans for settling into the right house, etc. and answered one contemporary question by saying: "I don't know anything about women's' lib. It's just that there are problems in the world today; such as a woman alone. Ten days ago I was willing to marry the plumber — not that he asked me."

She told an anecdote about her son Tim, then 26, who was working in the music department of Jay Bernstein's public relations firm. "Tim began in the mail room for 90 minutes. Then he went on to handle performers. He hated performers. He thought they were crazy. I said, "Maybe that's because you grew up with one.""

Her sons were trying to find a husband for their mother. Marty, and Helen Rackin knowing how lonely Susan was, were attempting to do the same in their own way, "Hey, Hooligan, we got a guy for you," Rackin enthused over the phone, "an Italian, a very good looking man in the wine business."

Helen continued, "It was a blind date. She gave in and said, 'Oh, alright!' He picked her up and brought her over to our house for dinner. She looked just beautiful. He was younger, a man in his 40's. Susan was in her 50's then. I called her up as soon as she got in the house and asked her how it went."

"Helen, I think I'm too old a broad for him: she said rather tiredly, "he probably would have wanted somebody younger anyway!""

Susan was back seeing some of her old Hollywood friends, in addition to her brother and his wife. However, something was wrong with her condition that she was trying to ignore or not admit to and perhaps she thought if she kept herself busy it might even go away.

Early in 1972, she reported to work on *Heat of Anger* for the first day of shooting and in her dressing room were two dozen long stem roses. Her heart skipped a beat and for a moment, she stood motionless, then she picked up the card and read, it then telephoned the sender. "Who told you that yellow roses were my favorite flower?"

"Nobody told me," replied Nolan Miller, "You just look like yellow roses to me."

She hesitated, "That's incredible," she said faintly. "When I get depressed or unhappy I send myself yellow roses." She explained about Eaton's yellow roses, always there, when she began something new or needed them.

"I honestly didn't know it," Nolan said, surprised at the coincidence, "so from then on I sent her yellow roses once or twice a week."

Nolan was on the set with her continuously for the next three weeks. "How's Miss Stanwyck?" Susan asked him the minute he walked in. "Have you called the hospital?"

"After awhile when 'Missy" Stanwyck was well enough to be aware of anything going on, Susan said she wanted to send her flowers and asked what were her favorite. I told her she liked anything pink, pink carnations, pink roses — pink or red."

Susan phoned the Beverly Hills Florist Harry Findley and told him to send some pink roses to Barbara Stanwyck. He asked if she wanted maybe two or three dozen.

"No Harry, I said I would like to send roses!"

"What does that mean?" he said not quite understanding.

"At least 12 dozen," she explained.

"They were not allowing Missy to keep flowers, there were so many coming in", Nolan said, "They couldn't let her have them in the room. They took the cards off and let her see them and sent them, as she requested, to the wards."

Susan Hayward's flowers arrived looking like a huge rose bush as they were carried in by the two deliverymen. On seeing the display, Barbara Stanwyck pleaded with her nurse, "Oh please couldn't I keep them." It was necessary to set up a special table in her hospital room to accommodate them."

The headaches Susan had been suffering for months were getting worse. Now she was never free of them. Her vision became blurred and she seemed to squint more than ever. She had a strange feeling in her right arm and the cigarette burns on her fingers, due to a lack of sensation in her hands, could no longer be ignored. She still consumed an unreasonable amount of alcohol and smoked incessantly through many sleepless nights. What she tried to keep secret was noticed by some people around her, Nolan Miller for one. He saw her lack of coordination and noticed her dizzy spells and occasional losses of equilibrium. Susan, who didn't like to talk about her health, would soon have to face up to it. For the time being, she was too busy to give it very much attention.

Through a decorator friend of Nolan Miller's, she found a house atop the highest hill in Beverly Hills. It stood at the end of a winding road on Laurel Way and was fronted by palm tress and Italian Cypress. Beyond its two huge oak doors were spacious rooms all on one level that looked onto a swimming pool which sat on the edge of a startling drop overlooking the whole of Los Angeles.

A long hallway led to a sunken living room with a round fireplace in its center. The property was priced suspiciously low for such a valuable site with its spacious dwelling. She had to find out why it had been on the market for such a long time and a shadow fell across her joy when she learned that the previous owner, a homosexual man, had shot himself and his nude body had been found floating in the swimming pool.

Somehow, Susan — will all her superstitions, which included some rather odd ones such as a fear of walking into a room which had peacock feathers as decoration — brushed aside the idea of any form of jinx on the house. With new furnishings and her own strong vibrations, she felt she could exorcise any bad omens.

When she was settled in, she made plans to have her usual annual check up and to catch up with Father Brew after two years.

"It was March in 1972 when she came to Washington to see Dr. Kellerer, an old friend of mine," said Father Brew. "We were in the same class in High School. I induced Eaton to go to him when he first started having his sickness (the ulcer trouble and hepatitis). Susan was very impressed by him. He is without doubt a top flight internist — a Doctor's Doctor. All his life he was crippled from infantile paralysis."

Susan had flown to Georgetown University Hospital to see Dr. Kellerer. As part of his extensive examination, he injected a dye into her bloodstream to enable him to check for growths, using a scanner. She was familiar with the procedure, although this time it was taking much longer and the physician's manner was more guarded. To confirm his findings another dye test was done and it showed that a tumor was definitely growing on one of her lungs. If it showed a malignancy, the lung would have to be removed. Susan sat frozen with fear and disbelief as the doctor talked about major surgery, the possible removal of her lung, the prognosis for total recovery, and cancer — a word that struck terror in her heart. Horribly frightened by her prospects she left the hospital to return to her new home making a stopover in Ft. Lauderdale to see Ron Nelson.

She fled to escape, however temporarily, the fact of the encroaching malignancy. Her nerves were very much on edge and though she didn't want to admit it she couldn't deny what she had learned. She told Ron of Dr. Kelleher's findings. Her life was threatened and could only be pro-longed by prompt action. Dr. Kellerer had urged with her to deal with the tumor immediately. When she left (at her request), he sent her hospital records to another doctor, Dr. Davis in Los Angeles.

On her return to Los Angeles, her brother called her with the news that his wife Carol was ill. She had tuberculosis, from which she suddenly died when complications arose. Susan put all concern for herself aside to help her brother through this sad period. Carol was to be cremated and her ashes were to be scattered over the Pacific Ocean.

Wally said, reflecting on this time, "It was arranged by the funeral director. First, they said they had a single engine plane, but Susan and I told them, 'we're not going up in a single plane.' When we got to the airport, the guy had a twin engine Cessna and we flew out over the ocean. The pilot had her ashes in a cloth bag." According to safety regulations, the pilot himself had to sprinkle the ashes over the ocean, but he asked Wally if he wanted to hold onto the bag until the last moment. "OK," said Wally indifferently, "it's just a bag of ashes as far as I'm concerned. He told us that when he got to this spot he would open the little side window and 'out it goes.' The wind from the propellers made everything open, I guess. That was it."

Later, Wally took a test for tuberculosis and was relieved to find that he had not caught it.

Dizzying headaches now plagued Susan and she drank to relieve the pain but it only increased. She just hoped it would miraculously go away as she approached the start of her next TV movie pilot, *Say Goodbye, Maggie Cole*. However, she was not sufficiently concerned to fly back to Georgetown University Hospital for another examination.

The news this time was critical. X-rays revealed growths in her brain as well. By the time, she returned to Los Angeles, she was already showing a loss of weight and was pale and unsteady. Determined not to back out of a commitment she made it through the filming of *Say Goodbye, Maggie Cole*, giving a remarkable performance considering the circumstances. "I can't hold up the whole crew. It cost them money," she told her brother. Hayward fans, however, could see a change in Susan, particularly as her hair, her proudest possession, was constantly covered over with various wigs. It could only be surmised that it had been cut for the hospital tests. Ironically, in *Say Goodbye, Maggie Cole* she was playing Dr. Maggie Cole, who saves a patient by operating on a brain tumor.

By the end of the year, she was back in Georgetown and during the Christmas season, she had a convulsive seizure. For the first time she faced up to the truth of her dangerous illness and she was sent home to L.A. under medical supervision.

For the next few months, she didn't know what was happening to her body. She continued to drink, and she continued to use the prescribed painkillers. The first sign of changes was in her hampered movements. At times, she had difficulty walking and she would drop things. Then she couldn't light her cigarettes.

With no particular sign of panic or depression Susan appeared to have faced up to the facts when one day, as Wally said, "'I don't know what brought it about,' she said to me, 'don't you know I'm dying.'"

"Oh, come on, quit your kidding," was all that Wally could reply. But he fell silent and though nothing more was said he began to brood over it. It was quite a shock to him.

Early in 1973, director Henry Hathaway celebrated his 75th birthday. The Rackin's attended the party; "It was at the Beverly Hills Hotel. They invited all the big movie stars who had appeared in pictures directed by him, Cary Grant, Bob Mitchum, John Wayne, Susan — everybody. That was the night when it started."

Henry Hathaway recalled seeing her that night, March 12, 1973, at his birthday party; "She was sitting at a table with Rita Hayworth and both of them were drunk."

In front of a crowd of her fellow stars, Susan had her first seizure. Medically it was much like an epileptic fit; the brain growths had caused a cerebral "electrical storm." Her body jerked spastically. Her hands became grasping claws and her face grimaced and went through agonizing contortions. When the seizure ended, she went into deep sleep.

She was taken to Century City Hospital where rigorous tests uncovered no less than twenty tumors growing at an incredible rate in her brain. They were inoperable and only immediate massive chemotherapy and radiation treatments could possibly save her from immediate death.

She was told that she would not leave the hospital alive without the treatments. If she could endure them, to Susan this was a way to fight back.

The nightmare began.

Monstrous machines circled her body, menacing needles jabbed her flesh, vile pills were forced down her throat, and gadgets were stuck on her head with trillions of wire tentacles running to scopes. She drank potions to kill the things in her brain. She was drugged and nauseous most of the time, and between two worlds.

Rumors quickly spread all over Hollywood — "Susan Hayward was dying." The switchboard at Century City buzzed with incoming calls to doctors, staff and Susan, all looking for news — some scoop, some last words. She was secretly moved to Cedars of Lebanon Hospital under the name of Margaret Redding.

Six weeks later, she was released, still alive but looking as though she had returned from the dead. Her five foot one inch frame held a mere eighty-five pounds and the chemotherapy and radiation treatments had caused all of her gorgeous red hair to fall out.

Dr. Lee Siegel, her doctor, told Ron Nelson, who had flown in from Ft. Lauderdale, that she soon would be dead. "It could be a week, a month, but she won't be alive by July 4th."

On the 4th of July, two months after Susan was released from Cedars of Lebanon, Wally's brooding over Susan caused him to have a heart attack.

He had continued his daytime job as a page at the racetrack and spent every evening with his sister on Laurel Way, keeping her company and having dinners with her.

"When we had dinner at her home, she was having trouble cutting her food. She then had to have a nurse. When we went out to dinner, I would have to get on one side of her with the nurse on the other side. We'd park our car and going into the restaurant, she would move real fast, each of us holding her up on either side. She would go like fire."

Wally's feelings of helplessness about his sister caused him to literally worry himself sick. He collapsed while on duty at the Hollywood Rack Track and was rushed by ambulance to the Intensive Care Unit of Centinela Hospital. His condition was labeled as stable. Susan, who wasn't permitted to see him immediately, telephoned him first thing the next morning. The nurse came into Wally's room to tell him they had a call from him from a woman, 'who said she was Susan Hayward, the actress — Susan Hayward the movie star.'

"Fine, she's my sister," Wally said, smiling at the surprised look on the nurse's face.

"Wal, don't let this get you down," Susan said. "When we're on our feet again you and I are going to take a trip around the world. Just us — and nobody else. We'll show 'em they can't keep a Marrener down."

"I didn't know I had heart trouble," Wally said. "When Susan came to see me she brought me stuffed animals, the first time, it was monkeys."

She went often and each time brought him a stuffed animal until he had a menagerie. Wearing her inevitable dark glasses, she made her unsteady way to the hospital room to cheer him up. They were alone and needed each other, as in the old days some forty years ago in Flatbush, when they had clung to each other to get through the disheartening family hardships of their childhood — when — little Edythe had helped her brother to deliver his newspapers and, stopping to rub his hands warm, she would say, "Come on Wal, let's get goin' sooner we'll be home,' giving his wagon a push from behind. Now, both in middle age, and both weak from illness, it was again Susan who gave Wally 'that push' to get him up and well enough to leave the hospital.

When he returned to his apartment, his condition required that he move to a more convenient place so he had to make a change, leaving the place where he lived with Carol.

Susan insisted on apartment hunting with her brother to make sure he found the right place for himself, in the same neighborhood. They liked a building on Hauser Blvd. and found an apartment there that was just about right. She checked out the lease with Wally in the rental office. Worried about his heart condition, she helped him carry things from his old place, piling them onto the elevator and scolded him if he tried to exert himself, while he was anxiously watching out for her. Patricia Morison, who lived in the buiding, met them on the elevator. Morison had achieved great success on the Broadway stage, creating roles in what now have become classic Broadway musicals, and hadn't see Susan since their early days at Paramount. When she saw her carrying a shopping bag full of clothes she couldn't help herself and said, 'Why Susan you're looking so well.'

"Did you think I wasn't?" Susan chided her as she introduced her brother to the singer.

Susan sent over some of her own furniture to the new apartment and bought herself a small sofa bed to sleep on when she stayed overnight. They would go shopping at the Farmers Market just across the way from the apartment building, with Susan pushing the heavy shopping cart around, in the early mornings when it wasn't so crowded, breathless, but determined that her brother would not have to exert himself. He allowed this so not to upset her, worried all the time that she might lose her balance and fall.

Susan, wearing big dark glasses, a scarf covering her red wig holding onto her brother's arm went unrecognized.

"She would buy a leg of lamb and have it cut in half," Wally said. "She gave half to me to take back and told the butcher to cut the other half up for lamb stew. She loved to cook. She didn't like to clean up 'cause she used every pot and pan in the kitchen. She'd pile everything in the dishwasher. She loved hot stuff — Italian and Mexican food, which I can't eat. I'd go out with her and order something else — but it didn't seem to bother her," he said as he shook his head.

They drove around in Wally's old car to all her old favorite places, Nate and Al's on Beverly Drive for corned beef sandwiches, or Senor Pecos in Century City for guacamole (near 20th Century Fox where she had worked for so many years), Howard Johnson's for breakfast, the Tick Tock off Hollywood Blvd. for lunch, and Frank and Musso's for dinner.

Eventually, a nurse had to be hired, for despite Susan's independent front, she needed constant supervision. Louisa was an attractive dark haired woman of Italian descent. She had an authoritative manner and when she moved into the house, she began to take complete charge of Susan. Her professional expertise was added to by growing devotion, as her interest in her patient became more and more a matter of deep personal concern. She wanted to provide the strength that Susan was quickly losing and accompanied her everywhere, jealously guarding her every moment.

"She smoked right up to the end," said Wally. "I would light her cigarette for her and I had to watch her so that she wouldn't drop it. She lost the feelings in her fingers. I cautioned the nurse up there about it. I told her to please watch that she didn't drop it in bed or on the couch."

Susan, now approaching the end of her life, was asked to appear practically everywhere. As is often the case many people wanted to be able to talk about seeing her during the last months of her life. Desperate to make her time count for something and fearing loneliness, she went out as often as she could. Wigs to compliment her gowns were set off by pieces of dazzling jewelry from her extensive collection. An experienced hand at make-up, she still managed to create a glamorous illusion. Fortified with drugs, including the necessary Dilantin, to help ward off any possible seizure, she made every effort to get out while she still could.

Her sons were constantly alert for news of her condition. Greg would fly up to visit his mother from Florida, and Timothy watched and waited for any reports from his home ground in L.A. having witnessed his mother's seizures at Hollywood parties. Behind the scenes, he had been working to gain control of his mother's estate, on grounds of incapability of reason and suffering delusions — irresponsibility. On March 30, 1973, he filed a petition with the courts, through his lawyers, Gerald Lipsky Inc., to gain control of her cash and property holdings claiming that his mother was unable to care for herself or her property. Susan had been served a summons prior to her long confinement at Cedars, but was so seriously ill that at the time that she had not understood the meaning of the papers ordering her to appear in court to defend her competence. Upon her release from the hospital, and when she realized what Timothy had been trying to do, she was outrage and angry and proved that she was as competent as she had ever been.

She challenged the original petition, through her lawyer, Charles Beardsley. On May 1st· her son gave up the fight by filing a petition of Termination of Conservatorship with the Los Angeles Court — but not before asking in the same document that his mother pay his attorney feels and other costs, amounting to $3,725.00.

Susan was to face yet another heartbreaking conflict with her son when on July 1st, 1973, she saw herself in a shocking photograph on the cover of *The National Enquirer* with the caption — SUSAN HAYWARD NEAR DEATH.

The National Enquirer had contacted Jay Bernstein's office for a story on their client Susan Hayward's condition. Timothy who still worked as a publicist at the office made a deal with the publisher for an exclusive scoop on his mother and arranged to have a photographer take a picture of her at a party during one of her seizures. For this, he would be paid $5000. And for the estimated 20 million readers of *The National Enquirer*, 26-year-old Timothy Barker talked, "Nobody can hide this anymore. She has multiple brain tumors and they're inoperable. My mother could live for only a few more days or she could live for another six months. No one can answer that question — not even the doctors. It's in the hands of God. My mother knows, but she hasn't accepted it. She keeps telling me she's going to beat it. But in her heart, she knows…When I saw my mother, she was alert. But under the circumstances because you're dealing with a portion of the body that controls everything else, sometimes she's in, sometimes she's out. She fluctuates….She forces herself to stay awake for long periods. She's in good spirits. She's a fighter."

Susan Hayward was at death's door as *The Enquirer* went to press — they editorialized — and because there is a time lag between printing the paper and getting it onto the nation's newsstands you may have heard of her death before you read this story…they warned their readers.

Susan fought to survive every hour of every day. She also fought to have the article of her impending death denied. The whole world had seen the ghastly photograph of her; somehow, she had to erase that picture from their minds. In someway she would find a means to leave the world with the impression of the Susan Hayward they had come to know and admire. She would get that chance and grab at it before the next twelve months passed.

Louisa hated Timothy for what he had done to his mother. Her attentions toward Susan now became overtly possessive and she displayed her feelings to such an extent that others around them could easily see that her feelings went far beyond her duties as Susan's private nurse. Whether Susan herself sensed this was not known, but Louisa's devotion, her emotional commitment and loyalty gave her a sense of protection and encouragement. Lou, as she was called, gave her hope daily for some kind of recovery. The radiation treatments had controlled the metastasizing of the brain tumors. Louisa herself a Catholic, prayed with Susan, reassuring her of a Hereafter, and bathed her in holy water shipped from Lourdes.

Ron Nelson remained as close as ever, even more so, but this time the nurse stood between them. Timothy was received at the house with considerable trepidation by Louisa, she accepted him only because his mother wished no lingering estrangement from her son at this crucial time. As for the unassuming Wally, Lou struck up an immediate rapport with him. Wally and Ron had nothing in common and could barely communicate, each holding on to his private and separate concern for Susan.

In the center of all this was Susan slowly being torn apart by the self interest of those she loved, but through her faith in God and with what she had learned from her years with Eaton, she held on with uncharacteristic control for someone in such critical health.

She had already lived past the date predicted for her demise by her doctors. She wanted now to look for help from another source that had helped guide her through her life.

Ron and the nurse helped a thin, drawn, confused Susan up the steps toward the front door of the home of her old and trusted astrologer friend, Carroll Righter. He too was older, but as bright as ever, with a twinkle in his eye, and a very active, wry sense of humor. Tall and slim, Righter, welcomed the tiny, frail woman into his living room as her companions went out to sit by the pool, leaving them alone.

After some of the usual social trivialities, she came to the point. "Do I have cancer?"

He avoided the question by saying her chart showed a "professional decline," but added, "I see you will be alive in January 1975."

Instantly, her depression vanished and her face lit up with excitement, "I'm going to get well!" she cried.

In that moment, she knew the doctors to be wrong and Carroll Righter, who had never failed her, to be far more accurate than they.

The professional decline he mentioned probably had to do with her next scheduled TV pilot, which could possibly be cancelled. What did that matter she would be alive for at least another year and a half, and maybe for years after that. As she was preparing to leave Righter's home, her escorts stood on either side of her to help her down the stairs — "No!" she said firmly. "I can do it alone." With her spirit renewed, she held herself straight and for the first time in months took off her sunglasses and waving goodbye to her friend, walked unaided down the front steps.

Believing the doctors to have grossly miscalculated her condition, she made plans to have further tests done at Boston's Massachusetts General

Hospital, to get a completely different point of view and, hopefully, some different results. Ron Nelson had flown back to Ft. Lauderdale and she would join him there after her tests. Wally moved temporarily into her Laurel Way home to be close to his sister in case anything happened very suddenly.

On the other hand, Susan was worried about her brother being alone after his heart attack. She was alone too, and would see that he had care and rest.

"I still rented this place," said Wally, referring to his apartment on Hauser Blvd. "I would come back weekends to check the mail and things. There was a day nurse on duty as well. I gave up my bedroom at Susan's to the nurse, who stayed full time."

Susan wanted to go back to Carrollton for a visit before her stay at Massachusetts General Hospital. In October of 1973 with Wally and Lou in company, she arrived in the town that had once been her home.

It was really to be a long look at the past, her last one, she must have suspected, despite her desperate hopes. When the plane landed in Atlanta, they checked into the nearby Hilton Hotel. Susan called Monsignor Reagan, now pastor of Our Lady of Perpetual Help, and Mary Williams and Ann Moran.

"I was working in a beauty shop in White Springs when my daughter called and said, "Mother, Mrs. Chalkley is coming and she wants banana cake. I got chilled when I knew she was in town," remember Ann Moran. "I didn't have any banana cake — and it was strange because I just bought bananas that mornin'. I had put them in my car thinking well, I'll just make a couple in case I see her. I'll have them in the freezer."

Ann told the beauty shop owner that she, 'had to leave suddenly — cause Susie was comin' over to my house." The proprietor knew Mrs. Chalkley from the church and sent Ann off with get-well wishes for Susan.

Susan hired a limousine and, with Wally and Lou, made the journey toward tiny Carrollton, along the avenues of great elms wearing their autumn colors and arching gracefully over the roads, and beyond to the spacious woods.

T.S Elliot's October his 'cruelest month' could not have referred to the sleepy, timeless town that Susan came back to.

The limo drove another five miles to Ann Moran's house. Ann was waiting and watching by the window as the car pulled up in front. Ann knew of her illness, but, no matter what, she would not say anything about it. As soon as Susan walked in the front door, heavily bundled up in furs, Ann hugged her and saying she still looked very pretty, but too thin.

The two of them chatted, Susan asked about everybody they both knew and Ann told her of all the local gossip. Susan showed her snap shots of her new house in Los Angeles. Then Ann fussed about the kitchen making them coffee — she told Susan she would bake that night.

"I'll make a banana cake and a fruit cake," she told Susan.

Susan's eyes lit up. Ann turned to Wally and Louisa; "Susie loves my fruit cake and Eaton my banana cake," then looking over at Susan's sudden downcast expression, realizing what she said she quickly added, 'my fruit cake doesn't have all that gook in it, right Susie?'

Susan looked up, smiled and nodded. Before Ann went ahead with the cake preparation Susan suggested they all go along to Harvey Hester's for dinner.

On their journey back towards town, many memories were stirring within Susan. They drove along Main Street, then on Dixie Street, passing the places where she and Eaton had shopped together; and the post office, the library, the courthouse. Wally had never seen any of it and Susan kept saying, "Look Wally there's so and so and over there, that's so and so..." They passed placid old homes with their white picket fences set back from the wide sidewalks and marking out the big front lawns.

Wally was sorry he had waited until now to see his sister's land of treasured memories; Susan, in her grief over Eaton, had almost forgotten the beautiful, gentle peace of Carrollton.

They drove down the lane to the ranch house and the land that she and Eaton had owned and cared for together. They got out of the car and strolled for a while in the late autumn air, still warm, but with a perceptible nip in it. They stood in front of Monsignor Reagan's rectory across the road from the little red gatehouse, from where the road led down the lane to the big house overlooking the lake. The house was now owned by strangers and Susan looked at it for only a moment. She took Wally inside to meet Monsignor Reagan.

The affable Irishman welcomed them at the door with huge Irish Wolfhounds by his side. Susan rested inside for a few minutes, in front of the fireplace — 'Wally that fireplace is exactly the same as the one we had in our house.' When she talked it was yesterday again, and Eaton was by her side, he had, 'brought this from Europe and he wanted to build this, and would one day add something else.' There was so much they had planned to do — then she became silent.

Susan's eyes wandered over the grounds as Lou joined them and they made their way to the church. Animals and creatures of all sorts roamed the yards. There were dogs, cats, hamsters, chickens, peacocks, donkeys; it was as though Noah's Ark had landed there. Monsignor Reagan opened the church doors and the first thing she saw was a number of statues of different saints standing on pedestals near the altar. She smiled, remembering her words to Father Morrow; "You won't always be pastor here Father and someday I'll get my statues in."

The October wind was rising and the air filled with leaves as the twilight hour brought a melancholy glow. She left her brother and Lou with Monsignor Reagan and walked over to Eaton's grave. The beautiful autumn background of the countryside was almost a stage set to the once beautiful dying woman as she stood quietly looking at the tombstone — "F. Eaton Chalkley 1909-1966" — for what she must have known would be the last time. These moments brought back overwhelmingly the happy life they had shared. Tears filled the corners of her eyes. She slowly and painfully kneeled down and with the palms of her hands pressed against the cool grass she leaned forward and kissed the earth, and then she placed some fresh flowers on the grave and struggled slowly to her feet. In Eaton, she had found herself and had found her peace with God, which had led her finally to enter the Catholic faith. It was the only consolation she had left. She looked at the place next to Eaton, where she would join him.

She turned around, put on her dark glasses again and was ready to leave. They walked toward the waiting limousine, entered and drove off as the sky darkened and the wind started to turn chilly.

Ann Moran called Susan the following morning. It was another windy day and now the wind was cold.

"I don't think you ought to get out in that wind," Ann told her over the telephone, regarding her plans to meet at Aunt Fanny's Cabin restaurant.

"Ann, God bless you," Susan said. "I was thinking about it too, but I don't want to renege on the invitation."

"No!" Ann said firmly, "You just stay and eat dinner there at the hotel and I'll call Mary Williams and we'll come over and have cake and coffee." Susan now realized that Ann must have known about her illness.

Ann Moran put down the receiver and cried, but she would never mention a word about it to Susan.

After Carrollton, Susan flew to Massachusetts General for more probing, more robot machines, more needles, chemotherapy, radiation, nausea and the cold clinical eyes of another team of doctors.

The moment Ron Nelson saw her emerge from a plane in Ft. Lauderdale International Airport; he knew what the news from Boston had been. She had waited until all the other passengers had left before attempting to leave the jet with Wally and Lou. Dressed in a sable coat and wearing

now once again the inevitable dark glasses she held on to the nurse, dragging her right foot as she moved.

He reached forward to embrace her. "Don't touch me," she said.

That night, after they were all settled into his house on Fiesta Way he
offered her a drink of her favorite Chivas Regal.

"She can't have that," snapped Lou.

"Who the hell says I can't drink!" Susan shot back. "I can do anything
I please!"

After a couple of drinks, she collapsed from exhaustion and was put to
bed. As the days passed, Nelson could see that her condition was growing
worse. The dragging of her left foot was the result of one of the tumors
in her right brain lobe growing large and beginning to paralyze the left
side of her body.

Back in her Laurel Way home, after three weeks with Ron in Florida,
Susan saw what was happening to her and made some decisions not to
undergo any further chemotherapy and radiation treatments, and she
would only accept narcotic pain killing drugs now in moderation. The
painful, nerve racking effort to save her life seemed increasingly futile,
robbing her of the relative peace of what had to be her last months. She
appeared to be giving up the fight.

"I don't want any more life-saving crap!" she cried out to Wally.

She wavered, between courage and terror, conviction and uncertainty.
Despite her brave words, she told Wally and Nolan Miller, "If I thought
it would help, I'd travel anywhere, take anything, even rat poison."

Laetrile was just beginning to be known in the United States so she
begged her doctors to give her some laetrile treatments — which were
illegal — and they refused. Still it could be gotten illegally from Mexico
if you had the right connections.

Lou knew how to get it. She would do anything for Susan and she
purchased the drug (manufactured from the insides of apricot pits) and
began giving Susan injections, knowing that she was risking her R.N.
license, her career, even a jail sentence. Her love for Susan came before
all of this.

Whatever happened, there was a remission in the early months of 1974.
Was it the miracle Susan had prayed for? Was it the results of the laetrile
treatments? Whatever it was, it happened — to the absolute amazement
of her doctors. Susan was once again filled with hope.

LONELINESS

I know it well.

CHAPTER 12

Susan had heard that astrologer Walden Welch was staying at a Redondo Beach Motel and made an appointment to see him.

She talked about business matters, discussed the effects of laetrile and repeatedly asked for some kind of conformation about life after death. She asked questions about reincarnation. When he told her he was a Catholic, she again wanted to be convinced in the belief of a Hereafter, through her faith.

Welch, like so many others, was surprised at how petite she was. He felt that she was gracious, but there was a wall she kept up in front of her. He never forgot her telling him that when they were shooting a scene for *David and Bathsheba* she was lying on the ground, looking up at Gregory Peck, with her arm at her side when suddenly she realized her hand had invaded an anthill. She jumped up in fright when she saw the huge red ants crawling about.

"You know," she said to Welch. "I've put my hand in anthills all my life."

Katherine Hepburn had never met Susan before her illness, yet was one of the first to call on her when she knew of her condition. Once Hepburn followed Wally's car into Susan's Laurel Way driveway and as she stepped out of her 1961 Thunderbird, in blue jeans and jacket, she spied Wally's license plate KHH and laughed when she told him he had her initials — Katherine Houghton Hepburn. Wally opened the front door with his key, to Hepburn's surprise, "Oh, I'm Susan's brother," he explained. From then on Hepburn always brought with her a bouquet of flowers from her own garden — because as she told Susan, "The florists around here are a rip-off." Susan adored it and her visits did wonders for her as they talked honestly, as few could, to each other.

Barbara Stanwyck had not forgotten the flowers Susan had sent when she herself was in the hospital and sent frequent notes to the younger actress, even though they still had not met.

Nolan Miller, another of Susan's visitors and Stanwyck's friend, carried messages back and forth between them. He told Susan about a visit to the Getty Museum that he was planning with Stanwyck.

"When Susan found out we were going to the Getty Museum she asked if she could join us. We said of course. Her limousine arrived ahead, with her nurse. Susan and Missy met and said 'Hello! Wonderful to meet you' — very casual about it all. We did the entire museum. Missy was constantly saying to Susan, 'Are you tired! Susan, do you want to sit down,' like best girlfriends. After we had spent the day there, we had lunch. When we got to the parking lot the two of them were in tears, hugging and kissing goodbye. You couldn't believe it was their first meeting. Every time we talked after that Susan kept saying she wanted Missy and I over to dinner. But it never happened."

Susan would not see many people, but she was always pleased to hear from Ruth Gilette, her Mrs. Burnside from *Mame*, and Helen Rackin.

Ron Nelson was a constant visitor and one time when he was there, with another loyal friend of Susan's, Loretta Swit arrived unexpectedly. She walked in, sat on the floor at Susan's feet, crying crocodile tears and pressing her hand and saying, "Oh, my beautiful, Oh, my darling," and went on and on. Someone present that day was moved to say afterwards, "Save your performance for the stage, Loretta I've had my fill."

Susan would usually be most conscious around 5 o'clock in the morning and Ron who was by her side that morning asked her, "Did you know Ruth Gilette came to see you today?" She mumbled, like a child — "Yes" — "Did you know that Loretta Swit came to see you today?" — "Yes — she's full of shit!"

When another friend heard this she said, "That shows you she was not out of it, for a woman half dead to get that."

It was rumored that Jess Barker had reentered Susan's life, that he had been seeing her on and off since Eaton died. There were those who said he was after something, possibly an inheritance. Barker himself said, "I never stopped loving her." Diana Baffer recalling all of the times Susan and she talked to each other said, "Susan never put him down." If Susan heard that Jess ever needed anything, she quietly found a way to help him. Someone close to her reported, "I don't know if she was seeing Jess Barker. At one time, his teeth were going bad and she foot the bill for new dentures for him. She didn't want her sons to see their father in that condition, with bad teeth."

Susan was receiving mail from all over the world. Fans sent her religious medals, cards, rosary beads, various relics that were intended as cures and letters, which Wally would read to her. One came from Richard Nixon at San Clemente. Susan was moved by the fact that, despite Watergate and his own health problems, which reportedly including drinking, he cared enough to call a mutual friend in Hollywood for her address. He and Pat were praying for her and hoped she would visit them as soon as she was able. She made only one comment about his troubles — "he got a raw deal."

Evangelist Kathryn Kulman told her TV viewers that she could save Susan Hayward. She also sent her a tape recording of some very special healing prayers.

Nolan Miller received a mysterious phone call from Susan, at his Custom Gown Salon on So. Robertson Blvd. She made an appointment to see him.

"She came with her nurse, we sat down and I waited for her to speak," said Nolan.

"I am going to make a public appearance," she told him.

"You're what?" he said.

"They have asked me to be on the Academy Awards, What do you think I should wear — how should I look?"

Hollywood had learned of Susan's remission and the Academy had sent her a formal invitation to appear live on television to present the 1974 Best Actress Award with David Niven, at the April 2nd Oscar ceremonies. The Academy was well aware of the risk of a seizure in front of the audience and the millions of viewers, but the spectacular effect of Susan stepping, Lazarus-like, up from her deathbed to make this appearance was the kind of drama from which Academy history was made.

Nolan, recovering from the shock, looked at her, "Let's get you the goddamnest Susan Hayward wig they ever made — lots of red hair." Then I did some sketches for her. As soon as she saw this dress (sketch) she said, 'this is what I want.' We were sitting here in the salon looking over fabric when she said she had no jewelry with her! It was all in Florida in the bank."

"So I called Huey Skinner at Van Cleef and Arpels and told him we were doing a gown for Susan and is there anyway you can loan her some jewelry (they never do this). He said to bring her over and let her pick out what she wanted so we drove over to Van Cleef and Huey put out three trays of diamond necklaces, bracelets and earrings in front of her, 'pick out what you want,' he said. She made every effort to look good that night."

Well aware of what was happening, she said, "This will be the last time the public will ever see me so I want to look beautiful."

She now had the chance that she had been waiting for to erase from the public's mind the grotesque photograph on the cover of *The Enquirer* nine months earlier.

The day of her highly publicized appearance before 53 million tele-viewers, she began to decline. Unhappy and worried over the way she might come across, she had second thoughts about being on the show. She told Lou to call the Academy and tell them she had changed her mind — but Louisa spoke to someone else about Susan's decision and then Katherine Hepburn was asked for advice. Hepburn rushed over to the house to bolster Susan's flagging spirits and to encourage her, insisting that she must go on. "Why?" Susan asked, "You never did."

Katherine Hepburn had never appeared at the Oscars not even to accept her own awards. Invited once again by the Academy this time she agreed to go to present the Irving Thalberg special award. She promised that she would be backstage to help Susan through her ordeal.

Make up artist Frank Westmore of the famous Westmore Brothers of Hollywood went to her home that afternoon and seeing the ravages of the cobalt treatments was shocked to find only the remains of the former unique look that was Susan. Only his knowledge and experience in recalling the Susan Hayward he remembered could bring back a transformation. Westmore literally reconstructed her as she had been 30 years ago.

Nolan Miller's dress would go up to her neck and arms with glistening sequins; Nolan added, "She was going to treat herself to something and she bought this sable coat and paid about $40,000 for it. She referred to it as the 'goddamnest sable coat anybody had ever seen.'"

She was very nervous. It must have been hard for any woman who had been that beautiful facing the facts that it had taken a real toll on her. When she was ready to leave, she said, "Well, I guess that's as much as anybody can do to help out, so we might as well get on with it."

Dressed in her black sable and holding on to the arm of her agent Jay Bernstein, Susan made her way through the side entrance of the Pantages Theatre.

Groucho Marx had the dressing room that was reserved for her and reluctantly gave it up. Her nurse, Lou, Ron and her doctor — who gave her an injection of Dilantin to prevent an on-camera seizure — were hovering around her. Frank Westmore was checking her hair and make-up and Nolan, the beautiful gown he had designed. A concerned Katherine Hepburn kept an anxious lookout.

The most awaited moment of the evening arrived, with the audience wondering whether she was really going to appear. David Niven introduced her and her co-presenter Charlton Heston.

"Mr. Heston has created many miracles — just illusions on the screen. But in presenting our next award, he brings with him the real thing — Miss Susan Hayward. She is no illusion."

Susan, leaning on Heston's arm was welcomed with a respectful, warm and restrained ovation. "Don't stop for a moment when you hear the applause," Hepburn had whispered to her just before she made her entrance, realizing that any over excitement might bring on a collapse.

The suspense backstage was gripping as everyone held their breath. Susan looked beautiful through the color cameras. There were no close-ups, the cameras kept a respectful distance.

Dr. Siegel's wife, Noreen, who was sitting in the audience never forgot, "The biggest recollection I have is the night of the Academy Awards. I was so furious — whether people were just stunned when she walked out, looking so pretty, so lovely, I don't know." Noreen Siegel felt the applause was not what it should have been. For so many people it was like watching a beautiful ghost, and they were dumbstruck they were so busy staring they kept applauding almost as though in a trance."

"I shall never forget the sight of Susan walking bravely out on that stage, in her high heels, straight and proud, holding her head up as if to say, 'I'll show the world,'" said Noreen Siegel.

In her dressing room, she was helped off with the 30-pound dress and the wig. She looked at herself in the mirror, seeing her bald head with some little tufts of hair beginning to grow back, her skinny arms and wasted body, and laughed as her friends stood around her watching, "If they could only see me now." She said cynically. "That's the last time I pull that off." She called it 'a miracle of faith.' Fifteen minutes later, she collapsed. She was carried out of the Pantages on a stretcher.

The Enquirer ran a story some weeks later — SUSAN HAYWARD'S MIRACULOUS RECOVERY FROM EDGE OF DEATH — 'I knew my faith in God would pull me through" — was the captioned quote, "Don't believe what those doctors are saying," she said. "I don't have cancer. Believe me, they're wrong. I know they think I have cancer in my head and that I'm going to die, but it's not so. The public will know how well I am when they see me working again."

Susan was gratified at last having vindicated The Enquirer story of July 1st, 1973.

Norman Brokaw remarked, "I think Susan demonstrated just how well she's feeling when she made the presentation of the Best Actress Award at the April 2nd Oscar Awards."

Stanly Musgrove was interested in her doing a television special about Sally Stanford — the infamous San Francisco Madam. Sally Stanford's first choice was Greer Garson, but Musgrove said he didn't think she would be quite right and 'what about Susan Hayward?' Stanford replied that she would be acceptable. Musgrove talked to Norman Brokaw who said it sounded great and to keep him posted.

Jay Bernstein told the press, "She's now reading TV scripts and even considering doing some TV commercials."

"As for Susan," *The Enquirer* noted that "*I Want To Live* has now become more than just a movie title — it is, for her, a very personal credo."

Susan the consummate actress had scored again.

Shortly after this news, Susan's remission ended. The tumor on the right side of her brain was enlarging again, causing further paralysis of her left side and occasional comas. She had to use a wheel chair, crutches, and leg braces to keep the partially paralyzed and wasted leg from breaking under the weight of her body.

"I had to build a ramp from her dining room into the living room," Wally said. "There were three steps and I got a friend of mine to get some plyboard and nail it in place. This way she didn't have to be carried back and forth. We used the wheelchair."

Wally, who was there practically 24 hours a day, did all he could for his sister, with the help of the two nurses — Lou overseeing the routines. As for her sons, Greg flew in from Florida every so often — when things were looking bad and Timothy, though she had a few hassles with him, was always forgiven — "blood is thicker than water" — she would say.

Timothy would stay away for weeks at a time and then would suddenly show up at the house with his wife Ilsa, and their young daughter. Susan called Timothy's German wife "The Kraut." Lou, who found Timothy abrasive, was not pleased with his sudden visits. She felt he was protecting his inheritance and was most interested in that than anything else. The nurse stood between Susan and her son shielding her from whatever might occur between them. The tension between the nurse and Timothy came to a climax when he arrived at the house one day and she would not let him in. He phoned later and she told him that Susan was still too tired to talk to him and hung up. He became infuriated and called back screaming and demanding that he be allowed to speak to his mother. The nurse coldly refused, reminding him that his mother was under supervision, and she would not risk her having another — possibly fatal — seizure.

A witness to this altercation watched the battle over the dying woman with horror.

Looking for revenge, Timothy went to the police to report the nurse who wouldn't allow him in the house. But worse, he also reported the illegal laetrile injections, which he had found out about. The police could only act on the charges if he would file a suit against the nurse and give evidence. His reaction was to call Lou and threaten to expose her, thereby having her license revoked. The nurse quickly flushed the evidence down the toilet and when the police came the next morning with a search warrant they found nothing.

Spurred on by this, Timothy found another way to get rid of the nurse. He contracted the testimony of one of the doctors, gained his father's support, his brother's and oddly enough even Wally's to declare his mother incompetent, to break Louisa's authority.

White uniformed men arrived at the Laurel Way house, waving official papers at the distraught nurse. They gave the helpless Susan a sedative and trussed in up in a straight jacket as if she were some hopelessly insane person. She tried to resist and told them that she would go, but must have her black onyx crucifix, which was always near her. She grasped it protectively as they carried her out on a stretcher to a waiting ambulance that sped off to a sanatorium.

Susan, who wavered in and out of comas, suddenly became alert sensing the danger. Propped up in the hospital bed strapped in the straight jacket she watched the doctors and nurses rushing around, nervous and uncertain as to what they were doing. The moment she was alone with one jittery nurse, she asked for a cigarette.

The frightened nurse obtained one from her belongings. Needing a light Susan pointed to a cigarette lighter in her bag. It was a rather large one, used by arthritics, that was built to operate at the touch of a fingertip. While the nurse was trying to operate the unfamiliar lighter, Susan, using her free arm, reached for her crucifix, lying on the night table next to the bed, she swung it will full force across the nurses' face. The nurse fell backward as blood smeared her cheek. Susan screamed for help, shouting for a telephone.

The attendants came rushing into the room followed by doctors. She threatened them with lawsuits, charges against the hospital; she would bring the full force of the press down on them all.

"I know my legal rights," she yelled at them. "I want my lawyer. NOW!"

They stood frozen before the wealthy and powerful actress. In control of herself, coherent and articulate her demands were met. Her lawyer secured her release and she was back home soon after.

Susan, wary of her son, at the same time tried to understand the actions of all involved. She would now have to be even more on her guard.

On her last birthday, June 30, 1974, she was 57 years old. She was very weak but she surprised everyone when she asked for a chocolate birthday cake. After a quiet dinner at home, Ron and the cook brought out a big chocolate cake aglow with candles.

She ate almost half of it. She looked at the other half and sympatheti-cally suggested they drive over to her estranged son Timothy's house with it, to share the remainder of her birthday evening with him. Later that evening, mother and son, reached an unspoken truce.

On the 4th of July, Susan wanted an old-fashioned cook out, like the ones she and Wally went to in Brooklyn when they were kids. They planned an all-American party celebration with hot dogs and hamburgers on the grill, corn on the cob, potato salad and all the fixings. She asked Dr. Lee and Noreen Siegel, Marty and Helen Rackin, Timothy and Ilsa, and her very special friend cinematographer Stanley Cortez and his wife to join her, Wally and Ron.

In the later part of July, Susan, in need of more treatments, went back to Emory University Hospital in Atlanta. She again phoned Mary Wil-liams, Ann Moran and a few others.

"I went to the hospital with a banana cake, paper plates and plastic knives and forks," Ann said, "and I went up to the information desk and said I'd like to see Susan Chalkley."

"There is no one here by that name," the nurse on duty told her.

Ann told her the room number, Susan's private nurse's name and other identifying information, assuring her that she knew she was there.

"Just a minute," she said, and phoned Susan's room.

"There is someone here with the right answers from Carrollton," she said into the telephone. Then she turned to Ann and told her that Susan had had a very bad night.

"I see. Well, that's all right. I understand. If someone will just come down and get this cake," Ann said to the nurse. When she wakes up, she can have it. I know she will want some."

Ann left the cake, with a note, and went home, knowing that Susan would call her as soon as she could. As she walked into the house, the phone rang. It was the nurse, "Mrs. Chalkley wants to talk to you."

"She balled me out for leaving," said Ann. "She was very upset when she woke up and saw the cake and knew I had been there."

Ann, not wanting to say how much she really understood simply said, "Susie you didn't feel good and you needed your rest more than you needed company. I'll see you again, some other time." Susan went silent for what seemed a long time.

Then she asked Ann if she would please come back to see her that Wednesday. Ann asked that she have her nurse leave a message at the desk giving her permission to go upstairs to visit with her.

"Moma's leaving Friday," Susan told her, "and — I'm gonna be fine."

"Good for you Susie — we'll keep you in our prayers."

That Wednesday, Ann went back to Emory Hospital. She inquired at the reception desk if there was any message for her, any word from Susan Chalkley's nurse. The nurse on duty said no, there wasn't. Ann Moran paused for a moment then turned around and walked away.

Father Brew, who had not seen Susan since their last meeting in Washington in 1972, met her again that September of 1974.

"She had been at Tufts Medical Center in Boston. Then she came down to Emory in Atlanta. She had to wait a couple of weeks to get the results of this test, so she spent some time in Ft. Lauderdale and asked me to come down. I arranged to make the trip and she said she would meet me at the airport. When I got there I didn't see Susan."

At the Miami airport, a man walked up to the priest and asked him if he was Father Brew, he was then asked over to the waiting limousine. Susan was seated in the back with Lou and Father Brew sat in front next to the driver. As they drove off to Ft. Lauderdale, the priest turned to Susan and started a conversation.

"From a distance she looked as she always did. Only later did I see that her red hair was a wig. She asked about mutual friends in Washington, all about Eaton's friends. I had no reason to suspect things were as bad as they were. In other words, she was really putting up a front. It wasn't until we got to the place where she was staying down there that I realized," Father Brew said. "The driver got out, opened up the back, took out a wheelchair and lifted her into it. She had not said anything about it. She had reserved a room for me at Pier 66. It was about two blocks from where she was staying in a private house. There was nobody there, just the two of them. She suggested that we have dinner that night and asked how soon I could be ready. I was still in shock about the wheelchair and her condition. I didn't want to let on to her. The way she presented it, well that's the way I was going to take it."

Susan told him she would pick him up around 7:30 this Friday night and they would have dinner at MacDonald's Sea Grill. The owner was from Washington and both Eaton and Father Brew had known him from there. It had been one of Eaton's favorite fish restaurants in Ft. Lauderdale. At 7:30, they called for Father Brew and drove over to MacDonald's. Again, she was lifted into the wheelchair, and taken inside the restaurant. From there she pulled herself to the table.

"After dinner I could see she was tired so I said I would see her the next day — when she called and told me we were going out to dinner that night. I said, 'Again?' But she insisted. This time she was with Ron Nelson."

Nelson made all the arrangements for dinner that Saturday night at the Tower Club atop Ft. Lauderdale's Landmark Building. The Tower management placed American Beauty roses at a corner table and printed special Miss Susan Hayward matches. The room was softly lit and there was an air of expectancy as the staff watched the Tower elevator doors.

When Susan arrived in her wheelchair, all beautifully done up in a long gown, with her buddy Ron and Father Brew walking on either side and the nurse pushing the wheelchair, the combo which featured an organist, began to play 'With A Song In My Heart,' 'No Foolish Heart,' and other songs from her motion pictures, as she was wheeled through the candlelit room. A hush fell over the room as she passed the other diners.

"She was clear in everything she said," Father Brew recalled, "I remember her signing a couple of autographs, but at the same time the people in there didn't embarrass her. I don't know what she was suffering, what she was feeling. There was no indication. I thought this girl has got a lot of courage. It was a pleasant dinner.

"When we left there and drove back to Pier 66 I said, as I got out of the limousine — 'good night, wonderful dinner, see you tomorrow.' 'No,' she said, 'we are going to have a nightcap.' She was put into her wheelchair and we went to the revolving roof cocktail lounge."

The four of them spent another hour or so there before they said goodnight to Father Brew in the lobby. As he went to his room, he wondered why she would put on a public performance like that for his sake? They could have dined privately at her home. He reflected on the time he was in England in 1962 with Eaton while Susan was making *Stolen Hours*, the story of a woman dying of a brain tumor. The dramatics of the evening left him pulsed — and then he recalled Eaton's words, "It's difficult to tell when the acting stops."

The next day Father Brew went across to Susan's home. From there they went to Holy Cross Hospital — where Eaton Chalkley had been hospitalized with his final illness. Father Brew was to say Mass at 2 p.m. that afternoon during which Susan received Holy Communion at the last Mass she would be able to attend.

Four days later, she was flown back to Emory. Neurosurgeon Dr. George Tindall performed a biopsy after telling Susan that if the results were positive there was no hope for a prolonged survival. With the biopsy procedure completed, she waited in her hospital room. The reports were back from pathology and Dr. Tindall and his associates came into her room.

According to Ron Nelson, who was with Susan, she looked at them and said to him, "If he's gonna tell me what I think he's gonna tell me, you'd better leave."

Standing outside in the corridor, he heard a heart-rending scream — then dead silence. The physicians left and he went back into the room.

A brain scan showed rapid brain tumor growth. Doctors concluded she would soon lose her speech and memory, then her swallowing reflex. Because she had explicitly forbidden any intravenous or other lifesaving devices she would die once she could no longer swallow.

"I don't want anybody to push me over," she said, "and I don't want anybody to hold me back."

Susan returned to Ron's home in Ft. Lauderdale, but by the end of September, she became so feeble that further care was needed and she was flown back to Emory in Atlanta, on October 5th. She went into a coma and doctors were now certain she would not regain consciousness and notified the family. Monsignor Reagan from Carrollton brought her Holy Communion.

On October 21st, she rallied and regained consciousness. The doctors were amazed. She simply refused to submit. With only a few months at best she did not want to go to Ft. Lauderdale with Ron because Eaton had died there. She wanted to go back to California, to her own home and Ron rented a plane to fly her back to Los Angeles.

Ron told Susan that his doctors had detected a mild heart condition and before Susan boarded her plane, she said to him, "Look, they think I've got cancer. We know you've had a heart attack. Make a deal? We won't talk about this anymore, but let's keep this special thing we've got til one of us kicks the bucket. If it's you, I'll try to be there — If it's me you goddam well better be or I'll haunt you."

Before she left him, she looked back and smiled, "I'll see you in the funnie papers."

Back home in L.A., Lou would sometimes carry Susan into the living room and place her on a chaise lounge, where she would greet visitors such as Kate Hepburn, Ruth Gilette, Nolan Miller and her sons.

Susan would wake up from sleeping and see yellow roses and say, "Oh, they must be from Nolan." Lou called Nolan at his salon and asked him if when he finished working for the evening to drop in for a while. It would cheer Susan up.

"I would go and have something to eat with the nurse, Susan would sit there. Sometimes she was propped up in bed, sometimes in a wheelchair. She wouldn't eat with anyone looking at her."

"One night I was at the house and one of her early films was on television — *Reap The Wild Wind* — and we watched part of it. 'Dear God, how did they ever give me a second chance? The way she threw her head around and rolled her eyes,' she said about herself. 'I can't imagine they would ever give me a second chance…'"

Susan refused to see Marty Rackin and many others who wanted to call — probably because of the way she looked. Helen Rackin tried many times to see her but, "she was sleeping most of the time. Some times I talked to her on the phone, but she couldn't talk too well as the paralysis had really taken hold."

"I'd say, 'Susie, can I come up and see you?' She'd say, 'fine Helen, but call first.' By the time I got there, she was already asleep. I would always leave a little note for her."

Most of the time Susan was heavily sedated and she had a horror of old friends seeing her as she was, and a growing disinterest in the things outside her home.

She called Father Brew to arrange to see him just one last time. Eaton's friend was her closest link in this world to Eaton and possibly, she might have thought it the next world as well. Saying goodbye to him would be in a way, saying goodbye to Eaton as well.

"In December she called and said she would appreciate it, if I could come to see her, she was pretty bad. So about the middle of December I went out there. She was heavily sedated and sleeping most of the time, but we had a couple of conversations. She still put on that brave front and kept her sense of humor. There was no indication of fear or rebellion. She went through each one of the stages that Elizabeth Kubler Ross wrote of in Death and Dying. On my last visit she accepted, and in her own way was consoled by, the catholic belief of life Hereafter. The sermon I made at the Mass (at her funeral) was all on the idea — that this is not the end."

The house was decorated for Christmas. There were poinsettia plants, wreaths, a big Christmas tree and there were four choir boy figures in front of the house with Christmas carol recordings piped outside. To the dying woman in her bedroom all of this could hardly have mattered but it was the well-intended idea of the people around her to make an attempt at capturing the holiday spirit for her — almost certainly for the last time.

Weeks later, on February 7, 1975, Susan phoned Ron Nelson and told him that 'it was time.' He left his job, once again, to go to her side. Ron arrived at the Laurel Way home for the death watch and found the household in a state of subdued hysteria. A strange interplay of intrigues manifested itself. Timothy approached Ron asking him to testify, at the right time, to help him break the will to have his Uncle left out. As it stood Timothy and Greg were to be left a million dollars apiece, their Uncle the interest from $250,000 held in trust for him for the rest of his life, the principal to revert back to Timothy and Greg only upon his death. Ilsa, who obviously distrusted her husband (later she would divorce him), also went to Ron to ask him to testify in court to have her daughter receive a share of her grandmother's estate.

Susan's estranged sister, Florence, knowing about the terminal illness, had been trying to see Susan for months to plead with her not to leave her out of her will. Susan hadn't seen her sister for 15 years and wanted no reunion now — it was too late.

It was revealed later that the desperate woman came to the house one day wearing only a barrel with a sign on it saying, in effect, my sister Susan Hayward won't give me any money and I'm starving. The publicity stunt was not recorded by the press, however.

Helen Rackin recalled that, "My husband and I had friends in the Real Estate business and they heard that Susan was very bad. They wanted to know if her house was up for sale and if my husband would put in a good word for them" (After Susan died they were all after the house — for when a movie star or personality has owned a home — the price almost doubles.)

Susan's poolside bedroom, which she seldom left during her last months, became the focal point of all the intrigues and often took on an atmosphere of frenzy. Ron, guarding the bedroom, finally not able to bear it any longer at one point yelled at them all, "Will you stop this fighting and let her die in peace."

Timothy at last won his battle with Louisa when the bookkeeper, who took care of Susan's taxes, files and checks, told him that he had discovered records of the payments for the laetrile. Now he had the evidence he wanted and his lawyer informed Lou that she must leave the premises immediately or he would turn the cancelled checks over to the authorities and see to it that she would never work again as a private nurse.

Louisa went to say goodbye to the woman she had deeply loved and cared for. With tears streaming down her cheeks, she pleaded with her, "Susan can you hear me? Can you hear me? They're forcing me out."

Susan turned her head toward Louisa's voice and slowly opened her eyes, looking at her with understanding, but unable to speak. Tears came to her eyes and fell down her cheeks as she realized Louisa's desperate position and enforced exile, and her own powerlessness to do anything about it.

Angry and hurt, Lou packed her belongings. Before leaving, she warned Ron, "If you ever try to make money on Susan, I'll take care of you."

Standing by the front door she turned and looked at Timothy who was watching her leave, "You'll pay for this," she said as she left them all standing at the open door watching her walk down the driveway.

In late February, no non-family members, apart from Ron, Katherine Hepburn and Ruth Gilette were allowed to see her — with one exception. One day a woman arrived dressed in a long black cape with a hood and said she wished to see Miss Hayward. The nurse answered the front door bell did not recognize the mystery woman as Greta Garbo, and replied, "Miss Hayward can't see anyone."

"I think she will see me," Garbo said softly and when she made herself known was led in immediately to see Susan.

The enigmatic legend flew in from Florida to share some personal health secrets she hoped might pull her through. Susan was her favorite star and she left very saddened after seeing her.

Ron kept his watch at Susan's bedside, taking his own sleep either alongside her on the same huge bed or in the big armchair placed close to it. He didn't get much sleep and hardly ever bothered to undress. Dr. Siegel prescribed Valium and gave him an insomniac's clock. It flashed the hours and minutes on the ceiling in hypnotic red digits.

Timothy could no longer bring himself to enter his mother's bedroom because of the foul odors. "I can't go in there. It makes me sick. I can't take it, the smell or look at her."

"Go in there!" ordered Ron. "She's your mother. She's dying." Timothy fortified himself with liquor before going into the room and when he came out, he turned a sickly yellowish color. "Don't ever ask me to do that again. I'll never go in there. Not even after she's dead."

Ron asked Dr. Siegel to let him know of some sign that would tell him when it was all about to end. He wanted Susan to die in peace, not to just hang on in this horrible way. Dr. Siegel instructed him on how to check various vital signs, like the pulses of the carotid artery in the neck, and the wrists, to listen to her heartbeats, to gauge the blood pressure, and to listen to the breathing.

Practically overtaken by nervous exhaustion he pleaded with Dr. Siegel, "When in God's name, when?"

"You'll know."

One tormented night Ron called Siegel at his Beverly Hills home, saying he had to talk to someone. "I called him at about 1:30 a.m. and talked to him until 5 a.m." Ron said, obviously much in appreciation of the Doctor's counsel.

After four days of unconsciousness, she roused on March 10th and called her son, Gregory in Jacksonville, Florida. Greg though fully aware that his mother was soon to die had never actually discussed it with her. It was to be their last conversation.

"You know I'm dying," she said.

Greg, who had been shuttling between his veterinarian practice in Jacksonville and her bedside for the past 30 months in response to the alarms of doctors, spoke affectionately to her.

"Is there anything I can do?"

"You're a veterinarian," his mother said, "I thought you might be able to fix up this old horse."

They talked about his wife and the practice and little bits of small talk, until finally she said, "This is my nickel — so I'm signing off now. I want you to remember something, though....remember that I love you."

Soon afterwards, she lost her speech.

Dr. Siegel visited her a total of fifteen times in the last 12 days of her life. Her bills were $100 a visit, to which Timothy objected strongly saying his mother would die whether or not Siegel was there and why did he have to come every day?

Louisa, who was friends with the housekeeper, called her to let her know that she was coming over to see Susan, and would she give her an all clear signal and let her in. The housekeeper was afraid to take the chance and when Lou appeared at the door, she told her she couldn't let her in.

On the night of Tuesday, March 11th an old speckled hoot owl perched on the diving board of the swimming pool under Susan's bedroom. When Ron saw it, he turned ice cold. He had remembered Susan telling him of the superstition that the appearance of an owl meant imminent death.

The hoot of the owl sound through the stillness of the night almost gave his heart palpitations, he was terrified that Susan would somehow hear it, but she lay still in her bed her hands clasping the crucifix that Eaton had held on his deathbed.

Stanly Cortez who had known Susan for over 25 years, the cameraman on so many of her movies, who had been very close to her came to see her for the last time, "Throughout it all, she was so brave, so typically Irish in her fighting spirit. I was in Susan's room to visit her a few days before she died. She was holding that crucifix in her hand, saying, in a faint whisper — 'Gotta work a little harder for me.' She looked up at me with that face that expression that always spoke a thousand words and breathed, 'Don't worry about me, Stan — I'll make it.'"

On Wednesday, March 12th, Susan was in a stupor all day and that night Ron was awake all night by her bedside and the same owl came back and sat by the pool on the diving board. When it began to hoot Ron

ran through the house practically verging on a nervous breakdown. He
found what he was looking for — an old shotgun. Standing by the pool,
he aimed at the owl silhouetted against a sky lit by a new moon. Ron was
shaking so badly from his nervous state that he missed the owl completely
and even the blast from the gun failed to frighten the bird from its post.

The echoing of the gunshot brought the Beverly Hills police to Susan's
home and after a bizarre explanation and knowing some of the circumstances of the dying actress — they gave him a warning not to fire the
gun again, and left.

The owl screeched relentlessly throughout the night and Ron stared at
it transfixed practically the whole time. He fell into slumber for a short
period just before dawn and when he opened his eyes, the owl had gone.

On Thursday, March 13th, the owl returned for the third night in a
row. Now Ron was waiting for its return, accepting it as, perhaps, some
form of mystic messenger, hooting its message that Susan would soon
be taken from the living, released from her pain and suffering. On this
the third night, the owl could again be seen by the light of the fading
new moon, and the following day, March 14th while Ron watched Susan
clutching the cross against her body he had a sense of time standing still.

The new R.N., Sidney Miller, walked in and out of the room, but Ron
was alone with Susan when the end came.

Suddenly, Susan was aroused from her inertia by a great inner storm
as a massive seizure seemed to grip every part of her body. The muscle
spasms that attacked her face, and clamped her jaws violently together,
caused her to bite off part of her tongue; though much of it had been
bitten off during several other seizures. With eyes bulging, her head
wrenched sharply one last time and the spasms came to an abrupt halt.
Ron paused a moment then checked her pulse. It was gone and the
breathing had stopped.

Edythe Marrener Barker Chalkley, known to the world as Susan Hayward, rested peacefully at last. Ron's eyes were drawn to the 'insomniac's
clock' it read 2:24 pm. For some reason he remembered that in the TV
movie she had made, *Say Goodbye, Maggie Cole*, Susan, playing the part
of a doctor, wrote down the time of death of her patient in the last scene.
The time had been 2:24 pm.

Her films had involved many excruciating reprieves from moments of
death and she had played a woman dying of a brain tumor, — a tormented
alcoholic, a woman on crutches…and on and on — now that was probably all she would be remembered for, since she was always bound to lose
this last fight in the end.

Ron picked up the bedroom phone and dialed Dr. Siegel. The doctor ordered him not to tell anyone. Just guard the body and let no one in the bedroom until he arrived.

Ron dipped his fingers in the bowl of Holy Water, which had been kept near Susan and administered extreme unction, according to instructions given to him by a local priest. He made the sign of the cross, gently touching her and closed her eyelids.

Then he sat in the armchair near the bed staring at the tiny figure wrapped in a pink blanket with her right arm stretched out clutching the cross and her heard turned to the left. She was still beautiful.

Now that she was laying there lifeless, the cancer that had consumed the flesh of her body seemed not so much to have affected her face, which was now relaxed and peaceful. Her long lashes, enhancing her vivid eyes, had remained despite the loss of her hair. He covered the top of her head with a pink chiffon scarf to hide the baldness, reached for his camera and took a last photograph of her.

Dr. Siegel slipped quietly into the room within the hour and told Ron his plan. He wanted to have an autopsy done as soon as possible. He — along with others in the medical profession — was astounded that Susan had remained alive for two years with malignant brain tumors that medical science had said should have taken her life within two weeks. Possibly, they might find within that corpse an answer to some peculiar cancer-delaying process to advance their search in helping others. Ron, having been associated with the Heart Association for years, understood his meanings.

Even in death, Susan perhaps to throw out another lifeline.

Siegel, Ron and Nurse Miller devised a plan to get Susan's body out of the house before the press found out about her death. They propped her corpse in a sitting position in her wheelchair and the pink chiffon scarf was removed and replaced by a red wig. Dark glasses were put on her face, and a wrap pulled over her shoulders and the cadaver was wheeled out of the house and into a waiting ambulance. A neighbor peering from a window could only surmise that Susan was being taken to the hospital for some further treatments.

Shortly afterwards, Ron called Timothy to notify him of his mother's death, and he took over from there, being quite adept at handling the media a necessary part of this operation. Ron went ahead with the funeral arrangements for her burial in Carrollton, according to her wishes. Timothy told reporters the funeral would be on Monday in Carrollton and actually planned it for Sunday.

Wally was on the freeway driving back from his job at the racetrack when he heard on the radio the news that his sister had died hours earlier.

"I asked Ron, if anything should happen to call me at work and I would come right home. He never did. I found out on the radio coming home from work and rushed right up there," said Wally. "She died Friday (March 14th) and late Friday night we were on the plane heading for Atlanta. Gregory and his wife came up from Jacksonville and Timothy and his wife, Ron Nelson and myself were on the plane with the body."

The autopsy at the hospital room was prepared for the arrival of Susan's body. The pathologist's knife found, as they had suspected, that the cancer had developed in the right lung and had spread to the brain. Nothing unusual was discovered to explain her amazing remissions and survival. It was concluded that the answer lay in her incredibly strong constitution, and her strong heart, which refused to release her until the biggest of the multiple brain tumors had snapped the vagus — or cranial nerve, which originates in the part of the brain that keeps the heart beating. The final massive seizure broke the vagus nerve link. Not to be overlooked was Susan's strength of character and her determination to hold on for as long as she could; this surely had to be just as responsible for the miracle of her survival.

That night, with Susan's body in the cargo compartment of the Delta flight out of L.A., Ron sat alone in the first class section, numbed, silently ruminating — Susan would have told him, "Have a drink on me. Come on Ronsy-Ponsy — it's all yesterday's spaghetti."

When the plane landed in Atlanta, newspapers at the airport magazine stands carried the headlines — SUSAN HAYWARD DEAD. The limousine drove the party to the Wedgewood Inn, not far from town, and took Susan's body to the Almon Funeral Home.

Susan had asked that she be buried in the gown that she had worn for her last academy award appearance — the one in which she had been seen in public for the last time. She had also requested that Frank Westmore make her up once more. Ron had the gown prepared and took it to the undertakers.

The following evening at 9:00 pm, there was a rosary in the chapel of the Funeral Home. The casket was closed and Ron asked that it be opened so that he could see her again for the last time. She looked quite beautiful, recreated as the illusion she had been for the millions of filmgoers. Frank Westmore's artistry was just perfect, though the bosom — because of the autopsy — looked puffy, stuffed with a pillow. To hide this, flowers were placed over her bosom and she held the rosary blessed by Pope John. The casket was bronze and of the same style — at her request — that Eaton had been buried in. Nelson recalled Susan complaining about the inflationary price, whereas Eaton's casket had cost $5,000, to her, a few years later, it was now $8,000.

Talking about her own death one day, Susan had said, "I've never thought about it much, but I don't suppose people will remember me very long. There's a new actress coming along every day. As a person, though, a few people will remember me and that's all that's important."

It seems only fitting that this book close with a farewell from Susan in the way she would have preferred with an expression that she used when she was parting from friends. She would look up at you with those big sad eyes and smile, "I'll see you in the funnie papers," — she would say and put her right hand up to her forehead in a salute — a farewell.

She lived like a star, worked like a trouper, and died a heroine. She was buried next to her beloved husband on the grounds where they had built a Catholic church, in the red clay of Georgia.

EPILOGUE

THE CLEO MILLER INTERVIEW (NOVEMBER 1984)

The Beginning of Friendship

"I started workin' for her (Susan Hayward) in 1953 to 1957 — she was a doll. We moved down from one house to another house, 3737 Longridge ñ that's where the big battle took place, then she divorced him and we moved, a house away 3801 Longridge Avenue, and that's the house she tried to kill herself. They (other domestics) said, 'You working for Susan Hayward?' I said yes. 'You can't stay there. She threw a bowl of salad at one of her maid's head. That woman is the meanest one on the block. You can't stay there.' I said, she ain't thrown one at mine yet. I'll wait 'till the salad start to fly then I'll go. We got along beautifully, she loved me and I loved her. I went on location to Utah. I could have gone to many places (except) I was scared to fly. She wanted to take me to Hawaii, Florida, Hong Kong, all over and I wouldn't fly."

Authors note: Cleo had the very first flight in her life when Susan sent a car to her house, airline tickets, and had her brought to the plane, put on board and flown to Utah with her daughter Willie Jean.

Susan "The Breadwinner" and the Suicide Attempt

"We both ate together in the kitchen, smoke, the whole works. She talk to me confidential. She couldn't stand her mother, her mother was jealous, her mother thought she should give her more than what she was giving. Susan was the support. Wally was a small man, out at the race track. Florence wasn't doin' anything. Susan was the bread maker. The whole thing supporting Jess, the kids, mother, Wally and Florence...and he (Jess) said he got tired carryin' her bags for her on trips. She was doin' the payin' and he was doin' the carryin' — so he got tired of carryin'. He was a louse. He was never any good. His own kids don't respect him. He used her. Her son Timothy called me up, he said, 'Cleo I don't know what to do with this old man, he can't even go on unemployment.' No, honey he can't go on unemployment 'cause he never worked enough to draw on unemployment. He said, 'I don't know what my old man's going to do. She stuck by him for ten years."

"My (Cleo's) husband, Mathew Miller, and I were sleeping in the maid's room. 3 o'clock there was a horrible knock on the door, which I didn't hear because I'm way back; maid's rooms are always in the back. When I wake up I hear all this rumblin' goin' on, they (detectives) had broken in the den door. There was Susan Hayward laying on the floor, nuthin' on but a terry cloth robe…I jumped outta' bed, threw a robe on and ran through the kitchen…he said, (the detective) 'Why didn't you answer the door?' I said who are you? What are you here for? 'I came — Susan Hayward attempted suicide.' I said you gotta be kiddin'. He said 'yes, she's laying on the living room floor dying.' I ran into the living room and here she was, one leg stretched out on the floor, the other rockin' and I waved my hands over her eyes and said, "Miss Hayward, Miss Hayward, this is Cleo honey. This is Cleo baby." She just kept smilin' and lookin' up at the ceiling. She was goin' very fast. They said, 'where's the bathroom.' I showed them, there were three bottles of pills; she had emptied every one of them into her body. She called her mother and said, Mother if anything happens to me, you ain't got nuthin' to worry about. You got it made! This is unknown to me at the present time. They had to take her out in the police car rush her to Cedars Lebanon. She called me the next day and she said 'Cleo, I goofed! I've been to hell and back. I died and came back.' That's what she told me."

"She was depressed. She was terribly, terribly unhappy. She loved Jess Barker. He just weren't the man she wanted him to be. She didn't know much about men. She didn't play around like the others. She was interested in her career. She wanted to be a good actress and she were. She was the best. But she was lonely. She was shy and withdrawn from the public but with the ones she loved that she wanted around, she trusted, she was a doll.

They sent Bette Davis' limousine to pick up Susan when she left the hospital, after she committed suicide and Bette Davis was mad. She blast them all out."

Susan and the Twins

"Timothy would listen behind doors — overhearing anything. Florence would come over with her son. Timothy called me and he wanted me to help him with his book about his mother and he said, 'you know a lot that happened in that house Cleo. I was a little boy. I don't remember, you can enlighten me on a lot of things that happened that I was too young to understand'.

With Florence, the boys were quite young and when they seen her a couple of times with her son they never gotten along because her boy was born of a German father. He was really rough and nasty and they always fight. So then Florence didn't come with the kid anymore, then she came to see Susan maybe 3-4 times. Timothy could be quite nasty, we would take them up to school when Mama was away on location and we'd pick them up. One time Timothy wanted to sleep out on the hill, behind the pool. I went to Arizona, my daughter was there. I let them sleep out and they camped and everything. So he talked to me all the way into Tucson the next day. He said, 'Cleo can we sleep out again tonight?' I said no, you can't sleep out again tonight because I'm not there and Willie Jean can't be responsible for you sleepin' out on the hill. He screamed 'You bitch!' He threw the phone down he didn't hang up. I said, he called me a bitch Willie Jean, call him back to the phone. She said he will not come back Mama. I said, OK leave him alone I'll take care of him when I come home 'cause he was goin' to the Chapman school up in the Bowen Hills and we'd have to give them the limousine to take them every week. So when I came home from Arizona I called the school and I talked to the principal. I said, now Gregory can come home on the next weekend but Timothy can't come home. Why not Cleo? I'll tell you why, we had a little misunderstanding on the telephone. I was out of town. He called me a bitch. I said, I don't want him home this weekend. Ok she said. Whatever you say. I went up in the limousine, picked up Gregory, brought him home kept him the whole weekend and left Timothy there. That was his punishment."

"When he came home on the next weekend, the limousine went back up to pick them up, my daughter went up with him, brought them down for the weekend. Timothy ran into the house threw his books down, threw his arms around my neck and said, 'I love you Cleo. I'm sorry I called you a bitch'. He was 10-11 so I never heard a bitch from him again I heard him call his mother a bitch when his mother was messin' around with this guy and that guy after the divorce. Tim was Susan's favorite. She loved them both but she loved Timothy more. So he said, 'you bitch'! He had that down fine, he loved to say bitch. Susan didn't punish him, she just talked to him."

Susan and Jess Barker

"Jess was in the Valley, around Studio City, down Coldwater CanyonÖ.. the old house where they had the fight before the divorce. When I came back-from my day off — the house was a mess. Ok, I didn't know what's goin' on until Susan Hayward walks in with black and blue eyes, beat all over her body and the flowers was all over the floor so I knew somethin' terrible took place. The fight was over the money 'cause he had approached her, this what she told me. She told me he ask her to loan him $3,000 or so many thousands of money. He wanted to buy some shares in Dallas, Texas oil. She said, 'No, you go out and get yourself a job'. He said, 'I'm an actor!' So what do you want me to be a department store clerk or a filling station attendant. She said, whatever, if it's an honest living. But I am not going to let you have the money.' That's when the fight came. I was off that night. My sister worked in my place. Always had somebody to replace me when I wasn't there. When I was, then I'd get the kids off to school in the morning, make their lunch, get them breakfast, teeth brushed, the whole works, get them off to school. Then I get his note, on the cabinet, wake me up Cleo at one o'clock with my juice. I go to his bedroom with his juice, and he's in bed nude, of course he's covered, but he's nude. He comes in the kitchen and drinks two pots of coffee, sat there and yap, yap, yap, yap all day. He said to me one day, 'if anybody had said to me in Georgia, sitting under my grandfather's pecan trees that I would be sitting on my fanny today I never would have believed it'. I said, Really Now!"

"He'd get dressed bout 3 o'clock and go to the market and bring home the green stuff and the food for dinner. I'd prepare the dinner. He'd sit and read his paper and at 12 o'clock he'd go out and get the late paper and he'd read 'til 6 o'clock in the morning. He didn't go to bed until daylight. That was the whole time I was there — more or less. He had dinner with the boys, because Susan was often late coming home from the studio, very seldom she'd be home on time for dinner 'cause the boys had to be in bed by 8-8:30."

"He threw her in the pool, over the money, she had a terry cloth robe on, no clothes at all underneath. He threw her in and she swim to the other side. He go over and poke her down in the pool. The black girl next door who was living in also, it was her night on. She saw the whole stuff.

She was in court with us. She testified to it. I was in court but never had to testify. I was there every day but I was never called. She (Susan) aimed at him with a cigarette. The judge said, 'did you poke him in the eye with the cigarette?' 'No, I didn't but I aimed.' Like that — we smoked the same I'm a chain smoker too."

"He acted like a queer, in fact her mother called him a queer. She said, there's something wrong with that man with his swishin' butt. He was always swishin', so she thought there was something queer about him. The mother never liked him 'cause he was a bum. He was really a bum, I'm sorry to say it but he was a bum! He drank Vat 69. He'd start about 4-5 o'clock in the afternoon. No, not during the day, he drank coffee all day, then the booze in the afternoon. And all the rest of the night. No, the mother didn't come too often 'cause she and Susan didn't get along too well, and the mother didn't like him. She'd only visit when Susan went to New York, going to Europe vacations, or away doin' a picture. I was there with the children, the mother would come down to stay with me and be there on my days off. She was on the prejudice side. She thought I was a black gal takin' over Susan's home. But I had my chores, things to do, and Susan and me got along very well. When she was home I'd take her orange juice too and we'd sit on the bed reading dream books. 'What did you dream last night Cleo?' She'd ask so excited I'd dream so and so... What did you dream Susan? I'd dream so and so and we'd compare our dreams. Horoscope everything, look up the story...and she'd tell me all her secrets."

"She had quite a temper, she's a Cancer, Cancer people got a temper. She told me I didn't know men had big ones, short ones, medium size. She didn't know 'cause she never experienced it. She was only used to Jess Barker. Everything she knew about a man was Jess Barker until she divorced him. She just didn't play around with the other guys."

Susan and Superstitious

"Susan threw salt over her shoulder if she spilled it; said a man was coming if a fork dropped, etc."

"The cutest thing, when she was goin' for that Oscar for "I'll Cry Tomorrow" — she broke a mirror. I said, 'Miss Hayward let me go and bury this mirror', 'cause we were goin' to have our big party at the house, and catered it, she got a beautiful gown for the occasion and were goin' to have a big party afterward. The Academy thing that night 'cause she was so sure she gonna' win. So she breaks this mirror, I picked it all up and I said, let me take it down and bury it on its face, break the spell and you'll have good luck. You, Cleo, superstitious? I said, well you know you're up for the academy so you better let me go bury it on the face to bring good luck. So she said, 'No, on Cleo superstitions. Ok, I didn't bury it, threw it away. She didn't win it. She came home and cried on my shoulder and said, I should have listened to you Cleo. I should have let you bury the mirror the way you said'.

She was lookin' forward to it, she was sure she's gonna' win this time. This big party, in this $100,000 home, all the food and the people came and she came home and she had lost."

John Wayne, Howard Hughes, and Eaton Chalkley

"She wasn't too friendly with the movie stars; she didn't have parties in her home. She didn't like entertaining, she didn't like to go out to entertainments. No, John Wayne never visited the house. No movie screen in the house, just TV. She didn't glory in these fabulous things most people did. She threw away a $3,000 diamond in the desert of Utah. She went out riding in a car with John Wayne one night, and my daughter. She pulled it off 'cause she was in the process of divorce at that present time, A great big diamond wedding ring -square big diamond, she throw it out in the desert. No, Jess never gave her that, he never had that much money she bought it herself. And you can believe that me and my daughter walked down in 120∞ heat the next day. She said, maybe you'll find it somewhere on the freeway on the side of the road, if you can find it you can keep it. We didn't. We was in St. George, Utah, there's no black people, Indians, Mormons, and stuff like that. John Wayne and Susan had a house, he lived about a block from her, we had a lot of fun. She kicked him all the way to the house one night. You know he married Pillar, he and Pillar were shakin' together at that time, that was before they were married. Oh, yeah! Susan had a crush on him. We had a party at the Wayne house. Susan pulled off her shoes and said Pillar let's fight. She made him take her down to her house which is a block away and she kicked him in the butt all the way down. Then they got in the car, that night, the night she threw away the diamond."

"Howard Hughes, yes, I was in his company I'll say 6 to 9 months. I served him dinner in the dining room. He was kinda cold, you know, he's southern, not so hot on Negroes any way. (Cleo was born 125 miles from Dallas in a little town near Jacksonville). But he was nice — sometimes. Susan felt sorry for Hughes and always had Cleo bake him an apple pie and he would eat the whole thing. But Susan would pump him up. I had my little nephew out there and she said, 'Oh, Howard look at this nice little ole baby, isn't he sweet'. He went ohhhh, moanin' and held back like he was scared it was goin' to rub off on him. Honey, he didn't make it with any of those women. He couldn't make it with any. I don't know his story. He was shy. I don't know whether because of sex, but he was a shy, sexless man. He brought her yellow roses, beautiful yellow roses, dozens and dozens. Yellow roses, that were her favorite. Other than that I don't know what else she got (she laughs wickedly). She wasn't a flashy woman, she didn't deal in wealth like the others."

"My family came to visit and she said, 'invite them here Cleo, they can sleep in any bed they want to sleep in, cook them anything you want, there's a freezer full of food if not I'll order it.' She said 'your Mama and Daddy can stay here with you'. So my mom and dad and any of my relations come from out of state stay in Susan Hayward's home. Oh, she was a doll. (This drove Eaton mad and they had cutting arguments.) He was goin' around with Susan before they was married. He came to the house, stayed there. He'd come in from Georgia, spend maybe a week at a time. They would go up to Big Bear and spend some time there. He just couldn't stand her servants because we all was black. This one incident — Susan told my husband Matthew to have a beer, to go to the bar and get a beer, which she knew he liked, she always offered him one, and meanwhile open a bottle of champagne, 'cause they were leavin' that night for Big Bear. That night after they left they got into a big fight but not before us. He gave her hell, he said, 'I don't like your servants'. She said, 'Why? What's wrong with them? 'They are Negroes and I don't believe in negroes speakin' until they are spoken to. He was a bachelor and only paid his housekeeper $30 a month. They went to Big Bear, they had this fight and she left him in Big Bear. She came home and she told me, Well — it's all over between Chalkley and me. But it weren't all over because in a week they made up again. The next thing I knew she was announcing they were goin' to get married".

Susan's Gifts

"She had a heart of gold. She loved us so much. She loved my children, my daughter, Willie Jean, she was 17 years old. I said, Miss Hayward I'm livin' out here and my daughter is in the city and I'm worried about her runnin' around not bein' supervised. So Susan and I talked it over and she said, 'let her come here. She can take care of the boys. She can be the second maid. She can have room and board and I'll give her a salary'. She'd take the boys biking in the hills, go to the movies, she did all the small errands. So my daughter worked under me for 5 years. Susan gave me that break so I can bring my daughter from a rough city where I can keep an eye on her. Yes, she slept right upstairs with the boys. She look after 'em just like a second mother. No, Susan wasn't tough on the boys. Sometimes I'd tell her when they got me upset. She said, 'well Cleo, the kids gotta' throw off steam just like us grownups'."

"When my baby came, my baby Pamela was the first black baby that ever went to a doctor in Van Nuys. They didn't have no black patients. So she called up and got an appointment for my baby. She paid all the doctorr's bills, bought all the food, all the milk. She said, 'this is my adopted daughter'. So we goes down to Studio City and Susan says, 'Cleo let's go buy Pamela some clothes'. She's about 2 months old. She bought her a new baby bed. So, we goes to Studio City to Babytown. She bought little shoes, little clothes and this English carriage, great big beautiful thing, with the shield over it. So she goes over to the cashier, the sales girl says, 'Oh, Miss Hayward I didn't know you had a new baby. Susan says, 'Oh, didn't you know it honey. I had it by Sammy Davis, Jr.'

Gang, Kopp & Tyre — Attorneys arranged the adoption papers (April 4, 1957).

Pamela went around tellin' all these black kids Susan Hayward is my Auntie, these black kids in the neighborhood. You gotta be a nut, they told her, as black as you are, how can Susan Hayward be your Auntie."

"Willie Jean did sleep upstairs with the boys. We didn't have enough room. My husband and I had one bedroom, the maid's room. The first house was small, only 3 bedrooms, 2 downstairs. The second house had 17 rooms, pool houses, and dressing room, a whole hill, cost $100,000.

She didn't care about money, she never cared about money. One day she dropped $150 in the driveway in a paper bag. I found it layin' out there, this is your money, Oh, I guess I dropped it getting out of the car. She did some shoppin' and just dropped some money change in the paper bag…"

"I was at Fox, MGM, Paramount, I been on all these sets and Jess took me in one day. She was doin' Bathsheba, I was out there all day watching her and watchin' them kill each other. She wanted me to play the Negro part in "The President's Lady", the maid, the black woman. I wouldn't take it, even her mother got on me about that, she said, 'Cleo, why don't you accept it, Susan wants you so much'. I said, 'I don't think I can make it', but they needed a woman who could speak southern and I'm southern. I wish I had now, after I grew older. I must a been 'bout 33 at that time. I felt my education might not bring me up to the part. I was afraid I would embarrass everybody and myself. I was afraid I couldn't remember the lines."

Susan and Loyalty

Authors note: What was amusing was how Cleo would read scripts with Susan in the living room, often playing Gregory Peck, John Wayne or whatever co-star Susan co-starred with. Sometimes they would reverse roles and Susan would take the male leads and Cleo, in that southern way, would be Susan. Of course, they had a great time doing it, laughing, nevertheless Susan learned her part. Also Susan would help her with the big words and her reading.

"A little ole girl came from outta' state and sat on my back step for a whole day wantin' to get Susan's autograph. Susan was home that day. I say, Miss Hayward, please write somethin' on this piece of paper for this kid so she can go away. She said, 'when I'm home, I'm home. If they want to get in touch with me, they can go through The Screen Actor's Guild, the studio; all my fan mail goes there. I'm not taking it here. This is my house. When I'm home, I'm private; I don't want to be bothered with people'. Now, Susan Hayward was shy, very shy, she shied away from people and never wanted anyone to see her before she was made up. She was proud of her hair and her boobs. Nice figure, skinny legs like me."

"I took the children to the Baptist Church, she didn't go. I took them to be baptized in Van Nuys. John Wayne and his wife, Roy Rogers and his wife belonged to the same church in Van Nuys. Every Sunday morning I'd get 'em up and take them to Sunday school to the Baptist Church. I never know Susan to attend the church, she believed but she didn't attend. But she wanted the kids to have that background of religion."

"I got her juice one morning, and there was this old man at 6 o'clock in the morning on the couch, I never been so shocked in all my life. So she must have been really out of it that night in alcohol. She was drinking heavy, even went out to the car with no make up on, so this day she walked him to the car, he was all crippled, on crutches, she stayed down in the livin' room with all night. He worked at the studio, somethin' to do with the studio 20th Century Fox, but I forgot. That was the only one time. She eat very good. She liked steak, salad, fresh vegetables, desserts. She started on wine before she got goin' on another picture. She got off the heavy booze and got on the wine. She said wine kept her weight down."

"The last Christmas tree we had in 1956 touched the ceiling, she had a high beamed ceiling. It cost $55, the Christmas tree. We had a little lady named Martha Little. Martha Little was a doll. She came down every year to decorate; she was so artistic with her hands. She could make anything out of a weed, a flower, a branch, with her hands, so Miss Hayward would always pay her a salary to come down from New York to do our Christmas decorations. Oh, we had fabulous Christmas, the most gorgeous Christmas presents on the Christmas branch with a couple of hundred dollars in it, my name on it. Sarah came too and after her sister died, the last Christmas Martha was there, I made her breakfast, 2 soft boiled eggs, I'll never forget, a piece of toast and a cup of coffee. She said, 'Cleo, this the last Christmas I'll be with you'. I said, 'no Miss Martha honey'. I put my arms around her, we hugged and kissed. Sarah came after her sister died and she decorated the tree."

Susan and the final days with Cleo

Susan pleaded with Cleo to come with them to Georgia to be her housekeeper.

"I just refuse to go to Georgia. The farther south you go down south, the worse it got. Susan said, 'I'll change things, I'll change the law", in front of Chalkley. He said, 'They'll burn crosses on your lawn'. Her lawyer got me to sign a paper. I didn't read it. The next day she said, "Girl, I put you in my will."

"When she moved to Georgia she dumped everything. She didn't want to take with her, the old days, you know. She was married to Chalkley and got rid of the diary and she said, 'Cleo, anything you want here you can have, anything you don't want here dump it. I came across the diary so I collected it. It were a high school diary. She were 63 when she died. Jess looked through all my stuff. How'd you get all this stuff Cleo? This is all I want. I would love to have the diary. I don't have no use for the diary so I gave it to him. I didn't realize it — didn't mean anything to me at the present time, it was her private life. Yes she was 63, which the diary proved. 63 when she died not 56…63. I know how old she is, they quoted 55, you know how people do. They don't quote the real age. I saw the passport, the diary and she told me".

"I saw her on TV at the academy awards, you saw how ill she was. One day Jess called me from the Beverly Hills home and that was the last time I talked with her. He said, 'Cleo, I have someone I'd like to have talk to you'. I said, Oh, who? He said, 'I'll let you hear the voice. She spoke to me and told me how much she loved Chalkley and Jess were there. She said, 'Oh Cleo I loved my husband so much'. I begged her to let me come see her and she said, 'I'll let you know. I didn't want her to think I wanted anything from her; I wanted to visit her, be with her, comfort her, whatever I could do for her. She wouldn't let me — see her that way".

"We got boxes and boxes of fan mail and she said, 'Go ahead Cleo and dump it'. I said, is it all right if I open it. She said, sure-do anything you want with it. I found money — 50 cents, sometimes dollars, quarters, I collected much money out of the fan mail. Paintings, pictures, all kind of stuff. She didn't want no parts of it. They would send money for an autograph she never returned photographs. She didn't have the time but she had a studio girl to take care of all this but a portion of the mail come to the house. So we all collected boxes for them, there was money in just about every letter and if I hadn't just took the boxes I would have dumped all the money. I said, Miss Hayward these letters have money. She said, you keep it. I was opening mail like mad, every letter had change in it, and from all over the world".

"Susan gave me a bonus when she went to Georgia and with that I purchased a home in the San Fernando Valley. I saw her a few times after she left, she called me. He (Chalkley) was snobbish, he kept us apart. Timothy asked me to help him write a book on his Mama. He was so mad over the separation. He wanted to exploit his mother. I said to him, 'You don't want to do that honey. He said, yes I do'. I said I know a lot of dirty things that went on. He knew I knew. He wanted me to put in the loose ends, he didn't remember 'cause he was a little boy."

Author Notes: They — Jess and Timothy love to come to dinner. I make charcoal broiled steaks, or southern fried chicken, tossed green salad, apple pie, sweet potato pie, all kinds of pies, we do a lot of things. I'll get 'em here and you (this author) come over. I'll get them to talk to you, if I can find him. (This never happened).

Susan Hayward could never forget the depression years, the Flatbush neighborhood where she lived as a girl. Neither could Cleo: "She (Susan) goes down every day to get day old bread, she helps Wally, shine shoes, throw papers, that's how tough it were. Her father worked on the railroad. They were very, very poor livin' in Brooklyn. That's how tough her life was, that's how she came up. She was tryin' to make somethin' of herself."

Pulitzer Prize Winner Ed Montgomery. Twice President of the San Francisco Press Club, who†was also responsible for the story of Barbara

Graham which won the Academy Award for Susan Hayward in "I Want To Live", remembered vividly, when he went to stay with the Chalkley's in Georgia (in 1958). He recalled…"It's just possible that Miss Hayward had in mind the role she never got to play. Scarlett O'Hara, had in mind the home Tara, with the columns and all when she and Eaton Chalkley built their new home there in Georgia. Come to think about it it's very much like the plantation in "Gone With the Wind."

Possibly Susan was exorcising figments of her childhood. And as the Flatbush beauty who lost out on Scarlett but, finally, became a Southern Belle she wanted to recreate, in some way, a lost dream, a memory that lived within her, when she came to the home she really wanted with the one man she truly loved.

Grauman's Chinese Theatre, August 1951.

FILMOGRAPHY

Hollywood Hotel
December 1937, Warner Bros.
D: Busby Berkeley

Hello from Hollywood: Louella Parsons takes her radio program, and herself, to the screen. Highlights 30's Hollywood places of interest, including exterior of famed Hollywood Hotel on Hollywood Blvd. — Dick Powell, Lola and Rosemary Lane and Hollywood hopefuls, along with 19 year old Susan Hayward, as cinemaella to Louella's fairy godmother.

The Sisters
October 1938, Warner Bros.
D: Anatole Litvak

Good period piece. Three sisters and their soap-opera loves. Nice Bette Davis, naughty Errol Flynn, great Frisco quake. Susan unbilled as telephone operator, and unseen every time it's shown — must have been out to lunch. Anita Louise; Jane Bryan; Henry Travers; and Beulah Bondi. *(95 minutes)*

Girls on Probation
October 1938, Warner Bros.
D: William McGann

Prison and probation 'B' melodrama with Jane Bryan and Ronald Reagan — "a lightweight as District Attorney, is perhaps a little too soft for that kind of job." Susan got 10th billing and a pardon for inexperience. *(63 minutes)*

Comet Over Broadway
December 1938, Warner Bros.
D: Busby Berkeley

Faith Baldwin story fashioned for Kay Frances. Starlet Susan, a walk on. No billing, no mention. Ian Hunter. CAMERA: James Wong Howe.

Beau Geste
July 1939, Paramount Studio
D: William A. Wellman

Susan fifth billed as Bel-Ami to brothers Geste, and Bel-Amour to one — Ray Milland. A pretty and patient ingénue, had little to do and does it forgetably. Gary Cooper; Robert Preston; and Brian Donlevy. *(120 minutes)*

Our Leading Citizen
July 1939, Paramount Studio
D: Alfred Santell

A Bob Burns (Will Rogers type) vehicle. Paramount apprentice Susan decorative as his daughter. Romantic interest was newcomer Joseph Allen Jr., who went on to *It Happened in Flatbush*, and oblivion. Elizabeth Patterson; Gene and Kathleen Lockhart; and Charles Bickford. *(87 minutes)*

$1,000 A Touchdown
October 1939, Paramount Studio
D: James Hogan

What used to be tagged a lightweight programmer. Two of the biggest mouths in the movies, Joe E. Brown and Martha Raye, took up most of the screen, squeezing out Eric Blore and fourth billed Susan. *(71 minutes)*

Adam Had Four Sons
March 1941, Columbia
D: Gregory Ratoff

Warner Baxter had four sons and Susan, as nymphomaniac Hester, wanted them all. Susan a standout, under Ratoff's direction, as the scheming, conniving wife of Johnny Downs. Saintly Ingrid Bergman comes to the rescue, but not until 23 year old Susan and the audience gets their kicks. (80 minutes)

Sis Hopkins
April 1941, Republic
D: Joseph Santley

A Judy Canova hayseed special, with Jerry Colonna. Cooked up Canova corn for her fans. Susan 5th billed as snotty, society debutante until she finds her true hillbilly heart. Picture cost half million, "It Ain't Hay," one of the songs played by Bob Crosby and band. *(97 minutes)*

Among The Living
August 1941, Paramount Studio
D: Stuart Heisler

Picture a sleeper. Susan second billed over Frances Farmer. Susan, at 23, plenty sharp as Millie Perkins — a sociological study, as the clothes hungry sexy daughter, of a rooming housekeeper, who nearly gets herself strangled by the unsuspected killer Albert Dekker, as twins, who also got good notices. Richard Webb; Harry Carey; and Maude Eburne. *(68 minutes)*

Reap The Wild Wind
March 1942, Paramount Studio
D: Cecil B. DeMille

De Mille's 30th anniversary production. Susan, 7th billed, is Drusilla, secondary romantic interest to Robert Preston, left firsthand impression. Best acting honors go to giant rubber squid who wraps up the picture with all ten arms. Susan's first with John Wayne, and Technicolor — looking lush. Paulette Goddard; Ray Milland; and Charles Bickford. *(124 minutes)*

The Forest Rangers
September 1942, Paramount Studio
D: George Marshall

Susan third billed over Albert Dekker, this time, is pert and sassy snitching scenes from Fred MacMurray's fiancée Paulette Goddard. The threesome bedding down for the night just passed the Hayes office by a pine needle, in those days. Susan's red-headed spark and a forest fire keep the picture hot in color. *(87 minutes)*

I Married A Witch
October 1942, United Artists
D: Rene Clair

Veronica Lake, of the peek-a-boo-bang, is the witch; Susan, with hair pins in place, the bitch — a cool, society snob. Camera Witchcraft effects, best thing going for it. Fredric March; Robert Benchley. *(82 minutes)*

Star Spangled Rhythm
December 1942, Paramount Studio
D: George Marshall

A Christmas tree of 16 Paramount stars, to boost wartime morale, 20 featured players, including Susan, doing a swing shift number for defense. A swell movie, even more fun to watch today. Bing Crosby; Betty Hutton; Preston Sturges; Cecile B. DeMille; Bob Hope; Mount Rushmore and Old Glory. *(99 minutes)*

Young and Willing
February 1943, United Artists
D: Edward H. Griffith

Six stage-struck kids out to break Broadway. Susan fourth billed vamps producer/chef Robert Benchley — apartment below — for big chance. Interesting today, to watch the young and willing players on their way up. William Holden; Eddie Bracken; Barbara Britton; and Martha O'Driscoll. *(82 minutes)*

Hit Parade of 1943
March 1943, Republic
D: Albert S. Rogell

Susan is Jill Wright, a talented tunesmith. John Carroll a two timing plagiaristic lothario. Eve Arden is Eve Arden — a highlight. Variety show 'mostly colored'. Count Basie, Dorothy Dandridge and Harlem talent Freddie Martin, Ray McKinley orchestras. This movie is often shown, by Susan's friends, on the anniversary of her death because in it she appears so young, vivacious and happy. Retitled *Change of Heart* for TV, from the Oscar nominated song. *(90 minutes)*

Jack London
November 1943, United Artists
D: Alfred Santell

Susan's entry into a series of biographical ladies. Susan, as Charmian Kittedge, London's second wife, in period costume, upswept hairdo, is lovely and ladylike but on screen only last half of film, unfortunately. Mrs. Jack London visited Susan on set during shooting. Michael O'Shea; Virginia Mayo; and Louise Beavers. *(92 minutes)*

The Fighting Seabees
January 1944, Republic
D: Howard Lydecker

Susan with World War II hairdo is wire service correspondent Constance Chesley who gets her wires crossed between Dennis O'Keefe and John Wayne. Triangle gets untangled when Navy Hero Wayne gets killed fighting Japs. Plenty of action for Wayne fans. *(100 minutes)*

The Hairy Ape
May 1944, United Artists
D: Alfred Santell

Susan returns in role as snobbish, spoiled, selfish daughter of a steel tycoon, while travelling on a freighter, she sees stoker Bill Bendix, calls him 'a hairy ape', and engages in brain over brawn gutter dialogue. Good adaptation of Eugene O'Neill play, impressive Hayward 40's acting style. John Loder and Dorothy (Mrs. Citizen Kane) Comingore. *(92 minutes)*

And Now Tomorrow
November 1944, Paramount Studio
D: Irving Pichel

Loretta Young suffering from mastoiditis finds love with shanty town doctor Alan Ladd, who restores her hearing. Susan, as Young's younger sister, tries to be bad but script won't let her. Familiar tale well told, Beula Bondi; Cecil Kellaway; and Helen Mack. *(84 minutes)*

Deadline At Dawn
February 1946, RKO
D: Harold Clurman

Top billed Susan is June, a dime-a-dance joint hostess, who picks up a dumb but sweet sailor, Bill Williams, involved in a New York murder. The couple team up as Nick and Nora to find out who done it. Picture tries to be arty. Wise cookie Susan interesting to observe. *(83 minutes)*

Canyon Passage
July 1946, Universal
D: Jacques Thourneu

Walter Wanger's Technicolor western filmed in Oregon. Indian fighting with pauses for songs by Hoagy Carmichael. Susan, third billed, as Lucy Overmire simmers with unrequited love for Dana Andrews. In color she is competition for beautiful scenery. Brian Donlevy, Patricia Roc. *(90 minutes)*

Smash-Up, The Story Of A Woman
February 1947, Universal
D: Stuart Heisler

Susan's lost weekend. As chanteuse Angelica Evans, 29 year old Susan gets biggest break to date as girl who becomes a dipsomaniac to overcome her inferiority complex. Cast overshadowed by her histrionics — she steals everything but the props. Reward — best actress nomination. Lee Bowman; Eddie Albert; Marsha Hunt; and Producer Walter Wanger. *(113 minutes)*

They Won't Believe Me
July 1947, RKO
D: Irving Pichel

Weak married playboy Robert Young and the three women in his life. Susan is Verna, a file clerk, who fools around with Young, goes straight and gets killed in a car crash. A budget picture that scores, for all concerned. Rita Johnson and Jane Greer exceptional. *(95 minutes)*

The Lost Moment
October 1947, Universal
D: Martin Gabel

Demented in Venice. Susan, as Tina, goes schizophrenic over dead poet's love letters. When she's normal her hair is up, when it's down she becomes unbalanced. Fire, attempted murder, and 105 year old Agnes Moorehead add up to a moody yet fascinating movie. Beautifully lensed and scored. Robert Cummings; Joan Lorring; John Archer. Susan delighted in panning this film, but it's a lot better than she made it out to be. *(89 minutes)*

Tap Roots
August 1948, Universal
D: George Marshall

Mississippi belle Susan fights both the North and South during the civil war. As the neutral Morna Dabny, she uses sex as a sacrifice for the cause, and with tossing shoulder length red hair, in color; she plays it to the hilt. Van Heflin; Boris Karloff; Ward Bond. A Walter Wanger color epic. *(109 minutes)*

I Can Get It For You Wholesale
March 1951, 20th Century Fox
D: Michael Gordon

Scheming Susan in the New York garment trade, ambitious to the last stitch, she wises up before it's too late to a smooth finish. Dan Dailey; George Sanders. Filmed in New York City. *(91 minutes)*

I'd Climb the Highest Mountain
May 1951, 20th Century Fox
D: Henry King

Sweet Susan, as minister's wife Mary, in the Georgia countryside. Heartwarming episodes, in color, set against the red clay hills makes for charming family movie — the kind they hardly make anymore. William Lundigan; Rory Calhoun; Barbara Bates; and Lynn Bari. *(88 minutes)*

David and Bathsheba
August 1951, 20th Century Fox
D: Henry King

Susan and God. As Bathsheba Susan makes her biblical debut becoming King David's obsession. Susan looks more solemn than sinful. A peeping Gregory Peck eyes the temptress bathing, and from then on all holy laws are broken. Israel was never the same. Raymond Massey, Jayne Meadows. *(153 minutes)*

With A Song In My Heart
April 1952, 20th Century Fox
D: Walter Lang

Susan's 3rd biographical role as songstress Jane Froman, crippled in a plane crash, courageously returns to show business. Moving drama gave Robert Wagner, as shell shock soldier, his stardom. Thelma Ritter as nurse Clancy, from Flatbush, a joy. Susan punches over the vocal simulation of Froman's voice masterfully, received many awards, scoring her third Oscar nomination, at age 34. A Technicolor box office smash. Rory Calhoun; David Wayne; and Helen Westcott. *(117 minutes)*

The Snows of Kilimanjaro
September 1952, 20th Century Fox
D: Henry King

A travelogue in cinemascope and color of Ernest Hemingway short story. Gregory Peck and Ava Gardner, out front all the way, until the closing sequence where Susan comes wonderfully into her own. Hildegarde Neff. *(114 minutes)*

Untamed
March 1955, 20th Century Fox
D: Henry King

Susan, is Katie O'Neill, a kin to Scarlett O'Hara, who goes to South African, fights Zulu warriors and generally goes through hell, looking sublime throughout in period costume, with a follow-that-horse determination. This one would have been tough on any actress but gutsy Susan achieved the improbable. Tyrone Power, Richard Egan. *(111 minutes)*

Soldier of Fortune
May 1955, 20th Century Fox
D: Edward Dmytryk

Red China next stop: Susan's, Vinnie Holt, husband disappears on a photographic trip, she goes to Hong Kong to find him (on the back lot) while seeking help from Clark Gable. What should have been a hot team as seen in the studio tests, only steams in the final takes. Gene Barry, Michael Rennie. Cinemascope and color. *(96 minutes)*

I'll Cry Tomorrow
December 1955, MGM
D: Daniel Mann

This is it! Susan, as a soul in torment, plays alcoholic singer Lillian Roth, who came back. Susan's own song belting, powerful acting from the heights to the depths of skid row, at 38, gives the performance of her life. A can't miss Oscar — that did! Danny Mann's direction -superb. Jo Van Fleet; Richard Conte; and Eddie Albert. Susan wins foreign award. *(117 minutes)*

The Conqueror
March 1956, RKO
D: Dick Powell

Howard Hughes's version of "The Khan and I". A sex and sand camp classic. John Wayne, as the Mongol leader Gengis Kahn and Susan as his desired hot-blooded Tartar Princess, were never more marvelously miscast. Susan even does a hooch dance to stay in the mood. However tragic consequences, from filming near an atomic blast fall out, dissuade one's enjoyment. Agnes Moorehead, Pedro Armendariz, cinemascope and color. *(111 minutes)*

Top Secret Affair
January 1957, Warner Bros.
D: H.C. Potter

Susan tries comedy role in a light, harmless, slapstick quickie. As magazine publisher, Dottie Peal, she is out to bring General Kirk Douglas, "Old Ironpants", to his knees. Best scene, a tipsy Susan doing a balancing act on a diving board. Paul Stewart, Jim Backus. *(100 minutes)*

I Want To Live
October 1958, United Artists
D: Robert Wise

No other actress could have done it! Susan, as Barbara Graham, party girl, convicted of prostitution, perjury, and murder reached new stature as an actress. The gas chamber scenes make a powerful indictment against capital punishment, Susan's work, at 41, received unanimous acclaim including Oscar, after 5 nominations, and about time. Bravo! Simon Oakland, Virginia Vincent, Theodore Bikel. Incisive wise direction. *(120 minutes)*

Thunder in the Sun
April 1959, Paramount Studio
D: Russell Rouse

Susan is ridiculous as Gabrielle Dauphine, with a French/Flatbush accent burning up the road in a covered wagon with a cargo of grapevines. No greater love than she that lay her career, for Brooklyn school chum Jeff Chandler, who gives her the hot and cold Basque treatment. Susan with eyes flashing, bosom heaving, stomps out a wine festival dance, between Indian fighting and a grape crushing break. Jacques Bergerac. *(81 minutes)*

Woman Obsessed
May 1959, 20th Century Fox
D: Henry Hathaway

We now find Susan, Mary Sharron, in Northeastern Canada. As the angry widow who remarries for the sake of her fatherless son, all she has to do in this one is fight a forest fire, a blizzard, her new husband and the script. Nature wins out in cinemascope and color. Hayward and Hathaway square off again. Stephen Boyd, Theodore Bikel, Barbara Nichols. *(103 minutes)*

The Marriage-Go-Round
January 1961, 20th Century Fox
D: Walter Lang

As a college professor's wife, in Florida, Susan manages to keep their Swedish houseguest, a sexy smorgasbord amazon, away from her hungry husband. As the understanding, wisecracking spouse, content, Susan appears anything but. James, Mason, Julie Newmar. *(98 minutes)*

Ada
July 1961, MGM
D: Daniel Mann

Susan, as Ada Dallas, a trollop from down on the farm becomes lieutenant governor of Georgia by default — Governor Dean 'Bo' Martin's, to be precise. As the reformed prostitute and first lady Susan cleans up political graft and corruption, putting a high voltage charge into her lines, and figure as dressed by Helen Rose. Director Mann gambol's for fun. *(109 minutes)*

Back Street
October 1961, Universal
D: David Miller
Susan moves to a luxurious back street address for the love of gorgeous but wed, John Gavin, glamorous Jean Louis clothes, and career independence, which most women would kill for. But she's miserable because she had everything but a wedding ring. As the long suffering other woman she follows' her lover all over Europe, first class, in the artificial world of producer Ross Hunter. Women love its soap operatics and *Back Street* is popular TV fare today. Vera Miles, Virginia Grey. *(107 minutes)*

I Thank A Fool
September 1962, Metro-Goldwyn-Mayer
D: Robert Stevens
Susan's back in jail, this time in London, on a murder charge for unprofessional medical practice. Seems her mercy killing when as a Canadian doctor, who follows her lover to England is under question. So is the picture, an implausible mish-mash that foolish Susan had no one to thank for. Peter Finch, Diane Cilento. Cinemascope and color. *(100 minutes)*

Stolen Hours
October 1963, United Artists
D: Daniel Petrie
Susan now takes on a remake of the 1939 Bette Davis classic *Dark Victory*. Made in Britain, it is visually effective, as is Susan as the doomed Laura, a woman facing death as a result of a brain disease. In retrospect it cannot help but arouse compassion when viewed today. A fated irony of the real life tragedy to come of Susan's own illness. Unconditionally guaranteed — a good cry at the end. Michael Craig. Color. *(97 minutes)*

Where Love Has Gone
November 1964, Paramount Studio
D: Edward Dmytryk
Susan in San Francisco is, Valerie Hayden Miller, a successful sculptress with a lot of overtime for sex. Bette Davis is her aristocratic mother, and their scenes together sizzle. Plot thickens when Susan's daughter stabs her lover — a script out of the headlines of that famous movie queen. Susan pays for all the fun, she's had in the script, by stabbing herself with a chisel, which should have pleased Bette Davis. Michael Connors; Jane Greer; and Joey Heatherton. Cinemascope and color. *(114 minutes)*

The Honey Pot
May 1967, United Artists
D: Joseph L. Mankiewicz

Elegant sophisticated comedy set in Venice, about a fading fox and his three hens flocking to his bedside, before the scheming millionaire's will is documented. Susan, Mrs. Sheridan, does her best as the wisecracking, hypochondriac from Texas. Mankiewicz brilliance cannot be disguised by choppy editing. Rex Harrison; Maggie Smith; Edit Adams; Capucine; and Cliff Robertson. Cinemascope and color. *(131 minutes)*

Valley of the Dolls
December 1967, 20th Century Fox
D: Mark Robson

Slick gimmicky, guess-who about show-biz pill popping personalities. Susan, as Helen Lawson, comes over like a Sarah Bernhardt as compared to the others in the cast. She also belts out "Plant Your Own Trees" with the help of Dionne Warwick's voice. Trashy film, big box-office. Barbara Parkins; Patty Duke and Sharon Tate. Cinemascope and color. *(123 minutes)*

INDEX

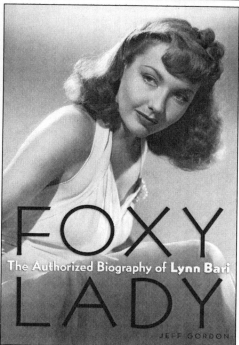

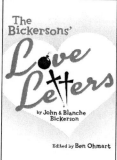